I Love You Anyhow

by

Marge Thompson

DORRANCE
PUBLISHING CO
EST. 1920
PITTSBURGH, PENNSYLVANIA 15222

Dorrance Publishing Co
701 Smithfield Street
Pittsburgh, PA 15222
Visit our website at *www.dorrancebookstore.com*

ISBN: 978-1-4809-0571-9
eISBN: 978-1-4809-0591-7

I LOVE YOU ANYHOW

Marge Thompson

DEDICATION

This book is dedicated to the One from whom I first received the liberating truth that 'Love Comes First'....Grace, freely given, before I knew, before I cared, before I loved Him back. Grace held for me in the spiritual bank account of my soul until I was ready to receive it. To the One who showers us with His acceptance and daily declares, "*I Love You, Anyhow!*"

I further dedicate this writing to those who, in the reading of this journey will be inspired by the Spirit to a new realization of how truly loved they are, enough to be healed, changed and empowered to offer, '*I Love You Anyhow*' to those around them.

ACKNOWLEDGMENTS

There are so many! How do I fit them all within the confinement of these pages?

Let me start with acknowledging that it is by the empowerment of the Holy Spirit that these words are written and without Him the pages would be blank!

Next, I must thank my husband for the many years of patience, love and support that he has given to me and our family and for his advice and encouragement in the birthing of this book. It will be obvious as you read that, without it there would be no book.

Thank you to my precious family for all of their love and inspiration. It is a wise friend who once advised, *"If you ever need a reason to go on pursuing God's purpose for your life, look at the pictures on your refrigerator."* Yes, they are all there, and along with the Lord, they are indeed my reason.

A special 'thank you' goes out to my editor, Kristi Dusenbery. Your love of the Lord, deep knowledge of the scriptures, and professional editing expertise has made this manuscript a more concise, enjoyable and compelling read. You are an incredible word crafter and I am blessed to have your partnership!

Ideas for the cover were just not coming for me….then you were inspired with an idea and put it all together Brenda and I love it. It so illustrates the heart of the book. Thank you so much.

When I reflect on so many who have freely shared their spiritual wisdom and encouragement, mentoring me throughout my journey, it's both difficult and dangerous to start naming you all, but I must make an attempt to lift the names of some without whose prayers and encouragement I would surely have given up.

God bless you Cal, Carl, Jean, Karyl, Russ, Marlin, Ken, Dave, and Mike. May God return ten-fold all that you have given me!

Thank you to my 'early readers' – Mike, Kevin, Bob, Leanne, David, Cal, Dale, Marv and Sue. You have all given so much time to read and evaluate my manuscript and to offer valuable feedback. You have shared great insights! This writing is better because of your feedback!

Pastor Mike, a special thanks to you for your friendship, instruction, and inspiration to be all I can be for the sake of the Lord. Your willingness to review this book for Biblical accuracy gives me great confidence that the Holy Spirit will use its contents to bless and empower its readers.

FORWARD

This book unfolds both a personal journey and the Biblical truths learned throughout that journey. It contains penned accounts of the lives of many, who have experienced devastation, healing, and empowerment, while on the road from broken relationships to the joy of giving and receiving a greater love....one that declares "*I Love You Anyhow.*"

Within each chapter you will find sections of *Personal Reflections*, revealing the compelling stories of dozens of people whose lives have been changed when God intersected their difficult paths with the golden nuggets of His truth. I have chosen not to reveal their real names, as the identities of the people are not mine to tell, but theirs.

At the end of each chapter you will find a *Personal Application* exercise, intended to help you apply the healing truths in your own life and relationships, bringing healing and strength for your journey. Scriptures used [unless otherwise noted] are from the New International Version of the Bible, published by Zondervan.

Also, after the Personal Application entries you will find a smattering of *Journal Entries* taken from over forty years of my jotting down inner-thoughts and struggles, most of which were penned after sessions of crying out to God and listening for His wisdom in return. They are, in essence, a vulnerable effort to put my soul out there between you and me. The road has been long, and not all together easy, but the victory is sweet, and still unfolding!

CHAPTER OVERVIEW

THE BEGINNING   Pgs xv-li
In *The Beginning* you will read of the 'journey,' a story of how God walked
along side, soothed a broken spirit, healed a broken heart, and empowered an
unworthy soul. This journey is likely not all that unlike the journeys of many,
moving from fear, insecurity, and lostness, to an understanding of God's
acceptance, and a love so great that it brings healing, and replaces pain and
hopelessness with expectations of victories to come.

CHAPTER ONE ...... LOVE – WHAT IS IT?   Pgs 1-20
Ahh, 'Love' - Such an all encompassing yet undefined word....I love my
Mother; I love my husband; I love peas, my dress, and my friends. Really! So
how is one *love* different from the other? This word is so over-used that it has
lost all sense of definition! The Bible gives us three different words to express
different kinds of love....*Eros*, *Phileos*, and *Agape*. How do they differ? We are
commanded to love, but when it seems we've run out of love, how do we
get more? Does your love lean to the hard side or soft side? What is your love
language? Is it really possible to express *I Love You Anyhow* under all
circumstances?

CHAPTER TWO ...... AFFIRMATION AND VULNERABILITY
                                                              Pgs 21-51
God gave His all to affirm us – while we were still yet sinners. Offering an *'I
Love You Anyhow'* kind of love demands a willingness to allow an open
vulnerability in our relationships, while at the same time striving to give honest
affirmation to others, even in the midst of difficulties.

CHAPTER THREE ...... COMMUNICATIONS   **Pgs 53-79**

When does true communication actually take place? Does your communication style embrace the listener, not allowing judgment, no matter what may be shared from a troubled heart? What do we say when there is nothing left to be said? Does elevating the volume of our communication help us get the attention we desire? What Biblical insights help our communications bring healing rather than hurt? How do our 'vertical' communications affect our 'horizontal' communications?

CHAPTER FOUR ...... FORGIVENESS   **Pgs 81-101**

What is the greatest example of forgiveness of all time? Who should take the offense to the cross – the offender or the offended? What is the difference in a *human* forgiveness and a *God- based* forgiveness? How many times must we forgive the same offense? Who is the real offender? Who empowers us to forgive?

CHAPTER FIVE ...... LIVING OUT LIFE'S ROLES   **Pgs103-126**

In our modern society, so quick to pigeonhole 'who' and 'what' we are and 'how' we are to function within that definition, there has never been a greater need to Biblically define our roles. What is the true Biblical definition of the role of a wife and mother? A husband and father? Does your family suffer from the consequences of *role reversal*?

CHAPTER SIX ...... AS BLESSINGS INCREASE - SO ALSO THE STRINGS OF STRESS

Pgs 127-150

Children are a source of pure joy, utter chaos, hurtful disagreements, and God's purest gift of love. How we each play out our responsibilities within our family dynamics shapes the world of our tomorrows. Who holds the true ownership of our loved ones? What is the difference in *teaching* and *training*? When more discipline seems our only hope for survival, does the *I Love You Anyhow* philosophy still work? How can we identify *strings of stress* within our families?

CHAPTER SEVEN ...... EMPOWERMENT   **Pgs 151-167**

Without fuel in our cars, try as we may to go somewhere we will go nowhere. In the same way, we must have God's empowerment of the filling of His Holy Spirit, and the guidance of His Angels in order to grow spiritually. How can we better understand the presence and purposes of the Holy Spirit and Angels? How does their existence interact with us, empowering us for victory? Have you ever had an 'Angel' encounter? Read about my sons and mine.

CHAPTER EIGHT ...... COMMITMENT AND GROWTH

Pgs 169-194
In this chapter we take a deep and vulnerable look at what it takes in personal commitment and growth, to strengthen our relationship with God and bring healing to our human relationships. We have been created and redeemed for a purpose.....what is yours? Too many of us remain baby Christians, trying to live a mature Christian life, and failing miserably because we are still being nourished only on baby's formula. What steps to Christian maturity does God reveal that equip us to offer *I Love You Anyhow* to those whom God brings into our lives, those which He desires for us to love for Him?

CHAPTER NINE ...... PAY IT FORWARD   **Pgs 195-224**
We have not been given the gift of life, love and victory only to savor it for ourselves. We have been commanded to *pay it forward*. This chapter challenges us to be like the ant who, after just finding a sugar cube crawls back to his ant hill telling all his buddies to come and taste of this sweet thing he has found, then leads the line that forms to the sweet prize. Marking a scriptural path to easily present the story of the presence, passion, and purpose of Jesus Christ gives us the tool we need to truly declare God's message of *I Love You Anyhow*."

THE BEGINNING

The beginning of the journey - A journey that birthed
this book - It's all about *LOVE*

"While we were still sinners Christ died for us."
The TRUTH that sets us free.....*Love comes first.*
Repentance, restitution, and reconciliation follow.

Jesus said, *"Father forgive them for they know not what they are doing."*
Thus God proclaimed – and still proclaims .... *"I LOVE YOU ANYHOW!"*

When miners search for gold, now and then they find a precious nugget.
Likewise as we thoughtfully mine out each page of the Bible, we will find
golden nuggets of truth that dramatically change our lives. Interspersed
throughout this book you will find 'Personal Reflections' - both tragic and
triumphant - through which God has used these golden nuggets of truth to
both challenge and soothe the spirits of the many whose stories you will read,
changing and equipping us for His purpose. The journey has been both
fantastic and frustrating - both victorious and devastating – and most of all it
has been a journey through which God has clearly revealed that He loves us
unconditionally and has created and redeemed us for His purpose!

I invite you to experience the reformation that takes place in our lives when we
are willing to truly take God at His Word - when we stop trying to 'play' God
and instead allow God to be God. When we do, He penetrates our lives with
the power of His very nature, a nature of Agape Love [a sacrificial and selfless
love] that generates a healing power, deep down in the very soul of our
relationships!

God, the very same God that created the Heaven's, the earth, and everything they contain, <u>actually</u> believes in you and me. And He loves us <u>just the way we are.</u> How refreshing! How unique! What an utterly mind boggling truth to grasp. How can it be that the Creator of the world sees us <u>completely</u> and loves us <u>anyhow</u>? Does it seem like too much of a contradiction to resonate with any truth at all? Can we truly be worthy of being fully loved, while yet still in the midst of our darkness? Or is that too much of an oxymoron?

It is this author's heartfelt prayer that this book will help you discover [or re-discover] the indisputable and irreversible truth of the cross – that 'love comes first' and healing, restoration and reconciliation follow - not the other way around. Romans chapter five plainly states that it was *while we were still sinners* that God sent a clear and powerful message, declaring "*I LOVE YOU ANYHOW,*" sealing it with His very own blood.

Digging out the golden nuggets of truth the Lord has given us, and applying the principles they present, turns our lives inside out with radical love. As you read, walk with me down a path from self-doubt, self-condemnation, and self-destruction, into a life of freedom, restoration, and healing. Discover the presence of a love so great, so unconditional, that it fills and frees you to pull out all the stops in your relationships, and love unconditionally as you are also loved.

Contemplate with me a few tell-tale questions.....

Does life sometimes feel really shallow, so superficial that when the 'party's over' your sense of 'aloneness' is too overwhelming to overcome? So crippling that you cannot bask in the joy of yesterday for the fear of tomorrow? Do the 'what ifs' and 'whys' disable the enjoyment of the here and now? Do you yearn for the freedom of true *I LOVE YOU ANYHOW* kinds of relationships?

Perhaps the journey recorded herein, revealing some of the inner-struggles the Lord has gently [and sometimes not so gently] pulled me through, will also help you as together we discover His *golden nuggets of truth* that set us free. With the reality that such a pure love has taken up residence in your heart, comes a healing in your soul that can't help but spill over to those whom He wants to love through you. You will want to pay it forward!

A Couple of Cautions:
* The journey into the depths of understanding of this kind of love can be long and difficult, sometimes accompanied by a pain that you will think you can no longer bear. But with His help you will. And with His help, your journey into the fullness of His love will bring new joys and new fulfillments that you would never have believed possible.

* Though you will reach a time when you are enjoying a whole new level of relationships, remember we will never really 'arrive' to such a state of perfection that we don't make mistakes. There will be times [even as there were for the Apostle Paul] when the only hope to redeem our relationships lies in God's continued forgiveness and work in our lives. We'll dissect this process more in the Commitment and Growth chapter, but for now take a look at a few excerpts from Paul's recordings in Romans 7: 15-25 [excerpts]....

> *"I do not understand what I do. For what I want to do, I do not do, but what I hate I do...For I have the desire to do what is good, but I cannot carry it out. For what I do is not the good I want to do, no, the evil I do not want to do – this I keep doing....who will rescue me from this body of death? Thanks be to God – through Jesus Christ our Lord!"*

Paul realized that the battles waging within us are spiritual ones, recognizing that we are all on a journey toward claiming God's promised victories. He 'got it,' the understanding that though the journey is rot with imperfections, <u>nothing</u> <u>can</u> <u>separate</u> <u>us</u> from the kind of love that Jesus poured out for each of us that day on the cross. Be sure to check out this awesome promise found in the Bible, in Romans 8, verses 37-39.

Along with Paul, I rejoice in the truth that God is not as concerned with where I am on my journey, as He is with where I am going. And I am determined that, though I am still not where I want to be, I will rejoice that I am not where I used to be. And I have great anticipation that, with His help, I am not yet where I am someday going to be! I am a work in progress. And I have the unwavering assurance that He will always be there to meet me on my growing edge. That golden nugget of truth leads me on!

In the book of Ephesians we are told that we were created long ago and for this purpose, that we might help one another. I John 3, verse 18, challenges us, *"Dear children, let us not love with words or tongue, but with actions and in truth."* Since we were created with the purpose of loving and helping one another, wouldn't you think that God would also equip us to carry out this calling? Yes of course He does! Yet, as a human race we spend inordinate amounts of time bickering, fighting and warring against one another. At best, we live in isolated harmony. But, we have been blessed to be a blessing, not an *acquaintance....a blessing.* To truly be a blessing begs for us to be vulnerable to deeper relationships, relationships that go below the surface of casually murmuring, "hi, how are you," as we hurry by the intended recipient of our insincere inquiry! When will we stop and really care how people are? When will we slow down and invest ourselves in the lives of others to the degree that we embrace them with a conviction that 'love comes first,' sincerely offering *"I Love You Anyhow"* even if they haven't lived up to our expectations? When we can truly do that - hold on, because the mind cannot conceive nor the heart begin to fathom the overwhelming return God has in store for us!

How can I be so confident of this?....because I've played it both ways. I have relied on my own resources, plagued with self-pity, anger, and resentment, not willing to risk being hurt [again] and finding each painful day of it unbearable. On the other hand I've walked with the Lord in reckless abandon of my human fears, and offered *"I Love You Anyhow"* in the midst of very difficult situations, resulting in indescribable blessings beyond what this pen can convey! This book is not intended to be only the story of my personal journey, but God's story, a story of His faithfulness in the midst of the human struggles, failures, and victories of the many whose journeys are told within.

It All Began in Middle U. S.A.

For me it all began in a mid-size town in the middle of the U.S. where I grew up with a younger brother and an older sister whom I loved dearly. I was the infamous *middle child*. As God formed me in my mother's womb [Psalm 139] it seems He equipped me with an incredible excess of energy, with which I totally exasperated my mother. One thing I was really good at was acting out your typical model 'tom-boy' character. When mom put me in pretty dresses and curls - all things little girls – she was compelled to keep a very close eye on me. If not, I would inevitably be out in the field to the north of our house, playing football with the guys, or catching caterpillars and butterflies. Or [you'll probably remember doing this] catching lightening bugs and smashing them on my fingers. Remember how neat it was to have all ten fingers aglow and then run around and flash them in the dark? Or not so much, whenever mom would come out to check on me to make sure I was remaining all cleaned up as she had instructed. [I was in 'time-out' a lot!] True, she needed the patience of Job just to survive me. But let me assure you, when I was found participating in such shenanigans, it wasn't pretty!

So what about my older sister? Well, she was my total opposite. She sported long naturally curly hair, flowing over the back of a slender beautiful body, and always – always, a perfect young lady, a mother's delight. After we were both prepared for an outing, mother would go off to get herself ready. When she returned to collect us, I had an ironic way of looking like a disaster, while my sis appeared without a hair out of place, prim and proper. Time and time again, comments rained, like; *"Look at you – you're a dirty mess. I can clean your sister up once for every 10 times I have to start all over with you, and look at those shoes! You go through shoes faster than anyone else in this house! And shoes aren't cheap you know!"*

I recall one painful day at a very young age, coming home in tears after a sad conflict with my girlfriend, feeling like my whole world had just crashed in on me, and desperately needing a hug. The first words out of my mother's mouth? *"What is wrong with you? Do you always have to be a neighborhood trouble maker?"* **Ouch**! She was right. My actions weren't always perfect, but my heart cried out to be loved in the midst of my imperfections, and instead my molehill failures were magnified into mountains.

Be careful how you approach the failures of your children, spouse, family and friends. Your words and actions have more impact than you might guess. Like another time when mom returned home from a shopping trip. Upon putting her purchases in the closet she determined that a box stored in there [which was holding my intended Christmas doll] was leaning at a bit different tilt then she thought it had been the last she saw it. I still carry a small scar from her attempts to get me to admit I had peeked. I had not. And I was way too stubborn to be willing to say I had, just to stop the pain of the palm of her hand against my face. She didn't understand. She thought she was teaching me the consequences of lying, but what I learned was that even the perception of a mistake meant I was not worthy of love and forgiveness. I never did get that doll.

Why are these issues worth a mention? Because it was a time in my life when lots of seeds were taking solid root, convincing me that I was anything but okay. Anything but worthy of being loved for just who I was. Instead of experiencing the healing power of unconditional love, I was filled with anxious failures, hurtful judgments, and rejection, fertile ground for the dangerous philosophy that began to take root: by *doing* things that please, we can earn the love we crave. As my dear brother so aptly put it, "We were always just *one good deed* away from being *okay*."

These incidents underscore the fact that, as reactions to my 'less than perfect' personality continued, the implications fostered the concept of, 'I love you, *if*' or 'I love you, *when*.' These concepts became so lodged in my psyche that the learned behavior that grew out of it was, '*if* I perform well' or '*when* I do as expected,' I will not be a disappointment, and then and <u>only</u> <u>then</u> will I be worthy of anyone's love.

Rebel child you say? Maybe. Problem child? Definitely. God's creation whom He loved anyhow? Yes. And I desperately needed to know that! I needed to know that His love for me was not based on my performance or the lack thereof. It was scary to think of how disappointed He likely was in me, and to contemplate what measures He may one day take to show me so!

Throughout life we all encounter hurtful incidents, when we allow someone else's reactions to our imperfections to devastate us, driving us inward to protect our sense of survival. If we are not grounded in the truth of God's proclamation that "we truly are loved anyhow," our spirit will become too bruised and broken to rise above the fray enough to offer those around us anything better.

At twenty years of age I became engaged to a man whom I was sure would take me away into a new environment of total acceptance, and love me perfectly - the way I had always longed to be.... *not so much*. You see, he too is human and my unrealistic expectations of him as a 'rescuer' were soon dashed with the reality that, try as I may, he too would be disappointed in me from time to time, as well as I in him. Imagine that!

During our young marriage, when I felt the most inept, I would think back to the discouraging reinforcement my fiancé got when we announced our engagement. Dad and mom loved him dearly, and mom assured him with, *"Well I hope you will both be very happy. One thing I know, if there are ever any problems, it will likely be her fault and not yours because she's not easy to live with."* Thanks Mom! I felt like the leading character in the Ugly Duckling story. After my mother's death, I remember saying to my husband of 46 years, *"Well, I made it. I never would have left you and given her a chance to say, 'I told you so'."* I followed quickly with, *"She may have been the reason I didn't leave, but love is definitely the reason I have stayed."* You see, though we don't think alike and our personalities couldn't be more different, he is a kind, faithful and generous man, with a sincere desire to be a man of God.

Having said all I have about my childhood family, I wonder if I should have told you before the revelation of the last few paragraphs just how very much I loved my mother. And I believe she loved me – just not my actions – which rendered her unable to affirm me for fear she wouldn't be able to change me as wanted to. God made it an inherent part of me to love her, no matter what, but it was truly hard for many years. I tried on many occasions to open up and share with her the love I truly felt for her, but it was such a challenge while harboring so much pain and unforgiveness. I felt like such a hypocrite, but didn't know how to bring myself to a point of being vulnerable enough to share my inside self with her, taking a chance of being devastated once again. That is, until one day when God 'transplanted' His kind of *"I Love You Anyhow"* love into my heart. Then loving her was unstoppable. You see, when we know what the true source of our love is, we know that it is never dependant on what comes at us, but what flows through us. And we find that His source of love never runs out! Be sure to camp for awhile on the Affirmation and Vulnerability Chapter [chapter two] and dig deep into the nuggets of truth shared there. God used them to release me to love like I never thought possible. But that's getting ahead of the story – let's move on from where we were and we'll catch up to the transplant experience later.

Though my childhood seemed filled with many moments of disappointment and devastation, I don't remember ever spending much time feeling sorry for myself, perhaps because we had many wonderful family times too, traveling, camping and spending time with our greater families. And perhaps because God used my active, social, resilient life to help equip me not to let the difficult times destroy my desire to do better. Yes, I felt lonesome and unlovable lots of the times, but I had really come to think that was just the way God made me. What a tragedy not to understand the truth of His unconditional love for me!

The other side of the coin? I was so very fortunate that in contrast to the "works" required from my mom, my father oozed with affirmation. He always had gentle hugs, and genuine interest in my well-being. God's gift to keep me balanced I'm sure! I used to think dad could walk on water, an absolute saint, with nary a fault. But now, as I have dug more and more into the truths of God's plan for a marriage partnership, I often wonder if it would have made a difference if Dad would have taken more initiative in helping Mom gain a deeper spiritual strength and understanding of God's unconditional love. I think so. Instead, the one solution which he enforced often was, *"Don't upset your Mom. We need to just do whatever is necessary to not upset your Mom."* He loved her greatly and spoiled her in every way he knew how. There is such a delicate balance between offering unconditional love and embracing unacceptable behavior, and only God can help us navigate through these tumultuous waters. And for my parent's commitment to navigate the course and stick together through it all, I praise God! It was a gift beyond measure to grow up and spend my whole life with my birth parents.

I think the significance of rehearsing this background is to help call attention to the fact that the totality of all your experiences go together to make up the inside you [the human you]. The 'you' that people seldom truly know. In fact the you and I that we don't even allow ourselves to dig deep enough to truly know. Thus, events from which our actions and re-actions are birthed, are often so buried in our sub-conscience that we 'act out' our relationships with feelings foreign even to us, completely un-aware of their origin. Instead, we get caught up in believing that our struggles are the fault of everyone around us, rather than understanding the root system from which they come and taking responsibility for them. As Andy Stanley puts it in his great series called, *Love That Lasts Forever* *"Others can only bring out of us that which is already within us."*

We would all do well to remember the admonition Romans 12:18 gives us; *"If it is possible, as far as it depends on you, live at peace with everyone."* This would suggest that no matter what comes at us, we have some culpability in maintaining peace within our relationships. To discover and deal with the reality that our feelings are most often internally driven is to begin the journey of being released from the control of those feelings.

When our actions are driven by our own insecurities we are unable to say *"I Love You Anyhow."* We can instead only offer I love you *when* or I love you *if.'* When driven by our insecurities, we find ourselves resorting to manipulation to evoke the attentions we think we need. To put it into the ever popular Dr. Laura's words, we become *'P P People.'* We *punish* and *pout* and *pout* and *punish,* assuming that those around us can fix the pain we feel if only they would. And maybe if we punish and pout long enough, they will. This imprisons us in a self absorption that ultimately eats us up and drives us to desperate measures in order to get the acceptance we crave. We withdraw, run, threaten to do oneself harm [my mother's pattern that evoked my dad's method of survival....'*don't upset your mother*']. It is ultimately a very controlling behavior and unfortunately I have been known to use this kind of manipulation from time to time, and I thank God every day for delivering me from the pain of it all!

Our family certainly does not have a corner on the market on this kind of behavioral pattern. Reuben Welch, in his book *We Really Do Need Each Other*, shares a similar story from his counseling experience....

> *"I know a dear family, and once in awhile the father gets his feelings hurt or is disappointed, or misunderstood – and when that happens, he just clams up. He handles this by total withdrawal from the flow of the family life. Oh, he says 'good morning,' 'pass the potatoes,' and 'thank you' – but he really wasn't there. And then everybody else starts walking around softly - "pussyfooting it" is the term I think - trying not to upset father and trying to keep peace. Father was miffed – mother got a migraine, and everyone paid for it. But one fine day father was alright again and everything was okay. He had some way of communicating this to the family – some word, some gesture, some small gift of conversation, that would signal the family that he was alright again and life would come back to 'normal' with never a word to indicate that anything had ever been other than perfectly regular. The migraine faded, the tiptoeing ceased – all as though nothing had ever been different and the incident was never mentioned – ever... Here is the detour – undiscussed – unconfessed – unshared – unrecognized – denial that it ever happened – AND GOD'S WORD SAYS, "NO!"*

Ever experienced a similar situation? Not truly communicating, just <u>expecting</u> others to know what you need, and then pouting and punishing when they don't deliver? Our relationships are often so shallow there's no one who really knows what makes us tick. We are neither vulnerable nor transparent enough to give insight to another in a way that they can effectively pray with us, hurt with us, find true joy with us, or help us face the emotional giants that cripple us. We may appear to be functioning well [as though 'all is well with my soul'] while all the while we are dying inside for a true sense of assurance that we are 'okay' 'accepted' and 'loved' for who we really are.

The truth is, no matter how much our loved ones and friends may try to fill this void we carry inside, they cannot fulfill the role set aside for Christ alone. The truth is, being loved with an, *"I Love You Anyhow"* kind of love is already yours and mine, my friend! It has been ours since the cross. And not until we truly grasp how wide and how deep and how high the Father's love is for us, will we ever experience the reality of the love we seek. But when we do, it is everything we ever dreamed it could be and more - enough to give some away!

Another insightful quote from Rueben Welch, in *We Really do Need Each Other*, claims that it was never intended for love to be held within, but rather to 'flow' out. God said that first.

Rueben puts it this way…

> "*It is no special blessing to come to the end of life with love unshared, selves ungiven, activities unactivated, deeds undone, emotions unextended…Isn't it God's intention that when we come to the end of the line – we're just about used up?*"

Yes, Rueben, I agree. It is my every intention to come to the end of my life all *used up*! I encourage you to read Ruben's writings. His insights effectively motivate his readers to action.

No human being will ever be able to give us enough love to fill the place in our hearts, purposely designated to receive the love of God. Nevertheless, He commands us to love one another in all circumstances, allowing His love to flow through us to all those around us. Too big an assignment? Sometimes it seems we run out, without near enough love to meet the huge demand for it. But in actuality we can never run out, because when Jesus takes up residence in our heart He brings with Him all we will ever need. We will touch on this concept again in later chapters, but it is such a foundational truth that it must be spoken of here. We have all we will ever need when we have Jesus, because with Him we are filled with the Trinity!

> "*For in Christ all the fullness of the Deity lives in bodily form, and you have been given fullness in Christ, who is the head over every power and authority.*"
> Colossians 2:9-10

So, when we trust Jesus with our lives, God deposits into our spiritual bank account [our soul] all we will ever need. The entire 'Godhead' – the Father, Son and Holy Spirit – takes up residence in our heart! When we feel we just can't go on, all we need do is go to the true source already deposited within us and withdraw His supply. Spiritually, many believers fall into a trap like one who dies as though they were a pauper, while in their bank account millions awaited them. They just never claimed what was theirs! When we received Christ we received 'all of the Godhead,' so indeed we are already filled with all we need. God the Father is there, and having created us, is aware of our every need. Jesus is there continually refining and cleansing us with His blood, shed for us. The Holy Spirit is there bringing us truth, and power, and healing. So, you think you've run out of patience? You think you have no more love left to give? No more compassion left to offer? Just go to the well of your heart and soul, where the Trinity has taken up residence, and drink of their supply! Your spiritual bank account awaits, and will always be full!

I implore you to claim the assurance that, no experience you will ever have will be significant enough to negate His love for you. This undeserved and unconditional love that He has for you is defined as 'GRACE - something we receive that we don't deserve.' In his book, *What's So Amazing About Grace*, Philip Yancey defines this love…."*GRACE means…there is nothing you can do to make God love you any more, AND there is nothing you can do to make God love you any less!*"

And as if this is not enough, He has empowered us with this same kind of love – the *"I Love You Anyhow"* kind of love with which He loves us - for the purpose of passing it on to those around us! Aside from His empowerment we cannot do it, but with Him 'all things are possible!'

So this is the journey on which we all tread. A journey during which the emptiness that so often haunts and cripples us, gives way to the filling of God's perfect love, bringing healing and fulfillment, and overflowing to touch those for whom God has planned ahead of time for us to love. Are you up for the journey? It will cost something. But the return is incredible! Oh that I would have known these liberating truths earlier. But it's never too late for God to reach us, redeem us, and restore us to who He plans for us to be. Because that's true my journey continued….and once again I've gotten ahead of myself, so let's go back …………

My journey to discover the true depth of God's love began when I was only a teenager [though I didn't really know what I was missing or what I was searching for]. I have always been a deep thinker and haven't ever found it easy to dismiss that which I consider the serious stuff of life. Thus I analyze life a lot. Some would say too much. As a result, in those earlier years of my life I spent a lot of time thinking about what God really meant to our family. Though we attended our home church regularly [Sunday mornings and nights and youth group on Wednesdays, where my parents were our leaders] it seemed ironic to me that this God of all creation whom we purported to believe in seemed so easily set aside whenever we were somewhere other than church. Outside of church activities, He was really rarely mentioned. As I look back, I don't know what kept Mom and Dad's faith so strong. I don't recall ever seeing them personally studying the Bible, and the only timed I observed them in prayer is when we all said table grace together before our meals. And even though it was clear that they absolutely believed in God and they were very dedicated to our church, they never seemed to discuss anything about their own spiritual walk. I wondered; shouldn't something as important as having a relationship with the God of the universe have taken a more prominent place in our family's communications – even when we weren't at church? It seemed so to me and the lack of it drove me deeper into my search.

I continually subdued 'dumb' feelings, feelings that I thought no one else could possibly understand, hang-ups that I was convinced 'well-adjusted' people just didn't have. One dangerously loses touch with oneself when life is lived out in an on-going state of denial. As I continued my pursuit for answers, while a junior in high school I begin visiting churches of all faiths, searching for one that truly demanded the 'whole' commitment that I thought God deserved from us.

During this same time I was sailing through school with good grades, good friends, and was involved in a myriad of school functions, mostly enjoying participation as an all-state debater, and a band and orchestra member. Wow, it would *appear* that I was the most 'all-together' kid in the world. It would appear – but *not so much*. Much of the time I felt like a robin in a snow storm…alone. I was constantly dealing with unfulfilled self-expectations, eliciting undeniable feelings of depression and withdrawal. But little did I know that God was using this time to help me find my rightful inheritance in Him. I had my life aside from God and my life with Him, but they were eons apart. The inner-conflict grew nearly unbearable at times. Anger management and self-discipline were difficult issues for me and I used to beat myself up every day, emotionally, for not living up to a standard that would be worthy of His Love.

I continued to drift in and out of about every kind of 'religion' I could find, trying to grab hold of something that would stick. Finally I thought I had found it, a religion whose teachings required *total reliance* on God – no human solutions – no exception. I climbed in with both feet. God would become the answer to all of life's challenges – as He should be. He would heal every hurt and give me the power to 'perform' at an acceptable level of His expectations and those of the significant others in my life. During my time in that 'religion,' I did experience answered prayer over and over again….just no personal relationship with Jesus. My journey continued to be solely about '*works*' – mine and His.

While still in my junior year of high school, I sat with my father in a hospital waiting room, anticipating the medical report of my mother's breast biopsy. The doctor came in, sat down and delivered the frightening words we so dreaded, *"Your mother has cancer. She will need radical surgery right away, and I'm afraid we can't guarantee her future."*

Instantly, I wanted to scream out the premise of my new found religion; "No No No – God heals and she doesn't have to have this!" I wanted to, but didn't, because I was being mentored that my willingness and ability to control how I responded to such challenges played a key role in God's willingness and ability to overcome the situation. I was given the premise that, if I responded with 'appropriate thinking' and behavior, He could work a healing. If not, I would get in the way of God's potential healing. Again it all depended on my *works*. Was I up to the task this time? I remained calm on the outside, collected and assuring to all around me. [I had already become an expert at playing two roles at the same time.] Oh how I worked to apply the teachings of my new religion, *to raise my thinking above the cancer claim*. I prayed. Oh how I prayed! Mom and dad were loved by so many people and so many were praying that I just had to believe He would hear and she would be healed. She was not. But a month later when mom came home, we still chose to believe that God had heard our prayers and used the skilled hands of the doctors and nurses [which was definitely not encouraged in my new found faith] to give mom what she needed. Yes mom had cancer. But we believed God had a hand in bringing her through radical surgery and back home again, and she was on her way to a full recovery. The experience seemed to validate what I was learning – if we can be strong enough to raise our thoughts above the circumstances, God will be able to heal and restore. At that point I really knew very little else about this religion. What I didn't understand then was that there was still a missing element essential to my relationship with God – *a relationship with His Son*. But I was on a journey and in His love and compassion continued to meet me on my growing edge.

I graduated with a 4 point and received a full-ride college scholarship. I was excited to visit the campus and meet my assigned roommate! I began planning my move. That summer, I had also been offered a great job in my home town. It came with a lucrative salary - for a woman and someone just out of high school. Mom thought it senseless to waste four years going to college, spending money instead of earning it. She reasoned that I could continue living at home and use the skills I had learned in High School to earn a very nice salary. As she put it, *"After all, women were meant to get married, stay home, and provide a good home for their husband and children, so really more education would just be a waste of time and money."*

She had come through the war and the depression, kept watch over three kids while dad served our military overseas, and times were tough. But she was tougher and she made it through some really difficult and scary times, keeping us all together. Her orientation of women in the work field was normal for that time in history, and I didn't want to be the one to give her any more grief. She had already suffered the anguish war time separation from dad, and she never really got over it. I didn't go to college.

Over the next two years I worked in my home town, lived with my folks, and spent a great deal of time with a very nice guy who would eventually become my husband [and unfortunately at that time - my god]. Because both he and I had only ever had a paper thin experience with *religion* and no personal relationship with Jesus Christ at all, during our dating life we became each other's whole life, security, and focus. We got married with the expectation of living happily ever after, I meeting his needs and he mine. We did everything together – great – until one evening when we didn't! He and his co-workers were to have an evening of bowling. Harmless enough wouldn't you say? But he didn't even ask me if I wanted to come along! I fell apart! Such insecurities. It was the first time since we had been married that I was excluded. It was not a good night. He felt terrible and I felt worse. That evening began a pattern whereby the more we set each other up as the 'god' that would meet each other's needs, the more responsible we felt for the other's happiness, or unhappiness, whichever the case was at any given time.

Lesson to be learned......when we allow this kind of scenario, permitting the people in our lives to become more important than God and more influential to our behavior than His Will for us, we place a responsibility on them to which they cannot possibly live up, nor should they even try. If you allow your spouse or any significant other to become your 'god,' their mistakes can shatter your sense of well-being and leaves you feeling desperate and alone, driving you to become more and more possessive and controlling. After all, who wants a god that isn't perfect; right?

Ask yourself, '*Who are the gods in your life?*' When you are feeling really happy and on top of your game, who gets the credit? When things are bad, who gets the blame? Who controls your condition? Often we allow the very people that we would least want to control us to do so, because we allow them to become a sort of god in our lives. When this happens, though from the outside it might appear we have a close relationship – candidates for the *couple of the year* - on the inside we are dying from the pain of unfulfilled expectations, reminding us that we may really not be loved at all. A relationship that depends on *performance* in order to maintain its validity has a shelf life only as long as its creative ability to do *good works* sufficient enough to prove it's worth.

And so it was with our young marriage. Our relationship often hung together by a thread....a very thin thread. Other things began to help 'fill' our lives. God blessed us with three beautiful children and many friends. We went to church whenever it was convenient. We continued to look for a church that would have 'all' the answers. None did. None ever will. As a good friend once advised us, "*If you ever find a perfect church, don't join it, because then it won't be perfect anymore!*" Such wisdom!

I continued to find a sense of fulfillment in the people around me. Never taking relationships lightly and having the nature of a 'fixer,' I often became deeply involved in the issues of those whom I befriended. Before learning the liberating truths we read about in this book, too often that 'connection' cost me more than I was emotionally prepared to survive. I still don't take relationships lightly. I still have the God-given nature of a 'fixer.' And to be sure, we are truly commanded to love one another as God loves us and show it by our actions. But it is important to understand that when we do we are putting our soul out there on the line. Thus, it is imperative that we invite God and His purposes into every relationship from the very beginning. Loving deeply and giving freely opens the heart to a great vulnerability. As C. S. Lewis so aptly puts it in his book, *Surprised by Joy*, *"If you love deeply you're going to hurt badly."* What a statement of truth. But in the end - it is so worth it!

I have always felt more mentally and emotionally healthy when my life is filled with making a positive difference in the lives of those around me. I guess all along my inner-being has sub-consciously responded to a combination of my need to do good works and God's purpose for us, to love and help one another. In a discussion with a wise friend one day we dissected the true incentive that drove us to get involved with helping others, determining that in all honesty, sometimes it's really for ourselves and the fulfillment we enjoy when doing so. In the early days of my life's journey I realized that my willingness to serve was often driven by misguided self-fulfilling reasons.

That said, as you may have guessed by now, my friends all too often became my security blanket. The church provided an arena in which I cultivated that which I considered to be meaningful relationships, with those whom I believed understood me and my spiritual journey. At that time, my husband didn't, so he became more and more excluded from what was going on inside me – down in the depths of my soul. This laid the ground work for misunderstandings and shallow connections. His frustrations often came across as a 'holier than thou' kind of judgment; and mine, as the 'victim.' Fertile ground for Satan to sow seeds of destruction.

Inside I was crying out for my husband to intimately connect with my spirit – to become my soul mate. It didn't happen and I resented it. I allowed myself to question; "Why doesn't he care as much about my well being as others do?" "What is wrong with Him - With Me?" Was this marriage worth the pain? More and more we lived as strangers under the same roof.

In Bruce Larson's book, *No Longer Strangers*, he shares a quote from a Priest, Samuel Johnson, *"This radical style of life in Christ has many pains, but anything less has few pleasures."* My heart longed for a radical love and my soul was not satisfied with anything less. Yet, I became too fragile to be open, too protective to be vulnerable, and I still didn't realize that this love for which I so yearned will never be fully found in human relationships. It can come only from its true source – the God who created us!

Bruce goes on to implore, *"The more we guard our lives and the more we protect ourselves, the more lonely and withdrawn we become. As we discover in Jesus Christ both the example we need and the power to live as He lived, we go through the pain* *into a life of <u>deep</u> <u>loving</u> relationships. Through this kind of radical obedience we discover that we are no longer strangers."*

We didn't really fight much. We didn't determine not to like each other. But as my husband and I became more and more guarded about being vulnerable with one another, unable to affirm each other in the way for which each of us were internally crying out, each day drew us further and further into a status of 'strangers.' The more we withdrew – the more we withdrew. Then as you will read in Chapter One, one dark and desperate evening, through an incident and a discussion that followed, God helped bring healing, and growth, giving us the incentive and ability to become vulnerable enough to begin affirming one another in the midst of our imperfections. If you haven't yet read *No Longer Strangers*, I encourage you to take the time to do so after you finish this book. It is chocked full of life-changing insights!

As the old saying goes, we become 'too soon old and too late smart'… Such has been the case in my life….so many liberating truths I wish I had learned sooner! Along the journey, as God has faithfully and patiently revealed His golden nuggets of truth, bringing me healing and restoration, I made a heartfelt commitment to Him that one day I would figure out a way to pass them along. It is my heart's driving desire that God would use me in some small way, that others might not find the journey quite so long or quite so difficult.

God has allowed such joy and fulfillment in giving me numerous opportunities to share the stories. One of those opportunities came in the earliest days of my Christian walk when I was able to come alongside an amazing Evangelist, and help him in the development of Biblically based family Bible studies. His friendship remains one of God's dearest and most precious gifts. Another has been the great privilege of participating in Christian film production, along with the development of a seminar which I have been blessed to teach in conjunction with film showings throughout the U. S. and abroad, helping thousands come to a relationship with Christ. In these most recent years the workshops and retreats I have been privileged to teach have thrilled my heart as God has used this imperfect vase to pour out His message that, *He loves us anyhow*! And now….the book you hold. May it bless you with new insights to receive the great love that God has for you, and the vulnerability to share it with others.

Let's get back to the journey….because all of the wonderful opportunities I mention didn't happen for a long time, and not without a lot of refining. Thank God He never gives up on us!

In an attempt to continue protecting myself, I remained very selective about when and to whom I would open up. On my husband's part [as with his father] *opening up* was never a part of his nature, so this was a comfortable life-style for him. As a result, we continued to systematically shut each other out. Our relationship vacillated from a satisfying and exciting physical relationship to a shallow nearly non-existent heart-to-heart connection. We began to become more and more sensitive to each other's looks and comments. *Performance* was everything. I knew how to play that game – I had grown up perfecting it. More and more I realized that the *soul mate* I longed for would have to be found elsewhere. This clearly is a dangerous state-of-mind, and only honorably managed when God is truly on the throne of your heart! I wasn't there yet.

I began to turn to others with whom I could share my heart - others who 'really understood me.' The problem? All others really understood about me was the *me* that I allowed them to see. How could they truly understand the real me, when I was carefully protecting myself from being open and vulnerable enough to let them see the real me? Honestly, I didn't even like or understand myself! I came across as solid, self sufficient, and in need of nothing, while all the while my 'self-concept' was traveling through life as though it were riding in the front seat of a roller coaster – with high peaks and deep valleys! I had not yet grasped the truth that, though life can sometimes rock our 'self-concept' to the core, our 'self-image' cannot be damaged by anything life throws at it. The truth is, you and I have been made in the 'image of God' and no life experience can ever change that. Josh McDowell has an electrifying series called, *His Image My Image*. Its healing message is dynamic, and it has been my great privilege to observe many hearts healed and confidence restored as a result of such a liberating truth. We will further 'mine' this uplifting and healing truth in a later chapter of this book.

Before understanding this profound truth, in my young adult life my 'self concept' rose and fell along with my sense of security in the relationships I had. Though the relational style I had developed brought me lots of desired attention [not always the healthy kind] and well meaning [or sometimes not so much] advice, it carried with it a false sense of fulfillment. Girl friend or guy friend relationships – no matter how significant they seemed at the time – in reality were all surface and based on 'need' rather than on a Christ-based, *'I Love You Anyhow'* kind of love. So, whenever a close relationship would crash – as one nearly always does when built on human co-dependencies – I came away from it worse than if I had never known it. That is until one day when God taught me how to face the ugly realities of a relationship gone awry, and still be willing to say, "I love you anyhow." When I did, we became life-long sisters in Christ. You will read more about this Holy Spirit led experience in the Affirmation and Vulnerability Chapter.

I had established a pattern of feeding my addiction – my need for affirmation and acceptance and my search for an unconditional love that I had grown up without, and which continued to be absent in my adult life.

In listening to others, I have become keenly aware that the quest for this kind of love is definitely not just mine alone. I have listened to story after story of men and women alike who have become like a leach, attaching to their current closest 'chum.' Some suffer unthinkable abuses due to their inability to walk away from an unhealthy relationship. Some have turned to the bar scene to drown their pain in the bottle. And for others, in their quest for that 'just right' person with whom they felt they could experience the kind of secure love they sought, they have resigned themselves to playing the dangerous intimate dating game – one that inevitably, though it may feel good for the moment, won't last long. I was tempted. But I could not – too much fear and guilt to carry through with it. Though my quest brought many moments of agonizing loneliness, I continued to cry out to the Lord for His help, and He continued to meet me on my growing edge, remaining my SOURCE and [as He promises] 'the object of my affections.' The assurance remains that His LOVE WILL NEVER RUN OUT!

As you will read in the ensuing chapters, time after time God has 'shown up' whenever there has been an impasse, not only in my marriage but in the lives of countless others with whom we have had the privilege of sharing His love. Though I was learning more about God – and about myself, the journey continued to be pretty bumpy as I pursued my walk toward Him. As I continued to search for God's Will for me, my involvement with 'religion' [the church scene] soon became a disaster. I found that using the gifts and talents God gave me, within the church, was a very fulfilling way to do *good works* and connect with like-minded people. All should be positive – right? Not always, because my deep-seeded motives were not always selfless, and because in the end my *works* were becoming my *religion* rather than depending on a *relationship* with God. Wayne Jacobson has authored a number of books, one of which is, *He Loves Me – He Loves Me Not*. In this book he sums it up brilliantly. *"….religion offers us elusions of earning acceptance, but it is only a cheap substitute for the reality of life in Him – relationship!"* Wayne is so right. Religious works will never substitute for relational fulfillment with God and with one another. Finding time to read Wayne's books is truly a worthwhile goal.

Not yet knowing all of these golden nuggets of truth at this point in my journey, I continued to find fulfillment in my religious works, and relational dynamics at home remained strained – physical connection less sought – conversation less existent – two people living alone, together. Something strange though, when I tried to address those things I assumed to be common struggles, my husband was clueless as to what they were. He was happy in our marriage, he insisted. Really? How could that be? This begged the point that perhaps it really was all me – or maybe not – perhaps it was only me that so desperately sought answers that I was willing to press on through the icky process to get them. And though my search for answers took me to about every 'self helps' genre available…church, seminars, workshops, books, it all seemed to present answers only to the symptoms, never addressing the real problem – the burning desire to know and experience a love so unconditional that I – yes even I – could not cause it to go away.

So what is this "I Love You Anyhow' kind of love?" I didn't know. In fact the first time a friend posed the concept to me I was very offended, wondering, 'What have I done now that requires the anyhow?' You'll read of that life-changing encounter later. For now, suffice to say that though the journey to its revelation was filled with pot holes and pain, the truths learned far outweigh the price paid to learn them!

One revealing golden nugget of truth that I learned along the way......every problem is a spiritual one. Therefore every *real* solution must be a spiritual one. Anything less than the healing of the Holy Spirit is a salve that temporarily sooths, but in the end delays the spiritual surgery God desires, the cutting out of the erroneous theology of I love you "when" or "if" or "because," and the implanting of a love so great that it cannot and will not be derailed from its intended purpose. The truth is, there is only one source for this kind of love and once discovered and accepted we cannot contain the whole of it. We are compelled to pass it on!

Still another golden nugget....
The fear of rejection is a powerful deterrent to experiencing the healing transformation of unconditional love, due to its inherent lack of transparency – even and especially with God. Dare we let Him where He can see the dark that exists deep down inside our soul? He already does! But while we are in a state of denial, we mistakenly think we have hidden our imperfections from everyone around us - even from Him. We haven't! I can't proclaim this often enough; He knows us completely, yet He goes on 'loving us anyhow!' We need not fear rejection from Him. He has already proven on the cross that His love came first – before our repentance, before our restoration, and before our reconciliation with Him and others. Once we stop fearing His rejection and return His embrace, His Holy Spirit is free to work in our lives, helping us clean up our act!

Jesus made sure that not only would we be able to *see* how much He was willing to sacrifice to prove His love for us, but we would also *hear* it. As He was dying, He looked down at those around the cross and declared to them, and to all generations to come, "*I LOVE YOU ANYHOW.*" It sounded like this: "*Father, forgive them for they know not what they do*" – a forgiveness granted *before* it was deserved, or any attempt was made to earn it. He proved loud and clear that, *love comes first.* In that one act, and through those affirming words, God loudly proclaims to you and me "*I LOVE YOU ANYHOW*" – even unto death!

Because He has already chosen to love us right where we are, we can count on the fact that He has also already prepared a plan for our lives....a 'good' and 'prosperous' plan....one that is seamless from this world to the next, because it is an eternal plan. I needed desperately to know that there was a plan for my life that didn't depend on my performance, one that no broken relationship, cancer, poverty, nor lack of any kind, could rob from me. We all yearn to be assured that God's plan for us is a good one and that He will be there to see us through it. And He assures us ....

> *"For I know the plans I have for you," declares the Lord, "plans to prosper you and not to harm you, plans to give you hope and a future. Then you will call upon me and come and pray to me, and I will listen to you. You will seek me and find me when you seek me with all your heart."* Jeremiah 29:11-13

This does not give us license to ignore God's instruction, living with no regard to His Will for us. But it does assure us that no matter how badly we mess up; He will still love us and He is always standing by to enable us to live in a manner in which we can receive His fullest blessings. He is never willing to give up on our coming to the realization of the depth of His love. And thus, He has never given up on me...so the journey continues....

Let's see, where was I...married with children and a paper thin experience with religion that found us pretty much giving up on going to church all together. We had sold our mobile home and moved to a new part of town where we bought our first 'real' house. We were very excited and though things were far from perfect, we settled in to be the best partners and parents we knew how to be – sometimes falling miserably short of our goal, and frequently verbally and emotionally beating up on ourselves – and each other - for those failures.

But remember, God had a plan. One day in the process of walking our two children around the block I looked up to see a longtime friend coming towards us, a friend whom I hadn't seen nor had contact with for well over two years. It was a happy surprise to discover that unbeknown to either of us, in our separate re-locations we had moved only around the corner from one another. It was great to have the opportunity to re-acquaint ourselves with one another. What I didn't know then was that it was all a part of that 'plan' God had in store for us. It was a divine appointment. She seemed genuinely excited to see us and since she had no clue we had given up on the church scene [in our earlier acquaintance it had been a significant part of our lives] she enthusiastically inquired about where we were worshipping now, asking; *"Can your daughter go to Bible School next week with my son."* What was I to say? I knew deep down inside that our children needed to be in church, that somehow even though it hadn't worked for us, our kids needed to know the things of God. I said *"yes."* But as I readied our precious daughter for the first day of Bible School, I really wondered why. God knew.

She loved it, and at the end of her great week's experience we were invited to her Bible School program. She was bubbling over with the idea that they would be singing for us and "we would be so happy to see how good they were." Of course we went. As parents we all tend to do things for our kids that we may not do for anyone else.

We were a bit nervous and protective about entering the 'church scene' again, however we found the experience very pleasant. We continued to go each Sunday thereafter. We listened. We observed. We heard and saw something different. In the car on the way home one Sunday we discussed one curious difference...they seldom ever mentioned God's disappointment in us as a human race. Oh they made it clear that He has expectations for our behavior and that there will be natural consequences for our actions, but they also proposed something new to us. Though God's desire is for us to live as He has instructed us to, knowing that there will be times when we fail to do so, He sent Jesus to pay the price for our failures and advocate for us before the throne of God.

Another emphasis was on a Biblical character named Saul [whom Jesus later renamed Paul] and whom we knew nothing about at the time. Paul was a New Testament Apostle who had once denounced Jesus, even killing those who followed Him. Later, having been radically turned around by the message of the love of God through Jesus, He took that message to crowds everywhere. According to these accounts, many who heard Paul responded to Jesus, receiving His love and forgiveness, even though they had done nothing to deserve it. In fact many had earlier stood on the periphery of the jeering crowds calling out in regard to Jesus' fate, *"Crucify Him – Crucify Him."* In Acts we read the account of their response to Peter's message after the crucifixion of Jesus'....

> *"Therefore let all Israel be assured of this: God has made this Jesus, whom you crucified, both Lord and Christ." When the people heard this, they were cut to the heart and said to Peter and the other apostles, "Brothers, what shall we do?" Peter replied, "Repent and be baptized, every one of you, in the name of Jesus Christ so that your sins may be forgiven. And you will receive the gift of the Holy Spirit. The promise is for you and your children and for all who are far off – for all whom the Lord our God will call...Those who accepted his message were baptized and about three thousand were added to their number that day."* Acts 2:36-39, 41

How great a love is this, that God would so fully accept those who had played such a key role in the killing of His own Son? And why?? I strived to understand and yet remained as one standing outside and looking through a glass at others who 'got it,' and not wanting them to know I didn't. Faking it, I yearned for a clearer understanding of what Paul's followers had found. I became an expert at appearing to *walk the walk*, and *talk the talk*. In my quest, I took advantage of every opportunity that might help me gain more insights. I attended (as well as taught) Sunday school, taught Bible School, and participated in every special church event offered, thinking it all might give me a glimpse into what I was missing. I couldn't seem to shake the deep desire within for true affirmation that God could love me – *just as I was*. I knew that, though the accolades I was receiving for all my serving efforts at church were great, they were still based on *performance*, and not really an acceptance of the truly mixed up person who was struggling for release within my soul.

So I continued the masquerade. After all, we don't volunteer to tell people where we fall short if we don't have to, not if we want to continue to receive their admiration and affirmations. As far as anyone could see I was just as devoted a 'religious' person as anyone out there. And, actually I was. But *religion* gives us no security and no future, only rules and judgments that no one can ever truly live up to. Religion is based on *dos* and *don'ts* and acceptable punishments whenever we fail at either ... something from which I had been trying to escape for years. It is a game too often played within church walls, preventing the nurturing of souls that God desires to redeem. So, not knowing the difference, I went along playing the game. No one confronted me personally with the truth of redemption from myself and my sin, and I wasn't about to dump all the skeletons out of my closet upon which they could then pass judgment. So I continued to make every effort to 'work out' my relationships with God and with others in a manner that would eventually bring peace. Sometimes it seemed to be working – but not really.

The Pastor in our new found church became one of our dearest friends. He was real and accessible. His love seemed to be genuine – the real deal. Whenever we had a family joy or tragedy he was there, not ever to pass judgment, but to either mourn or rejoice with us. Still today we walk beside each other in our personal and family joys and sorrows, enjoying an indescribable kind of 'Agape' love that does not depend on performance.

As this dear pastor continued to walk beside me, God continued to script me into His story, and so the journey continued ....

In the fall there was to be a retreat for the ladies in the church. I <u>Did</u> <u>Not</u> go to ladies retreats. I'd heard about such gatherings in 'Christian' settings and couldn't imagine it. Just to think about it, the insecurities it stirred up in me were overwhelming! Even recalling the battle being waged for my heart and soul back then wants to conflict my spirit yet today. What if I were to be called upon to really 'open up' and share my 'inner thoughts' and struggles? What if the schedule was to include a 'sharing time,' a time when we could all 'confess' our failures and humbly ask for forgiveness so we could pray for each other? No – I would not be going.

But Charlene kept gently nudging and assuring me that, *"she would really love to have me there."* Really? We didn't even know each other all that well yet. She seemed trustworthy. Finally, at the last minute, I decided to take the plunge and attend. While driving to the church <u>serious</u> doubts crept back in that threatened to turn me around, but since I was already packed and on my way, I kept going. And though I was oblivious to it, I was right on target with God's plan for me.

Saturday morning opened up with some wonderful devotional time, after which we were all challenged to go find a secluded spot in which we could meditate and fill out the questionnaire that had been handed to us. I remember thinking, *"Oh boy – here it comes. We're going to divulge all our issues and confusion on a piece of paper now, so we can come back together and have others analyze our condition and suggest yet more possible solutions."* I took my paper with a heavy heart, chastising myself; *"I told you so, dummy!"* as I trudged off to find my secluded spot.

It had been dark when we had arrived the evening before, so I had no clue of the beauty encompassing the whole place. As I walked through an open field on that incredibly beautiful morning, I found myself surrounded by a scene so breathtaking that one could scarcely take it in. Not until I found that big rock jetting out of the ground and begging to be occupied, did I realize that God Himself had also arrived, in that same very carefully selected spot, and was awaiting our visit. My face warmed with the morning sun and the cool grass snuggled up between my bare toes as I opened my 'questionnaire' and began a most indescribable, intimate experience with God.

Like a foretaste of Heaven, God sat there with me, seeing right through me - flaws and all - and I felt Him love me anyhow! As I worked through the questionnaire I realized it was not at all about my failures but rather all about His Grace - an unconditional love for me! I hadn't really ever given Him a chance, had I? I had been so busy protecting myself from hurt and disclosure that I had never been vulnerable enough to allow my heart a truly emotional connection with Him, nor with anyone else. I had been playing the 'religious' game and failing at it for so long that I thought my failures represented failure in my relationship with God. They did not. They never do.

The questions I answered reached deep down into my soul and begged for honesty. Was I truly committed to hearing God? I thought so, but as I reflected I had to ask myself: *"When I pray, how much time do I ever devote to listening to Him? Or do I just talk at Him, hanging up on Him with a quick Amen, as soon as I'm done speaking?"*

Next question: *"How willing was I to put Him aside whenever I went places, said things, or did things that I knew would disappoint Him?"* I had grown up with this, knowing in my heart it was not right, yet continued to conduct a good share of my life without consciously allowing Him to be a part of it. Did I really think He wasn't with me all the time; that I could hide from Him?

The Spirit dug deep down into my soul with His presence, as I pondered three pages of these kinds of soul searching questions. I still have that questionnaire tucked in my Bible as a reminder of that day – on the rock – wrapped up in the presence of God. And much of the journey He has led me on since is recorded on the following pages. As you read the accounts of God's faithfulness, I trust as He instructed, inspired and healed me, and the many with whom He has allowed me to minister, He will do likewise for you.

I began a new and authentic relationship with God that day, promising Him that I would partner with Him to do all I could to mesh the 'two mes' together into the 'one me' He had created me to be. In my new found enthusiasm I promised Him, *"God whatever opportunities you bring into my life that will help me know and follow you better, I will say yes."*

I had a renewed HOPE – a new kind of faith that maybe, just maybe, I was going to be able to live a life of open authenticity before Him and in my relationships with others. I've come to call it a, 'what you see is what you get' transparency, with no hidden agenda.

Riding high on the experience, I drove home bursting with the desire to better love my husband and share with him all that bubbled within, declaring how it was going to make a huge difference in the way I lived out not only my love for God, but also for him and for others. As I have since become aware of the character of the disciple Peter, I am more and more convinced that, in his unabashed enthusiasm for life [and the many blunders he made] he and I must have some of the same genes!

While God was at work in my life that day, His adversary was not standing idly by, and he was determined not to allow my new-found connection with God to make a lasting difference. He began planting thoughts into my mind...*After all it was just a 'high' right?* Be aware – if there's the slightest opportunity to do so, Satan will slip into the most vulnerable areas of your life in an attempt to steal the joy and assurance that God Wills for you. I thought I would never again lose that peaceful fully loved feeling of that morning on the rock. Wrong!

As I drove into the driveway and walked through the door, I was greeted with questions and reminders of how, once again I had not 'lived up' to expectations. *"Good grief, where have you been? When you left you said you were going to be home two hours ago* [back before the convenience of cell phone calls made it easy to update folks on your ETA while on the road] *and now we're probably going to be late for the ball game!"* My husband is really a good guy, but I was a constant challenge for him, and he was right. I had promised to be home in time to comfortably make it to our son's ball game. I hadn't. I had let him down. But instead of understanding his frustration to my broken promise, I responded on the defense, with anything but love. He was making a true statement - I heard judgment; *"you are not okay!"*

Why did I so quickly let these kinds of incidences overpower the message God poured out to me on the cross? The message of, 'you are okay – not perfect but okay, and worthy of love, even when you blow it.' Why do we allow what we perceive to be a negative to ring so much louder in our heads than the positive we know to be the truth? The Bible gives us a clue, because we battle not against flesh and blood but against the darkness of the powers and principalities of the evil one. Ours is a spiritual battle!

> *"For our struggle is not against flesh and blood, but against the rulers, against the authorities, against the powers of this dark world and against the spiritual forces of evil in the heavenly realms."* Ephesians 6:12

Communications can be a battlefield, won by the devil every time, if we don't find a way to apply God's principles in the midst of them. It would have helped our marriage so much if, in the midst of such scenarios, we had been aware of the principle of 'being generous in the gap.' Be sure to absorb this technique as it is presented in the Communications Chapter. Once again it is one of the many wonderful nuggets of truth from Andy Stanley's study on "Love That Lasts Forever." The peace you will find by implementing just this one communication technique will be a monumental gain in your relationships!

Since these truths were not yet a part of my experience [we grow too soon old and too late smart] my new little 'spiritual' world fell apart. And I truly resented the 'real' world crashing in on me so soon! I immediately employed my learned behavior, a way of protecting myself, clamming up and resentfully determining not to share any of my beautiful experience on the rock, protecting its preciousness from further damage. This is a common victory of Satan's, to discourage us from sharing how God has blessed us, so as to prevent the passing along of the blessing. His lie: others won't care or understand anyway. And he even attempts to make it seem as though the supposed blessing hadn't really happened after all. *God spoke with you? Really? I don't think so.* Yet in your heart you know He did. Now you're conflicted and unsure, easily thrown off track from the desired goal.

That would be me at this point. I hadn't stopped to realize that one who hadn't sat with me on that rock that day [not felt the warmth of the sun on their face and the cool grass between their toes, nor heard the voice of God in their soul] could not possibly be in the same spiritual place that I was. It wasn't fair to expect them to be. It wasn't all about me! It was about God pressing the truth into my life that He 'loves me anyhow.' And it was about His desire for me to pass that truth along to others – even in the face of disappointment. I didn't. Had I failed Him beyond restitution? No - He still loved me anyhow.

He continued His plan for my life. Over the years He has graciously allowed me to be used for His purpose. In doing so another great privilege He has given me is that of developing and teaching workshop called; "Created and Redeemed for a Purpose." What an incredible joy to get to encourage so many people that God has a purpose for their lives, and that purpose includes loving those around them with so great a love that He delivers healing through the process! Let's go on to what followed the day on the rock…the next step of the journey…

The next step in God's plan for me was an invitation in the fall of nineteen seventy one, to attend some Billy Graham counselor training sessions. A friend issued the invitation, telling me that attendees were going to be prepared to share the scriptures on how God sent His love to us through Jesus. He explained that, following the film, *Two A Penny* [to be shown in our local cinema] the counselors who had been trained to share their faith would be paired up with those who responded to the invitation to pray to receive Jesus, further declaring that I would be a great candidate as one of the 'counselors.' Are you kidding me! All I could think of was, *"if he only knew of my inner confusion he would never have even considered asking me to participate!"* I said *"no"* – adamantly and repeatedly.

Though my rock experience remained real and sacred to me – my sense of value did not. After all, I had blown it not ten minutes after arriving home! Let's face it; I had let Him down again and I was too confused to imagine helping someone else understand the unconditional love of God! Thus, the answer to my friend's continued plea remained negative. That is until one quite moment when God's gentle voice once again penetrated my heart, asking, *"Remember that day on the rock? The day we talked and you agreed that whatever opportunity I brought to you to help you know me better, your answer would be yes?"* I knew instantly that I had to go. I would go and learn what there was for me to learn, but with no intention of doing any 'counseling' – just for me to personally learn. I declared my intention on my registration, and the training presenters were okay with that.

Over three Sundays of sessions, I listened. I learned. I came home and did my homework. I read compelling scriptures about how God created us, how sin had entered the world through Adam and Eve, and how God had sent His Son, Jesus, to die on the cross to pay for that sin. Nothing new – really. I'd heard it all before. But it was so cool now. The little tract we used actually noted the addresses of where to find those claims in the Bible! I began to wonder, 'maybe now I had somehow 'arrived' at some sort of level of 'okayness,' one that I had been observing in others for so long. Now that I had enough head knowledge to actually sit down with someone and explain the Gospel to them. I must have broken through an important new level of religious experience! That felt good. Wow, it seemed now that I could almost be a preacher! So….I changed my mind and said 'yes' to volunteering to serve as a counselor.

I went to the showing, nervous, but willing to counsel responders following the film. But God was not willing, because He clearly says that '*He is not willing that any should perish.*' He is not satisfied with one's head knowledge, false sense of security, and paper-thin experience with religion. He wants us to partake in the *real deal*. Thus, that night, as counselors and seekers were paired up to speak with one another, I got no one! WHAT? My pride and sensitivity to rejection cried out inside of me; "*God, surely you aren't going to let all of my effort and vulnerability in making myself available go to waste, are you?*" God is not fooled with our self-righteousness. He is not blind to our ignorance. Nor is He satisfied with *head knowledge* that stands apart from a *heart transplant*.

It was not until I stood frustrated, feeling the pains of what I deemed yet another rejection, and eves dropping on others as they shared the plan of salvation with their seekers, that God allowed the scales to fall from my eyes and opened my ears to truly hear. As my heart began to listen, embarrassed and horrified, the thought rushed in that perhaps I truly was not yet a child of God. Impossible! I had been going to church for 30 years at this point. And hadn't I had that experience on the rock? I believed. Did I really need to tell God I was willing to *receive* His gift of salvation? But wait. I ask myself, "*Who am I really trusting for my salvation?*"

I quickly thought back to that questionnaire from that day on the rock, still tucked in my Bible. I recalled my answer to that very question - worded a bit differently, but now it screamed out to me! "*If I should come face-to-face with God and He should ask, 'why should I let you into Heaven, what would my answer be?*" The answer I had written on my questionnaire had been a long dissertation about all the things '*I*' had done and all the things '*I*' was willing to '*do*' for Him. Sure, it included how much I loved Him and how I wanted to be with Him. But even then, full of so many '*I*s! The glaring truth was absent; the truth that declared what *HE* had done for me in sending Jesus to die for my sin! I suddenly realized that with every "*I*" claiming a reason for why He should allow me into Heaven, I was in effect driving yet another nail into Jesus' hands. I was claiming credit for what He bled and died for that day on the cross. He had said, "*It is finished.*" Yet, I was claiming that it really wasn't! I was still working on all my reasons why He should accept me, when He had already declared loud and clear on the cross that He already loved me! My reasons for being acceptable were so full of '*I*s that I had sadly let the sacrificial work of Jesus done for me on the cross go unmentioned. What a travesty – and after thirty years in the church!

I wrestled with how this could be. After all He knew '*I*' was trying and that '*I*' believed in Him. Whoops; there I go again - more 'Is.' The truth is that the Bible says even the devils 'believe' that Jesus is who He says He is. And surely they will not be in Heaven! So my 'believing' didn't set me apart for the Kingdom, any more than it did them.

My mind whirled and my heart pounded as I struggled with the questions; If I was right and the claim of needing to 'receive' Jesus was wrong, then maybe going to church and striving to live right, doing good things and loving others were enough - right? But what if they were right and I was wrong? What if just *believing* Jesus is who He says He is, while yet *trusting* in my own efforts to make me right with God instead of what Jesus had done on the cross, failed me? What did I have to lose then? Everything!

That night on the way home from the film presentation, my mind whirled as I wept hot tears, mixed with confusion and regret. I had pretty much always maintained control of things, control of myself and all that I was able to control around me. To give up control and totally trust someone else – Jesus – with my eternal destiny was so frightening! Yet, as I continued to search my soul a strange kind of freedom and joy crept in. I confessed to the Lord that I was really tired, tired of trying so hard to live up, and failing. I was tired of being on the outside looking in. I was weary of trusting in myself and my own feeble efforts to make me right with God. Try as I may I always fell short. The load was too heavy. I struggled to give up my perceived control, but I determined that if trusting Jesus alone couldn't make me worthy of Heaven, it just was never going to happen. I was done. Sometimes when we come to the end of ourselves we make room for God to move in.

Unable to see through the river of tears tumbling down my face, I pulled off the freeway. Pouring out my heart, my confessions, and my apologies, I began telling Jesus that I wanted to receive His gift of forgiveness and salvation. I wanted to transfer my trust to Him, instead of relying on my works, to become right with God.

And as always, God was there to meet me on my growing edge. I may have come to the end of myself and cried 'done,' but as I resigned from tasking myself with the job of becoming 'right' with God, He continued His purpose, to love me just as I was, redeeming me, and giving me the right to become His child....

> *"Yet to all who received him, to those who believed in his name, he gave the right to become children of God."* John 1:12

Later, in sharing my faith walk with a dear friend, she summed it up quite brilliantly, saying, *"I think you were so inoculated with religion that you couldn't catch Christianity."* When I transferred my trust from myself to Him, I moved from 'religion' to a 'relationship' - a relationship with a Savior that had loved me too much to ever give up on me. He feels the same about you. If you haven't already, trust Him and His finished work on the cross. You will never be sorry!

As I looked back over my journey it was as though I had been sitting in church pews all my life awaiting some sort of transformation to take place that would one day make me into the kind of 'Christian' I perceived others around me to be…wondering, *"How long will this take, Lord?"* And now I smile thinking, *"How long would I need to stand in the garage before I would become a car?"* It's never going to happen! The church does not make Christians – Christians make up the Church.

The troubling picture that had played over and over again in my mind, of standing before God some day while He weighed my 'good' deeds against my 'failures,' and determined whether or not I was worthy of entering His Kingdom, no longer plagued me. Because, now I could join Timothy in his proclamation, *"I know in whom I have believed and I am persuaded that He is able to keep that which I have committed unto Him until that day!"* II Timothy 1:12

As a child, we sing of this declaration; *"Jesus loves me this I know, for the Bible tells me so. Little ones to Him belong. They are weak but He is strong."* Now for me, these words were real.

The Bible tells us that no one can pluck from the hand of the Lord those who belong to Him. Indeed He is able to keep us in the palm of His hand for all Eternity! Thus, I am persuaded to believe that when we trust in Christ alone to make us right before God, we are assured of spending eternity in Heaven with Him. And now I know that we don't have to wait until we get there to see if it all works out!

> *"….. God has given us eternal life, and this life is in his Son. He who has the Son has life; he who does not have the Son of God does not have life. I write this to you who believe in the name of the Son of God, so that you may know that you have eternal life."* I John 5: 11-13

The hardest part of this experience for me? Admitting that all those years of effort had not already made me a Christian. I had played the game well, fooled a lot of people, even myself on occasion, but not Him. For the first time in my life I understood the depth of the truth that Jesus proclaimed on the cross, "I Love You Anyhow." And I knew without a doubt that His words were meant for me personally. And I can declare today, without a doubt, that they are met for you also, because He has declared that it is not His will that anyone should perish!

Just as we can trust Jesus' finished work on the cross to make us right before God, we can also trust Him to help us live out His purpose for our lives. As we each pursue our own journey to fit into the plans God has for us, we need to be patient with ourselves. Gaining an understanding of God's Will and His plan for us takes time and a willingness to be open to His instructions and disciplines. We can't give up on ourselves. He will never give up on us. Even though sometimes our best efforts seem to result in poor choices that ultimately lead to regrets and undesired consequences, *He loves us anyhow*. Sometimes it may not feel like it, as we experience inevitable trials that the Bible refers to as His chastening of those whom He loves. But be confident that when this happens it is Him allowing us to experience disciplines that will redirect us back to Him. In the meantime, He never gives up on us. We may walk away from Him but He will always stand firm, awaiting our return. He will always be there to meet us on our growing edge!

In those first years as a 'new creature' [a 'baby' in Christ] I spent most of my free waking hours devouring the Bible and listening to Christian radio. I couldn't get enough because now it was no longer about a laborious religious effort – it was about a relationship with a God who loved and accepted me for exactly who I was. There were up days and down days. I learned very quickly that I hadn't been delivered from myself – only from my sin. When I failed, He was there to encouragement me. When I despaired, He was there to comfort. He sent brothers and sisters in Christ to stand with me – with us – in the laborious task of living out a Christian marriage, while still existing in human skin. In many ways life was not a lot different than in the past. Only now, I was not driven by fear and obligation, but by a deep sense of gratitude for the love He poured out on me. I yearned for all my family and friends to experience this liberating truth.

When I placed my trust in Christ In October of 1971, I also implored Him to give me the opportunity to tell my family and friends what I now knew to be absolutely true; God knows every good and bad thing about us, and he loves us anyhow. My heart bled for those like me, who sat inside the walls of the church searching for truth and hope but not finding it, often because Christians were too busy condemning and judging those who didn't live up to established expectations. They were often consumed with playing God instead of embracing hurts in a way that God could reach down through them and redeem the lost! I have heard the theory that, we are the only animal species I know of that actually kill their wounded instead of trying to help them. Why? Could it be that we have not yet grasped the truth of the love that Jesus came to bring? God has asked – no He's commanded – that you and I be in the business of loving, and leave the task of changing people to Him. In the 14th chapter of Romans, He chastises us a bit by challenging us to remember that others belong to Him and not us, and that He is perfectly able to cause them to do as He wants them to do. We need to pledge to get ourselves out of the 'changing business' and dive whole heartedly into the 'loving' business, to which we have been commissioned!

Not wanting to interfere with God's plan for the lives of my loved ones, yet yearning for them to know and understand His unconditional love for them and His great desire to have them trust Him with their lives, I pleaded with God to touch those around me. God began answering those prayers.

As I mentioned earlier, my husband was a good man, perhaps as insecure as I was, but faithful and committed to our marriage. His childhood, like mine, was void of true understanding of a relationship with Jesus, thus the "fruit of the Spirit" described in Galatians, was sometimes sadly missing in both of our lives. But, he too was on a journey, and God was there meeting him on his growing edge. Not long after my new awakening, during a Billy Graham Crusade in Minnesota, while chaperoning our youth group, he too placed his trust in Jesus. God is good!

Shortly after, I recall sitting on the edge of my son's bed one evening, attempting to adequately answer his nine year old inquiry about why anyone would continue to try to please God once they knew that no matter what they did He would love them anyhow. It was late October when our son posed this 'deeply theological' question, and Christmas was in the air at our house. The Holy Spirit led me to answer his question with another question in return – one that appealed to a little boy's anticipation of the gifts he anticipated seeing under the tree on Christmas morn…

Personal Reflection:
"Son, what if I told you that whatever you do from now till Christmas won't stop daddy and I from loving you and giving you all the good gifts on your Christmas list and more – even if you make mistakes and do things that you know we really don't want you to do —- how would you feel about still wanting to make us happy? Do you think you would deliberately want to do things that would hurt us?"

His eyes grew big as he excitedly blurted out, *"Oh no, mommy, I would really love you and want to make you happy. Wow I couldn't make you sad when you were going to give me all the things that make me happy."*

"That's how it is with God, dear. I really want to love Him and make Him happy too, because He has given me all I could ever ask for and more – He loves me so much He gave me Jesus, and because of Him, God forgives me and promises that He will love me throughout all eternity. And He did that even before I deserved it! God wants me to do what He asks me to do. That's called obedience, but He loved me first - even knowing I would disappoint Him by making poor choices sometimes. He is disappointed in me when I do things I shouldn't do, and He wants me to do the things He asks me to, but He will never stop loving me. And because I believe that Jesus died on the cross to pay the price for my sins, and have trusted Him to receive His forgiveness, I get to go be with Him someday. So I really want to love Him back the best I can, and do the things that will make Him happy."

Oh, that his kind of faith and growth would be as easy for all of us – for me! As a father of three today, our son continues to live with the joy and freedom of knowing God's unconditional love, blessing his family, his church, and his friends with the love that God has so freely given to him. Later in the chapter on the Holy Spirit, don't miss the truly electrifying story of his 'angel encounter' while yet a teenager. I think you will be greatly encouraged and blessed by it!

Not long after, praise God our eldest daughter also gave her heart to Jesus. Following her decision to trust Jesus, she has experienced many ups and downs in her walk with the Lord, allowing her sense of well-being to be governed too often by the misplaced judgment of those around her [often within a misguided church].

Personal Reflection:
As a beautiful, talented, and loving women, with a 'fix it' personality like her Mom, she drew people to herself who placed unreasonable expectations on her that she was not equipped to fulfill – only God is. This led her to a difficult and sometimes seemingly non-existent walk with the Lord. But you know what I've observed and what she has learned? He never leaves. He is always waiting for us to realize He is still there awaiting the opportunity to hug us in the midst of our pain. It's such a hard concept to internalize, especially when we have too many church leaders telling us, "If you don't perform as required, you'll bring down judgment and condemnation upon yourselves." Unfortunately, she has been the recipient of a lot of that. Has she made mistakes – yes – and she would be the first to admit that. Haven't we all! But like all of us, she has yearned to believe the truth that if we blow it, when we acknowledge our mistakes and humbly turn to Him, He stands ready to redeem and restore us for a new day of fellowship with Him – because He loves us anyhow! The resounding truth that has set her free is that His love for her came first – healing, restoration and reconciliation follow!

In her early adult years, totally dedicated to His Word, she filled the hearts and minds of her little children with the truth of His love for them. At just under two years old, after playfully singing 'Jesus Loves Me,' her daughter climbed up on my lap – only barely able to talk yet – and proclaimed to me, "Grandma, Jesus loves you too!" She learned that from her mother. And today, as that granddaughter raises her own four children, she continues to pass along the message, "Jesus loves you" to their little hearts. And praise the Lord they 'get it!' I praise God that even in the midst of so many disappointments, broken relationships, untold judgments, painful physical illnesses, our daughter chose to pass the truth along to her children!

Unfortunately, from time to time, the years have continued to bring various challenges and disappointments into our precious daughter's life. Perhaps some because she has believed the lie, that human relationships can fulfill our need to be loved unconditionally. They never will.

Time and time again when people have let her down [or she has let herself down] God has restored her and set her on her feet again. No matter what she faces deep down within her is the conviction that, ever since she asked Jesus to come into her life at eleven years of age, He has always been there with her. He has always loved her and He always will. What so many have seemed to try to destroy, with their 'holier than thou' attitudes, God did not allow. His unwavering love always has been and always will be the healer of our souls. And today her roots continue to grow deeper, as she seeks His voice through the church and through media messages from so many committed Christian teachers who fill her mind and heart with His golden nuggets of truth. Praise God for Christian media!

God's faithfulness is overwhelming! I was so full of gratitude for His answer to my prayers, making the message of salvation clear to me, my husband, and to all of our children, that I could hardly contain my joy. I had an insatiable hunger to learn more. I began spending all the time I could spare seeking God's instruction. It became my obsession. I couldn't get enough. I continued praying that He would lead me to more opportunities to help others know Jesus. During the next 39 years He allowed me the blessing of serving in a ministry where I had the opportunity of helping with the production and international distribution of powerful Gospel centered dramatic films, and teaching others how to use these films to share their faith in Jesus.

This became a very fulfilling time in my life. Slowly all the old tapes of "I love you 'when you stay clean' or 'if you do well' or 'if you meet my needs,' or 'you are worthy only when you serve in all the needed areas – at the church,' began to play a less and less predominant role in my reactions. There was still a lot of garbage inside, but I now had the assurance that someone – God Himself – stood by me, saying, *"I Love You Anyhow"* even when I fell short."

During this period of time, one afternoon a friend that had been spiritually mentoring my husband and I made a curious comment to me. As he walked down the porch steps to leave our home, he turned to me and said, *"I Love You Anyhow."* As I closed the door behind him it immediately began to bother me. What did that mean? I had to ask myself: what had I done that required the 'anyhow?' I called to inquire. *"What have I done?"* *"Oh nothing,"* he said. *"I only wanted you to know that if you ever did fall short, I'd love you anyhow."* Wow – Really? That was the first time I had ever heard such a statement and I'm sure he had no idea what an impact it would have on me.

As I contemplated the concept, God used it to fill my heart with the true intent of Jesus' words on the cross, *"Forgive them for they know not what they do."* I knew that He was declaring loud and clear to all those around Him, *"I Love You Anyhow!"* And later as I studied the story of the prodigal son I realized that I heard that same declaration. I realized that the story of the prodigal son is neither a story of one son's rebellion nor of the other's anger and frustration at the 'unfair' celebration upon his brother's return. It is the story of a father whose love never wavered! As with our Father in heaven, it is a declaration of a father who was willing to unconditionally proclaim, *"I Love You Anyhow!"*

In the early 70's, when our son and eldest daughter had both responded to faith in Jesus, I had made little effort yet to try to explain to our youngest daughter [five years younger than our son] about the message of the Gospel. She was so young. But the truth of it surrounded her and as we would soon learn, it had penetrated her little heart. It happened like this.....

Personal Reflection:
One day on a hurried mission, running indoors from playing, our youngest stopped in her tracks, and observing that I was 'marking' in my Bible, with the authority of one much older she exclaimed, "Mommy, we don't ever, ever, ever write in our books!" [Guess where she'd learned that from.] The incident opened up an opportunity for me to share with her about the purpose for the Bible and the stories it tells, and how God loves us so much that He wants us to learn all that we can about Him. I explained to her that sometimes that means writing in our Bibles when we are studying them, so we can more easily find important things when we want to read them again. God planted seeds.

On an evening not long after, having returned home from a school program, I went to her room to see if she was following instructions and getting ready for bed. She lay on her bed – her little head buried into her pillow, sobbing. I couldn't imagine the source of her distress. As I sat down beside her, she looked up and confessed, "Mommy, I need to tell you something." I was all ears. This was her story....

"Remember last week when I told you Rhonda and I didn't dump out your shampoo into the tub, that it just fell? Well, it didn't. We did dump it out, and I lied to you, and I'm sorry." I held her shaking little body as she got out all the guilt she had been carrying around inside her. I told her it didn't matter anymore and

that the important thing was that she realized it was wrong and that she was sorry, but that of course I still loved her – just like God does - assuring her that God always loves us even in the midst of the mistakes we make and the bad things we do. I strongly assured her that even while He waits for us to decide we are sorry, His love for us never changes. Her sobs began to subside as she listened intently.

"Mommy, my Sunday School teacher said that Jesus is like the key to Heaven and that, if we want to go in, He will open the door for us. Is she right?"

"Yes, my dear, when Jesus died on the cross, He was showing us God's Love for us- that He loves us so much that He was willing to let His Son, Jesus, die in order to pay the price for all the naughty things we do – they are called sins. So, when we decide to believe Jesus died for us, and receive the gift of forgiveness He offers us, He becomes like our key that opens up the door to let us in when we get to Heaven some day."

"I want Jesus to be my key too, Mommy. Can I tell Him right now that I want Him to be my key? Will you listen to me while I tell Him?"

She prayed while silent tears fell from my eyes. I had thought she was too young. God did not. The Sunday School teacher had not. The Holy Spirit reaches whom He will.

Within 15 minutes after she had prayed to receive Jesus, while out in the front room telling her daddy goodnight, one of our youth group kids stopped by. Our happy little angel ran and jumped into her lap, and pulling her long blond hair back, whispered in her ear. Then jumping down, with a huge smile, she ran off to bed.

"What did she say", I asked Deb. She responded joyfully, "Oh, that she had just asked Jesus to come into her heart and be her key to Heaven."

A 6 year old girl had just lived out the entire message of the Gospel, recognizing her sin, opening her heart to receive Jesus' love and forgiveness, and then telling another what He had done for her – all in about a half an hour! I was blown away!

Today, as a teacher of 'at risk' kids and mother of three military sons, she continues to pass along His love in a powerful and healing way!

Even as a child, when our hearts are open, the Holy Spirit helps us understand that God stands ready to pour His love inside! Once we believe in Jesus' free gift of salvation, trusting in God's unconditional love, He instructs, guides, corrects, and changes us into who He wants us to be.

Once we have received God's unconditional love, He commissions us to join Him in loving the world He created – helping reconcile others to Him and to each other. It's an awesome realization that the God of the universe not only created us and sacrificed His Son to redeem us, but He also counts us worthy to serve alongside Him!

The Holy Spirit opened up our little daughter's heart that day for a purpose beyond her redemption. And so it is with each of us. God redeems us for His purpose, to be His mouth and hands and feet, bringing His love and compassion to the world. He reconciles us to Himself through Jesus, that we might also help others become reconciled to Him, and to each other. Consider words from Paul, recorded in II Corinthians Chapter 5, verses 17 through 20.

> "*Therefore, if anyone is in Christ, he is a new creation; the old has gone the new has come! All this is from God, who reconciled us to himself through Christ and gave us the ministry of reconciliation: That God was reconciling the world to himself in Christ, not counting men's sins against them. And he has committed to us the message of reconciliation. We are therefore Christ's ambassadors, as though God were making his appeal through us. We implore you on Christ's behalf; Be reconciled to God.*"

A huge golden nugget of truth: God did not give us the assignment of changing people, somehow thinking we can help Him in reshaping them until they become worthy of His love. He simply asks us to share His love and His Word with them. There are dangers in the role reversal in which Christians often engaged, trying to do God's work for Him. When we fulfill our assignment to share Jesus with those around us and love on them for His sake, keeping ourselves out of the 'changing' business that tends to lead us into a condition of criticism and judgment, the Holy Spirit is released to change lives!

Does this mean then that we are not to get involved in helping others understand what God's Word says as to how we should live according to His commandments? No. On the contrary, He commands us to go unto all the nations and teach them all that He has taught us. In fact in I Peter 3:15b-16a, He tells us, "*Always be prepared to give an answer to everyone who asks you to give the reason for the hope that you have. But do this with gentleness and respect.*"

When we continue to judge and condemn those who desperately need to know God's love for them, we drive them away from Him instead of to Him. God's heart cries out to us; "*You love them….I'll change them.*" Not the other way around! Remember, God loved us first, before we were worthy, and He asks us to do the same, to love first, whether we think those around us may deserve it or not.

When we are willing to humble ourselves to love the sinner [while uncompromisingly hating the sin] we release His power to bring repentance, restitution and reconciliation into the lives of those whom He allows us to love [for His sake!]. Then and only then will we fulfill His purpose for us, the purpose of reconciling the world to Himself through us. This ministry of reconciliation, with which He has charged us, is both a huge responsibility and a gigantic blessing! Later we will dive into what this ministry looks like, in the chapters on Commitment and Growth and Paying It Forward.

Throughout the following chapters you will read true stories of lives changed, hurts healed, habits kicked, and hang ups abandoned, all for a life of freedom in Christ. You will read of the wonderful victories when people 'get it,' that God's message to them is, *"I Love You Anyhow!"* You will read the results of God's faithfulness when we simply love others and get ourselves out of His way, trusting Him with the business of molding them into what He wants them to be. As referenced throughout this writing, God says loud and clear throughout the scriptures, *"Love others to me and then I'll change them into what I have purposed for them to be!"*

I pray that by the time you get to the end of these incredible stories of God's victory in real lives you will be filled with the desire to go out and hug those you may have previously been unable to even like. I pray you that will be full of desire to give yourself to loving others to the Lord, instead of trying to drag them there, committing yourself to say without reservation, 'I love you' and really mean it!

So far this has been an account of *The Beginning* of a journey. There is so much more! I have been very blessed by those whom God has brought into my life, those who have loved me and whom I have loved, because He first loved us. Throughout these forty+ years since *The Beginning,* as it has been my great privilege to share God's revelations with thousands throughout the United States and internationally, I have dreamed of writing the wonderful stories of their victories in this book. Their stories are His story and thus it has been my great blessing to be scripted into His story. The ensuing writings reveal the liberating and powerful, yet often very difficult truths, which God has taught along the journey. May He anoint these words for the purposes of His Kingdom. I offer Him my prayer to this end....

"Oh, Lord, I know I have had a stubborn heart. Seems I have been through heaven and hell trying to grasp what you have been working to teach me. I've attempted to pen our journey together for the purpose of your glory. Now that it is nearly finished, I ask myself how I dare complete it when there are still unresolved relationships in my life. Doubts pour in....Perhaps it can never really be 'finished.' Perhaps it's a concept too illusive for the human mind to truly quantify. Perhaps 'saying' "I Love You Anyhow" is so far from actually 'living it out' that the attempt is futile. But then, you've taught me that just because we sometimes can't seem to find the wherewithal to live out the truths that you have revealed to us, it makes them no less true. God help me. Without the guidance and direction of the Holy Spirit, this book will never reach its intended audience.

1

Lord how passionately you long for resolution to our hurts and the pain of destroyed relationships – enough to give everything for us to reconcile. And still we just don't get it! We refuse the vulnerability of offering your "I Love You Anyhow" kind of love to those whom we desperately want to love and be loved by, holding hostage the freedom and joy that could have been. It must hurt you so much!

Lord, be with me – let your fingers guide this pen. Allow this long-time evolving story to find clarity on the written page. Lord, I am so human...so vulnerable...keep me pure, that I neither let anything creep in and muddy up the flow of your Spirit, nor skew the purity of your message. Unto that purpose, Lord, I dedicated this book. Amen"

CHAPTER ONE

LOVE – WHAT IS IT?

Ahh, love! What actually is 'love?' The word is so over-used it's almost a joke. With the same breath we say, 'I love peas" – "I love you" – and "I love God." This just isn't sufficient to express what we really mean. Surely we must have a different level of feeling for the significant people in our lives, and absolutely for God, than we do for peas!

LOVE = 'Phileo' – 'Aerous' – 'Agape'

Most current day languages give us only one choice for the word 'Love.' One word for such an expression is totally inadequate to convey our true inner thoughts. In the original Greek language there are actually three words for love, giving people an opportunity to better select the one that appropriately expressed what they were trying to really trying to say. Since we have only one choice, sometimes we flippantly toss out the word love, while other times we want the same word to convey a much deeper and more sacred meaning. For instance; if using the Greek words to express the various levels of 'love' it would sound something like this: "I love (aerous) peace, " love (phileo) my mom, or God loves (Agapes) you and me." Let's look closer at the meanings for these three Greek words for love.

- 'Aerous' expresses a feeling that is often a shallow and changing kind of love, one that comes and goes with our latest whims, tastes, or fashions…also defined as *romantic love.*
- 'Phileo' love is to say, '*I love you in the best way I know how*' [with a limited human capacity to love] perhaps slightly above the expression of *like* such as, '*I am your good friend.*' Also defined as *brotherly love.*

1

- 'Agape' love is a God-based, God-sustained, unconditional love....a love that is willing to express, *'I Love You Anyhow'* no matter what the circumstances – a love that never runs out.

As promised in the book of Colossians, when we invite Jesus to come into our heart, recognizing Him as our Savior, He brings with Him all of the God-head [Father, Son, and Holy Spirit] thus our source of 'Agape' love. Our problem is that though our hearts are full of all the love God has to offer, when we face difficult situations we tend to live as though we have run out of love. This happens because we are trying to love the unlovely without tapping into God's unending resource of love. Let us not live like paupers when it comes to our supply of love, when in fact in our heart's bank account of love, we are millionaires!

God is not satisfied to have us respond to Him or others only with an *Aerous* or *Phileo* kind of love. Though God is in favor of romantic and brotherly love, He clearly shows us that *Agape* Love is the best. Yet though He isn't satisfied with our oft times insufficient expressions of love, He loves us anyhow and uses us right where we are, until we mature enough to allow the Holy Spirit to sincerely express *Agape* love through us. His desire is that we *Agape* Him, and all those whom He places in our lives. Let's take a look at a Biblical example of this principle.

In the eighteen chapter of John, we witness an exchange between Jesus and Peter [then referred to as Simon]. Jesus had a special relationship with Peter, the first of his followers to recognize and confess Him as *'the Christ, the Son of the living God.'* [Matthew 16:13-16] However even before He was arrested and beaten by His accusers, Jesus knew that Peter would deny their friendship as soon as he was faced with fear for his own well-being. [John 13:38 and Mark chapter 14] And so it was that Peter denied Him not once but three times, actually claiming he didn't even know Jesus! [John chapter18]

So, did Jesus give up on Peter for such a selfish act? No. After Jesus' resurrection, through an Angel, He had a special message for Peter, making sure that he would know that he was forgiven and that Jesus loved him <u>anyhow</u>. Here's how it went....

When Many came to the tomb to bring spices to anoint Jesus' body, she found the tomb empty and instead an Angel of the Lord encountered her, instructing her; *"Don't be alarmed...You are looking for Jesus the Nazarene, who was crucified. He has risen! He is not here. See the place where they laid him. But go, tell his disciples <u>and Peter</u>, 'He is going ahead of you into Galilee. There you will see him, just as he told you.'"* [Mark 16: 6-7]

Jesus knew that Peter was heartbroken as soon as he realized that he had let Jesus down. He knew that if He didn't specify that the invitation was for Peter, as well as all the other disciples, Peter would assume He was no longer a part of Jesus' inner circle of disciples. How could he think he might be, after such a spineless denial of even knowing Jesus!

God holds that kind of 'Agape' for you and me. He wants us to understand that even though He knows we will let Him down from time to time, when we realize we have done so and our hearts long to be right with Him, He is always ready to receive us and restore us to Himself, just as He did Peter.

Not only is He willing to receive and restore us, He counts us worthy of serving with Him. Peter did go with the rest of the disciples to see Jesus in His resurrected form, and Jesus had a very special discussion with him. Remember, at this time Peter was referred to by the name Simon. Let's unpack verses 15-17 in John 21 to see what they reveal to us.

> *"When they had finished eating, Jesus said to Simon Peter, 'Simon, son of John, do you truly Agape me more than these?'* [Peter answered] *'Yes, Lord, you know that I Phileo you.' Jesus said, feed my lambs.'*

Peter had walked away from His life's work and all that was common to him in order to follow and serve Jesus, yet he now realized that for him to say that he *Agaped* Jesus the same way that Jesus *Agaped* him was not yet possible. After all he had abandoned Jesus in His time of need. Jesus asks Peter a second and a third time. Take a look ....

> *"Again Jesus said, 'Simon, son of John, do you truly Agape me?' He answered, 'Yes, Lord, you know that I Phileo you.' Jesus said, 'take care of my sheep."*

> *The third time he said to him, 'Simon, son of John, do you 'Phileo' me?' Peter was hurt because Jesus asked him the third time, 'Do you love me?' He said, 'Lord, you know all things; you know that I Phileo you." Jesus said, 'Feed my sheep."*

Notice that Jesus changed the word which he was using for love when asking Peter the third time 'Peter do you *Phileo* me.' In doing so, He was meeting Peter where he was in his human capacity to love. It hurt Peter to realize that, though he wanted to *Agape* Jesus, he was not yet able to promise Jesus that depth of love. He knew he had already blown it, denying Jesus three times. And this happened shortly after he had declared to Him, *"Lord I will follow you anywhere you go, even unto death."* [13th chapter of John] Peter didn't want to make the same mistake again, promising something of which he wasn't sure he could deliver. But Jesus was willing to meet Peter where he was, changing His request to 'Peter do you *Phileo* me', which allowed Peter to respond positively to Jesus' call. Jesus accepted Peter's response, continuing to issue the invitation to, *'feed my sheep.'* It was Jesus desire that Peter strive to offer an *Agape* kind of love, but He did not demand that he do so before He was willing to use Him.

He doesn't us either. He does ask us to strive to love each other with an *Agape* kind of love, but He knows we are on a journey, learning to do so. He asks us to strive to understand His kind of love and to offer it up to Him and to others as best we can. In the mean time, He promises us that, when we give all of ourselves that we are able, to all of Him that we understand, He will meet us on that growing edge, and He will use us for His purposes.

Human Love is Most Often Conditional

The kind of love with which we often identify is a conditional love. It depends on the boomerang effect … we must receive what we consider to be an appropriate response to our expression of love or we aren't satisfied. In fact if we don't get the response we are looking for, we often withhold our love from flowing in that same direction again, fearing that this relationship will never be fulfilling. There is a book by Max Lucado that I have to recommend here. It lends great insights about how we can break out of this insufficient conditional love we offer one another, and begin to experience the joy of offering one another the kind of love Jesus gives us. The book I'm referring to is, *"In The Eye Of The Storm."* Well worth your reading time!

God's Love Is Unconditional

God's love is *unconditional*. It doesn't count the cost and never goes away regardless of the response it gets. Unconditional love does not sort out its recipients. It has endurance well beyond human tolerance because its source and strength comes from God and flows over all who come near, not choosing to exclude anyone. Though we may not have experienced this kind of love in our human relationships, it is nonetheless available to anyone who seeks it!

God is the author and only true supplier of this *unconditional* love – a love that stands ready at every opportunity to say, 'I Love You Anyhow.' In fact in First John, the Bible tells us that God actually *is* love. His very nature is love. Thus, He has been the embodiment of love from the beginning of time and will continue to be throughout eternity. He doesn't just talk about how much He loves us. He demonstrated it with the painful sacrifice of His own Son!

> *"For God so loved the world, that he gave his one and only Son, that whoever believes in him, shall not perish, but have eternal life."* John 3:16

Soak in the astounding liberation of this truth, dear friend! He loves you right where you are, enough to die to give you life! Some might say, "Oh but He is God. He knew what would happen and He had a choice." Exactly! He had a choice! And He chose to make this painful decision because of His great love for you and me. This is the kind of love we are talking about in this book, the kind of love that screams loud and clear, "I Love You Anyhow!" Take a minute to do a little experiment with me. Read the next couple of paragraphs, and then do as they suggest.

Close your eyes for a minute and picture someone who holds your heart, someone who means more than anyone else in our life, the one who completes you. Now, can you fathom not only allowing, but actually deciding to send that person to suffer ridicule, flogging, and ultimately the painful death of the cross? And all the while you would know that he/she would then have to descend into the depths of hell in order to accomplish the task of taking all the world's sins and leaving them there once and for all. In order for that to happen you would have to turn your face away from your loved one and leave them to experience indescribable rejection! To make it even harder, the ones for which your loved one suffers this plight wouldn't even yet know or care about them. In fact as Jesus suffered His beatings, they spit and jeered and called for His crucifixion!

It is utterly overwhelming to grasp the fact that God would have sacrificed His Son just for you, [just for me] even if you or I were the only one in the world! Before He did this God knew that we were going to sin and fall short of His expectations. Sin cannot exist in Heaven and God knew that if He didn't go to this length to cover our sins, He would have no hope of spending eternity with us, His heart's desire! He loves us with that kind of *unconditional* love!

God's Greatest Commandment

In order to help protect us from ourselves, God delivered ten commandants through His servant Moses, defining appropriate behavior intended to help keep our relationship with Him and each other at the highest level. As important as each of these commandments is, there is an underlying theme that God wants us to hear. In a setting where Jesus was speaking with the Sadducees and the Pharisees, one of the Pharisees asked…

"Teacher, which is the greatest commandment in the law?" Jesus replied, "Love the Lord your God with all your heart, and with all you soul, and with all your mind. This is the first and greatest commandment. And the second is like it; Love your neighbor as yourself. All the Law and the Prophets hang on these two commandments." Matthew 22:36-40

Is the act of 'love' important? God certainly says so! This scripture places the task of loving our neighbor as ourselves as a high priority, suggesting also that God wants us to love ourselves because we are His and He places a high value on us! My husband and I once took a series of classes that challenged us to reach out to others with at least one good deed each day. It further challenged us that acts of convenience didn't count. Only if it cost us something, time, money or emotional effort, would it be given out of a sacrificial heart. We should never lose our desire to sacrificially love others as He commands us to do.

"Let no debt remain outstanding, except the continuing debt to love one another, for he who loves his fellow man has fulfilled the law. Love does no harm to its neighbor. Therefore love is the fulfillment of the law. Romans 13:8 & 10

In an attempt to produce harmony, think of all the 'dos' and 'don'ts' demanded in our world today, yet within nations everywhere there is constant conflict, as well as worldwide wars and rumors of wars! God says we only need one law…learn to say *"I Love You Anyhow"* to yourself and to those around you. It is the only law we need!

Soft Side vs Hard Side

Following are some great insights that will help us in determining how we as individuals tend to give and receive love. *We are all 'intricately and wonderfully made in our mother's wombs'* (Psalm 139). We are not all alike. We each have our own unique reactions that reveal the manner in which we give and receive love. Some of us lean toward the *'hard'* side of love and some, the *'soft'* side. Some of us feel especially loved when we receive gifts, others when we receive time and attention. We all have our own *language of love*. In the following few pages we will see just a quick introduction to some of these revelations.

First of all, let's review the following set of questions. They will help us determine our tendencies toward the *'soft'* or *'hard'* side of love. For each question circle the number that best expresses where you feel you are in relationship to that question, then add these numbers together to determine where you are on the Intensity Index … on the soft side of love? Or the hard side of love? This exercise reveals so much about how we give and receive love!

Knowing where we fall in this 'Intensity Index' helps us to see more clearly where we might need to make some adjustments in order to better love those around us. It is no wonder why sometimes we think we are adequately expressing love to another, yet we miss the mark so far. When we know where we stand with the hard/soft side of expressing our love in each given relationship, and have an idea where our family and friends stand, we will have a better idea how to adequately express the love we feel for them in a way that they are able to receive it. You will find that, depending on whose name you put in the blank, you express your love differently. We may lean toward the hard side of love with one relationship and the soft side in another. The goal is to try to find a balance in each of our individual relationships.

Feel free to take copies of this exercise for each relationship you would like to evaluate. Then circle the appropriate number for each statement, indicating how you feel you respond to each given relationship. Be honest!

When you finish each one, add up your numbers. Note on the scale below where your total falls. This will help you see how your reactions to a given relationship stack up – on the hard side? Or on the soft side? Perhaps you will determine to make some adjustments.

Intensity Index

Hard Side						Soft Side

20	40	60	80	100	120	140

Now take a minute to use the exercise on the next page to rate your special relationships....

Rate how do you tend to act in your relationship with _____

I. Take the Lead   Follow
1   2   3   4   5   6   7

II. Forceful   Non-Demanding
1   2   3   4   5   6   7

III. Energetic   Reserved
1   2   3   4   5   6   7

IV. Strive to Accomplish Personal Goals   Let Others Set Your Goals
1   2   ?   4   5   6   7

V. Self Controlled   Lack of Self Discipline
1   2   3   4   5   6   7

VI. Makes Quick Decisions   Hesitates in Making Decisions
1   2   3   4   5   6   7

VII. Want to Hear Facts   Want to Share Feelings
1   2   3   4   5   6   7

VIII. A Motivator   A Responder
1   2   3   4   5   6   7

IX. Hold Grudges   Easily Forgives
1   2   3   4   5   6   7

X. Set Rigid Standards   Set Flexible Standards
1   2   3   4   5   6   7

XI. Feel the Need to be Hard on Him/Her   Soft on Him/Her
1   2   3   4   5   6   7

XI. Hard on His/Her Problems   Soft on His/Her Problems
1   2   3   4   5   6   7

Love Languages

Another very telling exercise is to evaluate what kinds of other's actions towards you most make you feel loved. This would be your 'love language.' Once again, we are all unique. We all have our own way of responding to others. We all sense that we are being loved as a result of different kinds of attentions.

In the book, "The Five Love Languages," author Gary Chapman proposes that there are at least five specific love languages. He contends that if we can determine which of the five stated languages our specific love language is [and which is that of our loved ones] we will more effectively be able to sincerely show our love to one other. As a family of 28, including kids, grandkids, and great grandkids, we try to consider these guidelines in determining what kind of actions it takes to ensure that each feels loved. It is amazing to see the results! While our source of love is the Holy Spirit, and not a human manipulation of some kind, we can still help the process by better understanding how we and others best receive that desired love. Our family would encourage yours to read Mr. Chapman's *"The Five Love Languages"* and let it help you determine which love languages are experienced in your family.

Once you figure out your own love language, help your loved ones determine theirs. When we all know just what it takes to best help others feel loved, we will surely try to love them in the way that they will best feel loved. But when we don't know each other's love language, we tend to stumble around trying to express our love the best way we know how while all the while those we are trying to love are not feeling it and we can't understand for the life of us why!

Let's take just a glimpse at the five love languages suggested by Mr. Chapman as the most common way we express and receive love....

- *Words of Affirmation*
- *Quality Time*
- *Receiving Gifts*
- *Acts of Service*
- *Physical Touch*

Our daughter tells of how this understanding changed her marriage. While her love language is Physical Touch, her husband's is Acts of Service. Before understanding this concept, when he would come home from a long days work [or often week away on business] and go straight to the task of mowing the lawn, she felt unimportant, neglected. He considered he was showing his love via "Acts of Service." Once understood, they made the proper adjustments to both offer and receive their individual love languages in a way that better met each other's realities. The results?...they both feel more loved.

When We Are Willing to Try, God Willingly Enables

Yes, all of these insights will help us in our desire to better love one another. But try as we may, we all falter from time to time. From time to time, we are all tempted to compromise our principles. Sin is real and God knew ahead of time that we were frail, thus prone to it. But ever since the beginning of time, it has been His plan to willingly meet us where we are, enabling us to love as He commands us to.

> *"Above all, love each other deeply, because love covers over a multitude of sins."*
> I Peter 4:8

When I read this scripture, it's like reading God's insurance policy....how marvelous! Love actually makes up for some of the dumb things I do! So where do we go to draw from the well that supplies us with the sort of love God asks of us? Love has no boundaries – no end – when our source is Jesus Christ....

> *"Now that you have purified yourselves by obeying the truth so that you have sincere love for your brothers, love one another deeply, from the heart."* I Peter 1:22

There's a lot said in these few words! First of all, the very first word, 'now' gives us the assurance that our resource is available 'now.' We don't have to seek some priestly status or acceptance by a religious group before becoming worthy of the filling of God's love. 'Now' is the time!

With Christ as our Savior, we are filled with the capacity to love as God wants us to love – NOW! That doesn't mean that we will love perfectly. It doesn't mean that every time I want to react in love that I will actually be able to swallow my pride and do it. But when I cannot seem to muster up the unselfishness to react in love, I know I need to join King David in declaring, *"I look unto the Heavens from whence cometh my help!"* [Psalm 121] And though I'm sure there are times when God is disappointed in my actions, it's so reassuring to know that He never gives up on me. He is always there to meet me on my growing edge. And whenever I turn to Him and confess my shortcomings, asking for His forgiveness and help, He stands ready to declare, *"I Love You Anyhow."*

> *"God is not unjust; he will not forget your work and the love you have shown him as you have helped his people and continue to help them. We want each of you to show this same diligence to the very end, in order to make your hope sure."*
> Hebrews 6:10-11

As if the benefits of loving and being loved here on this earth are not enough; God has prepared for us the fullness of His rewards when we see Him face to face!

What Love Is Not

Love is not a 'free pass' that allows us a permissive lifestyle - in the name of love. To love another is not a willingness to agree with a sinful lifestyle. For as long as man has existed there has been a tendency to embrace the idea that love means 'anything goes.' This was the devil's first lie to mankind...duping Adam and Eve into believing that because God loved them He surely would not deny them. *"You will no surely die...For God knows that when you eat of it your eyes will be opened and you will be like God, knowing good and evil."* [Genesis 3:4-5] Adam and Eve chose to believe the serpent. Countless others have also chosen to believe this lie. Their philosophy is that, to require obedience and propose the idea that disciplinary consequences will follow disobedient actions is the opposite of love. Is it? No! This philosophy is the back-breaker of society's civility. Children are running, screaming, biting and kicking through the malls and in the classroom, because they want to do what they want to do. Moms and dads helplessly follow along because society has instilled so much fear that disciplining their children in any way is abusive. Drivers getting by with speeding, running red lights, road rage and in some cases even shootings, because law officers are afraid to carry out their duties for fear of vocational retribution. Husbands and wives are having 'open marriages' because they have no fear of any consequences, either for themselves or their damaged children. The truth is....living within the boundaries that God has set down for us is expressing the highest kind of love!

> *"Everyone who believes that Jesus is the Christ is born of God, and everyone who loves the father loves his child as well. This is how we know that we love the children of God: by loving God and carrying out his commands. This is love for God: to obey his commands."* I John 5:1-3a

Obedience does not bring suppression, but freedom. As a child of God we obey His rules, out of love for Him. As parents we set down boundaries for our children to protect them, out of love for them. As husbands and wives we have responsible expectations for one another to protect our relationship, out of love for one another. As a loving Father, God has set down commands for us to follow to protect us, out of love for us! Saying 'no' does not mean there is an absence of love. It expresses the presence of a love so great that one wants to protect the recipient of their 'no' from suffering the consequences of poor choices. God does not allow consequences because He does not love us, but because He does!

> *"If his sons forsake my law and do not follow my statutes, if they violate my decrees and fail to keep my commands, I will punish their sin with the rod, their iniquity with flogging; but I will not take my love from him, nor will I ever betray my faithfulness."* Psalm 89:30-33

"Endure hardship as discipline; God is treating you as sons. For what son is not disciplined by his father? If you are not disciplined (and everyone undergoes discipline), then you are illegitimate children and not true sons. Moreover, we have all had human fathers who disciplined us and we respected them for it. How much more should we submit to the Father of our spirits and live! Our fathers disciplined us for a little while as they thought best; but God disciplines us for our good, that we may share in his holiness. No discipline seems pleasant at the time, but painful. Later on, however, it produces a harvest of righteousness and peace for those who have been trained by it. Therefore, strengthen your feeble arms and weak knees. Make level paths for your feet, so that the lame may not be disabled but rather healed." Hebrews 12:7-13

God makes it indelibly clear that discipline is love. Let us lead disciplined lives so as to be protected from the evil one. In upcoming Chapters, Living out Life's Roles and The Strings of Stress, we will discuss more about this area, as it relates to parent and child relationships,

SO...What Is Love?

We have looked at what love is not...it is not an *'anything goes'* permissive pass, allowing us to get by with whatever we wish. It is not putting ourselves first and demanding what we want.

Though the Lord is saddened by our lack of love for one another, He knows we are a work in progress. He doesn't excuse our disobedience, but He does have compassion on us, forgiving us and keeping His promise to remember with love those who are remembering Him. The scriptures are full of definitive explanations of what love is.....

"The Lord is compassionate and gracious; slow to anger, abounding in love. He will not always accuse, nor will he harbor his anger forever; he does not treat us as our sins deserve or repay us according to our iniquities. For as high as the heavens are above the earth, so great is his love for those who fear him; as far as the east is from the west, so far has he removed our transgressions from us. As a father has compassion on his children, so the Lord has compassion on those who fear him." Psalm 103: 8-13

In His Grace, God gives us a glimpse of what Love is supposed to look like....

"If I speak in the tongues of men and of angels, but have not love, I am only a resounding gong or a clanging cymbal. If I have the gift of prophecy and can fathom all mysteries and all knowledge, and if I have a faith that can move mountains, but have not love, I am nothing. If I give all I possess to the poor and surrender my body to the flames, but have not love, I gain nothing. Love is patient, love is kind. It does not envy, it does not boast, it is not proud. It is not

rude, it is not self-seeking, it is not easily angered, it keeps no record of wrongs. Love does not delight in evil but rejoices with the truth. It always protects, always trusts, always hopes, always perseveres. Love never fails." I Corinthians 13:1-8a

"Love must be sincere. Hate what is evil; cling to what is good. Be devoted to one another in brotherly love. Honor one another above yourselves. Never be lacking in zeal, but keep your spiritual fervor, serving the Lord. Be joyful in hope, patient in affliction, faithful in prayer. Share with God's people who are in need. Practice hospitality. Bless those who persecute you; bless and do not curse. Rejoice with those who rejoice; mourn with those who mourn. Live in harmony with one another. Do not be proud, but be willing to associate with people of low position. Do not be conceited. Do not repay anyone evil for evil. Be careful to do what is right in the eyes of everybody. If it is possible, as far as it depends on you, live at peace with everyone." Romans 12: 9-17

If we will take these scriptures to heart, and guide our relationships by them, we will experience joy and fulfillment beyond words! Consider your most precious relationships. Measure your interactions within these relationships against the two previous scriptures. What do these scriptures reveal about areas that you might want to change in order to improve your love relationship with those important to you? If we are willing to apply these guidelines to the way we love, we will find a release that frees us to offer a radical love that heals and restores.

Agape [love] is Freedom

Learning to offer an authentic God-driven love brings the most liberating and empowering freedom to our relationships that we will ever experience this side of Heaven! This kind of love invites God right into the midst of our relationships, giving us the freedom to say, "I Love You Anyhow." Take a look at some excerpts from 1ˢᵗ John…..

"Dear friends, let us love one another, for love comes from God. Everyone who loves has been born of God and knows God….This is how God showed his love among us; He sent his one and only Son into the world that we might live through him….No one has ever seen God, but if we love each other, God lives in us and his love is made complete in us…And so we know and rely on the love God has for us….God is love. Whoever lives in love lives in God and God in him." I John 4: 7,9,12,16

It is my prayer that you will be empowered to give unashamedly of the love God has placed within you…. No matter what issues you have to overcome to do so.

From the Mouths of Babes

When asked by their classroom teacher to share with the class what they think love really is, kids from ages 5 to 10 share their unabashed vision of what they have observed……

- "Love is like a little old woman and a little old man who are still friends even after they know each other so well." Tommy – age 6
- "Love is when Mommy gives Daddy the best piece of chicken." Elaine – age 5
- "Love is what's in the room with you at Christmas if you stop opening presents and just listen." Bobby – age 7
- "When my grandmother got arthritis, she couldn't bend over and paint her toenails anymore. So My Grandfather does it for her all the time, even when his hands got arthritis. Now that's love!" Rebecca – age 8
- "When someone loves you, the way they say your name is different. You just know that your name is safe in their mouth" Billy – age 4
- "You really shouldn't say 'I love you' unless you mean it. But if you mean it, you should say it a lot. People forget." Jessica – Age 8
- "Love is when you go out to eat and give somebody most of your french fries without making them give you any of theirs." Chrissy – age 6
- "If you want to learn to love better, you should start with a friend who you hate." Nikka – age 6

I don't know in what version of the Bible these comments belong, but I'm convinced they belong in a concordance somewhere as descriptions of the kind of love God has in mind!

"Dear Lord,
We need your help. How do we love as you love us? It is just impossible without the empowerment of your Holy Spirit. Help us to better understand the love languages of others so we can better love them as they desire to be loved, and show it by our actions. We believe that with your help we can. We want to reach Heaven's door and be able to hear you say, 'Well done good and faithful servant.' Help us to show tough love with compassion and not with judgment. We want others to know that their name is safe in our mouth. We want to grow in our ability to show love, from an 'Aerous' love to an 'Agape' love, just as Jesus showed His love for us on the cross. Thank you for loving us so much! Amen"

Personal Application

TRUTH:

God has shown His Agape [love] for us in that while we were still sinners He sent His Son to die for us. God meets us where we are and empowers us to express Agape [love] to others.

1. Give personal examples, in your own words, of the three Greek words for love.

2. Did you concentrate on someone whom you love, and whether you would be willing to sacrifice them for the sake of others, as described in John 3:16? How did that exercise help you in grasping the vast love God has for you?

3. Explain the insights you gained in examining the hard side/soft side of love and the 5 love languages? How did these insights help you have a better grasp on action steps you might take to help communicate and receive love?

4. Reflect on the Corinthians and Romans scriptures that describe love. Based on these scriptures, in what areas would you say you need to improve to better love as God loves?

Journal Entry:

Loving God's Way

God, how should I love others?
From a distant mountain top
Where intellect and doctrine
Are all that I need to convey
I love you – but do not touch!

How I wish that you could be here today!
I want to know – to feel – to be
Sure of your way!

And, Lord, somehow
(forgive me if I'm wrong)
But, somehow, I feel
You'd hold me and not
Struggle with human plans
Or motives, or tomorrows,
But just today and this moment,
And my need for a loving hand!

Lord forgive me
If ever I say, 'I love you'
With a shallow sound
Or an empty intent.

Forgive me, Lord,
If 'I love you' ever becomes just words
Instead of feelings
From you – to me – to others.

How I wish you could sit here with me Lord!
I need your touch just now!

I don't mean to bring you down to my level Lord.
You're too precious and too wonderful for that.
But somehow I feel your Love so strong that,
Were you here, I just know…we could be one…
One in intent…and one in love!

Journal Entry: My Heart – A Mansion of Love-Filled Rooms

[Written after a tearful, soul searching outcry to the Lord for answers that seemed too aloof to ever come.....]

I'm troubled, Lord. I am sitting here asking myself, God how can I love adequately enough for you? Can I truly love more than one person at a time? How can I focus on loving others without short-changing my own family? Doesn't giving love to one rob a portion of another's? How can our love be equally given to so many who need it? I want to be fair, to be sure of your way. Help me understand, God. I am listening.

"Picture with me, your heart" He said *"A heart in which I have placed dozens of rooms. Each room is filled with my love, all awaiting release to those for whom it is my intent for you to share. You hold the keys to the doors of each love-filled room. I have placed all of that love there for a purpose that it might flow out to its intended recipient…from me, through you, to those I place in your life. What you do with our rooms full of love is up to you. Will you protect yourself, allowing your fear of being too vulnerable, or your unwillingness to forgive, or your self-focused life, to keep the doors locked and bolted, holding hostage the love within? I know my dear….you opened your heart once and someone betrayed your trust, squelching the love you poured out, and since then - you've determined never again. The pain of the emptiness you felt caused you to declare, "Sorry no more love left to give." My child, when you allow these chains of bondage to keep my love locked up within you, you move through life robot like, lonely and alone, even in a crowd. You've become like the Dead Sea, everything flowing in and nothing flowing out. It is a body of water that's lifeless within. So it is with you….your false outward appearance of self-confidence veils your inner-longing for the reality of deeper heart-to-heart relationships."*

Wow, Lord, what a revelation. How precious to sit quietly after talking with you and wait for your response. Thank you, Lord! I sense a new freedom to unload all of the love you have poured into me, and do it without fear of the results. Help me find a way to pass this incredible insight along to others that they too will find the freedom to love without fear of loss. At just the right time God, you prompt those who belong to Jesus to unlock each love-filled room in their heart and freely and unashamedly allow the love within to flow out for your sake. I see it all so clearly now….because you have given us quite enough love for each person, we don't have to steal from one person's portion in order to have enough love for another. Yes…thank you Lord; your love never divides – it always multiplies. It's clear now Lord, just as moms and dads quickly learn that they really can miraculously love their second child every bit as much as their first, I know I have quite enough love for each person you want me to love, for your sake!

And so it is that it becomes a privilege – a mission – to unlock the doors to the love-filled rooms within our hearts and allow the love reserved for each person to flow out to them, in His name. For many it may be the only touch of God's love with which they will ever come in contact. For some, the portion of God's loved spilled out from your heart to theirs will answer the cries of their broken lives, helping heal and restore them, and encouraging them to open their eyes to the truth, forgiveness and healing available to them through Jesus. For sure, It will be a series of miraculous loves — loves that will never run out, loves that boldly declare, "I Love You Anyhow!"

CHAPTER TWO
AFFIRMATION AND VULNERABILITY

Throughout this book there will be reference to these two critical areas - *affirmation* and *vulnerability*. In this particular chapter, we will more specifically focus on the crucial role these two principles play in enabling us to enjoy successful relationships. We all crave affirmation while it is difficult to be vulnerable, yet the two go hand-in-hand. With this in mind, I vulnerably declare to you my inadequacies to pen this book. My heartfelt desire is to somehow connect you to the powerful affirmation God offers us, so I admonish you...

> Don't follow me; I might not be a good leader
> Don't lead me; I might not be a good follower
> Just walk beside me and love me and be my friend

With that in mind, I recall a line in one of my favorite songs, performed by Bill Gaither, *"Put your eyes upon Jesus, look full in His wonderful face, and the things of this world will grow strangely dim in the power and the might of His grace!"* When we are able to fix our eyes upon Jesus, human deceptions that otherwise govern our relationships will yield to God's higher principles, and in doing so will bring victory into our relationships.

There's a certain paranoia when one sets out to encourage others with God's instruction, because there's always the chance that once we've shared what we feel God has laid on our heart, we may not be able to live up to those claims ourselves. And we fear, 'what will others think?' Does that make us a hypocrite? Or a failure? Perhaps that isn't the most important issue. Perhaps the most important question is, *are we willing to lift up His principles, not worrying whether or not we will always be able to live up to them ourselves?* That's vulnerability.

God Affirms in the Midst of our Doubts

As I struggled with this dilemma in the midst of some personal challenges a few years back, a dear friend encouraged, *"Remember, the fact that we may not always be able to live up to God's principles does not make them any less the truth."* Thank you dear friend. You released me from the fear of failure that would have paralyzed me from this writing. I now pray that God's declaration of "I Love You Anyhow," will flow so strongly through this writing that it will penetrate each reader, enabling and empowering him/her with the unfathomable depth of victory that God has planned for them...despite this author's shortcomings.

God's Purpose and Plan for Our Lives

From the beginning of time God has had a purpose and a plan for each of our lives. Foundational to our finding and living out His purpose and plan for us, is that we build upon the truths and promises reflected in God's Word, knowing that they are absolutely dependable! The scriptures reveal all that God holds for us. The goal of this writing is to help us unpack some of God's powerful truths. The affirmation of His love predominates throughout His Word. His call for us to be vulnerable to His plan predominates throughout as well.

So let's start by taking a look at an oft quoted treasure in Romans 8: *"And we know that in all things God works together for good ....."* Sounds pretty simple, doesn't it? He is working all things together for our good. Sounds like a pretty good insurance policy for happiness. Strangely, life often seems to play out very different from this truth, doesn't it? But wait – there's more. One mistake we often make is attempting to conclude what the Lord is trying to communicate by reading only a part of His instruction. I know I have done this...not fully accepting the whole truth, but rather only the part that suits my need. As a result, my response can also only be in part. Let us then consider the whole statement from Romans 8:28...

> *"And we know that in all things God works for good for those who love him, who have been called according to his purpose."*

I would choose to be 'called according to His purpose,' however how can I know Gods purpose for me if I don't have a clue what the purpose is? It's like navigating through rough waters without the proper tools to do so! Like beginning in one part of the country to find our way to another – which is unknown territory – without a map [or more recently a GPS] to guide our turns! One thing we can depend on is that God knows! His plan for us is not a plan for harm but for good! Once again let's review how He reveals His purpose and plan for us in Jeremiah....to give us 'hope' and a 'future.'

> *"For I know the plans I have for you, declares the Lord, plans to prosper you and not to harm you, plans to give you hope and a future. Then you will call upon me and come and pray to me, and I will listen to you. You will seek me and find me when you seek me with all your heart."* Jeremiah 29:11-13

Because it is God's desire to be with us always, His plan for our 'prosper, hope and future' is not just for this world, but for all eternity. Therefore, it transcends the illnesses, brokenness, and pain of this world. Allowing ourselves to be vulnerable to God's plan depends on the sense of assurance we have that His promise of 'hope and a future' is for real. As well, our willingness to be vulnerable enough to affirm others in the midst of their pain and trauma depends on whether we rely on God's promise of 'hope' for them, or whether we are paralyzed with a 'hopelessness' that comes from relying on our own limited understanding. God cautions us.......

> *"Trust in the Lord with all your heart and lean not on your own understanding; in all your ways acknowledge Him, and He will make your paths straight."* Proverbs 3:5-6.....

This is such a great affirmation! Whenever any situation appears hopeless, we can depend on God's promise, trusting Him to set things straight. Whenever we claim the truth that God's Word is more powerful than our experience, making every effort to find His purpose in a given situation, then [and only then] can we count on His promise that He will work <u>all</u> things together for our good.

God Knows the End from the Beginning

Sometimes due to the human frailty of our relationships we cry out, *"How on earth is this circumstance ever going to work out for good!"* Often, given our limited understanding, it doesn't seem possible. But, God knows the end from the beginning. We don't. As we trust that God is with us in our relational challenges, and acknowledge that He does have a plan for us that is designed for 'good and not for harm,' we are released from ourselves and empowered to reach out to those with whom we are experiencing anger and hurt. When that happens we allow the Holy Spirit to fill and heal us....and/or the situation. Allow me to share one such time.....

Personal Reflection:
We were good friends. As families we shared much of our lives with one another.
Trouble came into our friend's marriage and we shared their heartache, praying
for them and trying to help them work through some very tough times. On one
occasion God allowed me the special privilege of helping their young son trust Jesus
as his Savior.

But there seemed to be a distance growing between our families. As a Christian
father and husband, our friend began to act out in ways very uncommon for him.
For as long as we had known them he had been a solid Christian family man,
employed at a good job. Now his lifestyle took a dramatic turn. During this time
I spent a lot of time with the children, as well as in communication with both their
mom and their dad. As time went by, I began to sense some real strain and friction
between myself and my dear friend – their mom. Then I began to hear rumors that
she was really not very happy with me. I wondered - perhaps my involvement in
trying to be helpful was being perceived as interfering. Perhaps sometimes I can be
too vocal. := (

My feelings were not loving. Hurt and anger wanted to creep in, but my friendship
with her was so important, and through my tears I cried out to the Lord to help
me know what to do. He prompted me [but at the time it felt a bit more like a
command] to go and listen to her and tell her I loved her. I didn't want to. He
insisted.

I went – shaking all the way as to what I might be getting into....a shouting
match or a knock down drag out? Hesitantly I knocked. And then - the words
that came out of my mouth were not my words. I knew this for sure because I
wasn't 'feeling the love' right at that moment. But God was. I claimed His promise
to help us when we are willing to vulnerably speak out for His sake, and that
promise took precedence over my pride.....

"Just say whatever is given you at the time, for it is not you speaking, but the Holy
Spirit." Mark 13:11...

And again in Matthew: 10:19

"...do not worry about what to say or how to say it. At that time you will be given
what to say, for it will not be you speaking, but the Spirit of your Father speaking
through you"

And so He did....
I told my friend that I had heard and sensed that something was wrong and I
didn't know what I had done. I asked if she would please tell me what was wrong
and why she was so angry with me, so we could work it out. My invitation brought

it out of her and she let me have it fast and furious. Accompanied with loads of anger and tears, she accused me of many violations of our friendship, calling me nasty names that stung. I stood there as though my mouth had been stapled shut [not my normal response in those days!]. Had I really done all those things and been totally unaware of it? No, certainly not intentionally. Some had been blown out of proportion, probably due to not being addressed at the time they arose. After a long while of her dumping out all the vile nasty build up that had poisoned our relationship, she suddenly stopped – both of us in tears. And then what came next was most certainly not me. God was at work, putting into place His 'good plan' for both of us, and allowing the Holy Spirit to speak through me, because I could not possibly humanly have mouthed my next words. His desire was for me to be able to affirm His love for my dear friend, as well as mine for her. He knows the power of Godly affirmation.

I asked her if she was done getting everything out that had built up and needed to be said. She didn't speak. I told her that from my perspective many of the things she had spoken of had no basis of truth. [No, I had not purposefully intended to interfere with her spiritual responsibility to instruct her children in the ways of the Lord; nor had I in any way intended to take her husband's side against hers in their marital struggles, and most certainly I had never had any kind of inappropriate relationship with him.] But in those areas in which I had been insensitive to her feelings, I needed to ask her for forgiveness. I told her that I loved her. She was my Christian sister and I wanted a relationship with her, and nothing could ever come between us that would ever be more important than that. A moment of silence followed and I sensed that it was time to leave. We didn't offer hugs or any more words of explanation. We just parted in a kind of silent separate peace. There was a lot for each of us to process and I had no idea what the aftermath of our discussion might be. I had to give it to God and trust He would use it.

Within the next week, we received a phone call from my friend…she said that they had something they wanted to talk with us about, saying she had spoken with their attorney and wondered if we could come to a meeting on that next Saturday with her, her husband, and their attorney. Now what? My faith grew weak, along with my knees. When Peter was walking on the water, he took his eyes off Jesus and began to sink. I began to do the same, as I panicked over what may lie ahead. Had she thought things over and decided on some kind of retaliation? For what? My imagination soared. Satan was having hay day with my insecurities.

The day came. We went to their home. She greeted us with a guarded smile. I relaxed a little. As we sat down she explained that they had an important question they wanted to ask us. They had spoken with their attorney and were working through some details related to their family's future. And then she asked if we would we be willing to accept the responsibility of becoming Godparents for their children. What!? My heart nearly burst, knowing this meant a restored relationship with her. Of course we would agree to be Godparents to these two precious young people. We loved them like they were our own. God is so faithful! We can be sure that where He guides He will provide!

Shortly after that day, though the kid's dad left his family and began a new relationship in his life, we maintained contact and I continued to pray for God to use us in a positive way with all of them. The kid's dad came by shortly after the break up and shared with me that he had received some news from a Drs visit that was a bit alarming and asked if I would accompany him to the hospital for some more tests. I did and the tests confirmed a brain tumor. Long story short, when they sent him to a specialty hospital about 150 miles away, I accompanied the children to standby with them while their father underwent very serious brain surgery. Sadly, the area of the brain that governs our ability to reason right from wrong had been compromised. That explained so much about his recent behavioral changes. Sometimes we are at a loss to understand the 'whys' of this life. We just have to continue to rely on the ever-present hand of God to guide. It was my privilege throughout that day to sit with our Godchildren and affirm God's love for them and their dad and mom, assuring them He would see them all through this difficult time.

While the kids and I waited in the surgical waiting area, we experienced the opportunity to come alongside and encourage a new acquaintance. We visited with him awhile about his reason for being there, learning that he was awaiting word about the outcome of his young wife's surgery – a last attempt to turn her condition around and save her life. We prayed with him for her well being. We asked if we could share some scriptures with him that might help encourage him that God cares about them and wants to stand with them in their need. So there we sat sharing from a small New Testament that I had marked with the story of the Gospel. What a privilege to be able to share this holy time with Tom and assure him that God was there with him and his wife, and that whatever the outcome of her surgery, He would see them through this time. What a joy to be there as he asked Jesus to come into his life and give him the strength to carry on. And later that day, when we looked up and saw Tom come running down the hall toward us with a huge smile, we all rejoice together. His wife's surgery was successful. She would live. God is so good!

The kid's dad came out of his surgery with a fairly good prognosis for recovery, though his future would require some extra help to navigate life, he was going to be okay.

Yes, God is good! All of the time; God is good! Because of His ultimate plan for good and a purpose for each of us, He had restored a broken relationship. Little did we all know at the time what lie ahead! But because He restored that relationship, these precious kids were provided with all of the love and counsel He could pour through this very unworthy servant during a scary and difficult time. And in the process, they got to experience the exciting birth of a new child of God!

Reconciliation vs The 'Blame Game'

When we allow God's affirmation to flow through us, so that instead of playing the blame game we can be reconciled to one another, *love wins out over adversity*. When we don't, sin wins out and the price we pay is far too high! If we and our friends had spent all our time blaming each other for the difficult situations we were experiencing, we would never have been able to stand by one another through a very difficult life experience, and two children would not have had the opportunity to see God's power to heal and restore! Be sure to hide these liberating truths in your heart. Later, in the Communications Chapter, we will read an account of the devastating consequences we experience when we insist on playing the blame game.

God Declares, 'Here Take Mine'

When God first created humankind – Adam and Eve - He gave them everything they needed to live a blessed and beautiful life. But even in the center of the beautiful garden in which He had placed them, they rebelled against Him, not willing to be vulnerable enough to believe that He had their best interest in mind. As a result, sin entered and began to eat away at the world – like a cancer on the rampage. God gave His children principles to live by so we wouldn't destroy ourselves or each other. We mostly refused to listen, but He continued to love us anyhow, calling us to Himself with message after message, through Prophet after Prophet, over thousands of years, imploring us to give ourselves to Him. Still, a sinful humankind continued to turn away. We refused to yield our hearts and accept His invitation to reach up and give Him our hand allowing Him to pull us out of the mess we had created for ourselves. We refused either because we didn't feel worthy of His Grace, or because we couldn't bring ourselves to believe that we could ever reach high enough [or become good enough] to earn His love. Or maybe humankind made a deliberate choice to enjoy sin rather than surrendering to God and becoming vulnerable to His good plan for us.

Then one day a baby was born in a manger in Bethlehem and the story of the New Testament began to unfold. Instead of God continuing to plead with us, *"give me your hand so I can help you,"* He reached down through His Son Jesus, right into the heart of humankind, while we were still in our sinful condition, and said, *"Here - take mine."* No more stretching up to unattainable heights, keeping all the hundreds of laws laid down by the Sanhedrin in order to be accepted as 'okay' in the eyes of the religious leaders of the day. No more trying to reach up to a lofty God, too perfect to ever accept us right where we are, with all of our failures and imperfections. Through God's Son, Jesus, His loving hands now reach right down into our souls, and standing at the door of our hearts He declares:

"Here I am. I stand at the door [of your heart] and knock. If anyone hears my voice and opens the door, I will come in and eat [fellowship] with Him, and He with me." Revelation 3:20

While God never forces His way into our lives, He stands as close as our hearts door, waiting to be invited in. As the famous painting of Christ knocking at a door depicts, there is no doorknob on the outside of that door. The door represents our heart and the intended message is that the only doorknob is on the inside. If we want intimate connection with God, it is up to us to accept His plea and open the door of our heart to His knock, and invite Him inside to live within us and fellowship with us. When we do, He comes in to stay for all eternity.

A little story comes to mind - told on an Oral Roberts afternoon radio show ....

There were these two men walking along a river bank. One man: a very selfish person, so selfish that he would give no one anything. All who had one time befriended this man had dropped away from him, save this one last friend. Suddenly the selfish man slipped over the river bank and fell into the raging current. He could not swim. His kind friend began to implore the selfish friend, screaming, "Give me your hand – give me your hand!" To which his friend paid no mind. He panicked in face of his plight and made no attempt to let his friend save him. But then, as the selfish man was being swept further and further downstream, his friend who was running along the bank still pleading with him to give him his hand, thought about the fact that this drowning man had been so selfishly looking after his own interests all of his life that he had never reached out to give anyone anything. So, instead of insisting that the drowning man give him his hand, the kind friend leaned down over the edge of the river bank and stretching out his hand as far as he could, switched up his plea, imploring, "Here for heaven's sake take <u>my</u> <u>hand!</u>" to which the very selfish man finally took the hand of the one reaching out to save him.

And so it is with God. He loves us so much that, even in our selfishness, He reaches down to save us. We are no longer implored to reach unattainable heights to find Him. We no longer must go through sacrifices, and Priests, and ceremony, to reach Him. As Christ died on the cross, the thick strong curtain that blocked off the entrance to the room of the Holy of Holies to all but the High Priest was miraculously ripped from corner to corner. Ever since, we have had an open invitation to join Him in entering into the very presence of God.

In dozens of stories recounted throughout the New Testament we see evidence of this truth, of God leaving Heaven in the person of His Son, Jesus. These stories tell of scenario after scenario and Him extending His mighty arm to humankind, saying, *"Here, take mine."* He calls sinners to come and follow

Him; *"Here take mine."* He calls the sick to be healed; *"Here take mine."* He calls the discouraged to be filled; *"Here take mine."* He called the wayward woman at the well to repent and be restored, giving her a glimpse of her future Heavenly home, *"Here take mine."* Through His Angel, even after Peter's denial, Jesus declared to him, *"Here take mine."*

We have no record of Jesus ever refusing a soul who was willing to receive the love that He offered them. And He continues to reach down to us today, in the midst of our failures, our pain, and our trials, saying, *"Here take mine – I love you anyhow."*

God Commands: Do As I Have Done

He asks us to be willing to do the same - to reach out our hand in His name and offer love and compassion to those around us. And, even if they have hurt us, He asks us to be willing to ignore our pride and our 'rights' and offer forgiveness and unconditional love, without waiting or demanding that our offenders grovel at our feet first. To be vulnerable enough to offer 'I Love You Anyhow' in the midst of hurt, affirming those who are drowning in their own circumstances, is to offer the hand of Jesus, in His name and for His sake.

When we employ this nugget of truth, we give a 'bad' situation the benefit of the doubt, for a 'good' outcome. This attitude fosters hope, patience, and kindness, in the midst of what may otherwise result in total brokenness. We are more willing to let go of control and affirm others when we know that in doing so we are affirming God's plan for good, even if we are unable to affirm the behavior of the one with whom we are experiencing conflict.

Allow God to Script You into His Story

God will use every situation to further His purpose, when we are willing to invite Him into it. Sometimes He even ignores our unwillingness and uses us in spite of ourselves. In allowing God to reach through us to touch those whom He brings into our lives, we are allowing ourselves to be scripted into His story. We read a clear example of this when we read the Biblical account of Esther's story. She had a choice to make…trust God and allow herself to be used of the Lord to save His chosen people…or flee from possible imprisonment just because she was a Jew. But what if He didn't come through for her? Her uncle Mordecai challenged her with the possibility that God wanted to use her seemingly impossible situation to secure the salvation of the Jewish nation, and when he posed the question, "What if you were born for such a time as this?" She gave herself to the Lord, trusting in His purpose. The Jewish nation was saved and she became Queen Esther, the King's favorite wife, even though she was of Jewish decent – the race he had intended to annihilate! In doing so, Esther vulnerably allowed herself to be scripted into God's story, instead of succumbing to fear or insisting on following her own plan and then asking Him to bless it. Read her whole fascinating story in the book of Esther. Ask yourself, "Am I willing to be vulnerable enough to submit myself to God's plan, allowing Him to work through my circumstances to ultimately bring about His purpose?" When we are, it is amazing what He will do with our obedience!

The Best Is Yet To Come

Do you recall Jesus' first public miracle, the changing of water into wine? He didn't do that for the convenience of the wine drinkers at the party. He did it to demonstrate a critical truth. It was the custom of the day to impress the guests by serving the good wine up front. And then when everyone became too inebriated to know the difference, the host would pull out the cheap wine to finish the evening. But as often is the case, God's ways are the opposite of ours – He saves the best for last! As we work through tough situations, when we are willing to believe in and act upon this *golden nugget of truth*, vulnerably standing firm on the promise that '*God's best truly is yet to come*,' He will affirm His plan in the end. Many times we don't get to experience the 'best' that He has planned for us because we bail on Him before He has a chance to show us His intended blessing. If we will just vulnerably trust Him on this principle, we will find the wherewithal to stand strong in the current storm for the affirmation of His future blessings!

Wouldn't it be a tragedy to give up on a relationship just one day short of a miracle! When we hold these truths in our hearts – that God knows the end from the beginning and He saves the best for last - we begin to see how relational stumbling blocks can become stepping stones to victory! Then, instead of insisting on instant gratification and falling on our faces, difficult situations become opportunities to grow spiritually; thus allowing our relationships to be lifted to new heights.

Risking Radical Love

God has affirmed His love for us loud and clear. His love is greater than any challenge we face. The fact is, no matter what our victories or failures in either our vertical relationship with Him or our horizontal relationships with each other, when we trust His principles and affirm one another in the midst of our hurts, we are released to risk radical love, for Jesus' sake!

C. S. Lewis records his understanding of this principal in his book, "*Surprised By Joy*," declaring, "*To love greatly is to hurt badly*." Mr. Lewis made it very clear later in his life with his wife, Joy, that being willing to 'hurt badly' in order to enjoy the indescribable joy of 'loving greatly' was well worth the vulnerability it took to serve and affirm her and her children throughout her devastating terminal illness. Watching the film on this story will tenderly move your heart to action when it comes to offering this kind of radical love!

Risking radical love allows us to break down the barriers and embrace one another in the way Jesus embraces us....as intimate friends instead of strangers. In his book, "No Longer Strangers," author Bruce Larson quotes Priest Samuel Johnson: *"Marriage has many pains, but celibacy has no pleasures."* He goes on to explain: *"This radical style of life in Christ has many pains, but anything less has few pleasures. The more we guard our lives and the more we protect ourselves, the lonelier and more withdrawn we become. As we discover in Jesus Christ both the example we need and the power to live as He lived, we go through the pain into a life of deep loving relationships. Through this kind of radical obedience we discover that we are no longer strangers."*

Unfortunately, many of our human 'authorities' in such matters claim differently. They would have us believe that, for all kinds of psychological and psychiatric reasons, God's ways are not really sufficient – maybe even harmful. Instead of encouraging us to work through our relational difficulties with God's principles, people like Margaret Mead have told us that marriage as we've known it cannot and will not survive into the future. Society listens to such predictions and drifts that way – and a self-fulfilling prophecy emerges. Thus as Christians, when our own relationships begin to face challenges, we buy into the idea that hopelessness is 'inevitable.' We give up instead of clinging to the truth we know in our hearts that 'Greater is He that is in us than he that is in this world!"

God implores us to trust Him, being vulnerable enough to affirm those around us with the power of His *'I Love You Anyhow'* kind of love. Instead, all too often we give up on relationships just short of the healing God has in store. We have become a society full of compromised, abusive, non-traditional, shallow marital relationships. It doesn't have to be that way!

When we are willing to be committed to His ways, vulnerably affirming those around us with His kind of love, God is willing and able to heal and restore us to unconditional love, with our spouses, our kids, and our friends! Do you yearn for deeper, more meaningful relationships with those in your life? Love unconditionally. Accept others as they are. God will do the rest! I've experienced this miracle over and over again!

The Journey is Rocky – But the Rewards are Out of This World!

My journey has been filled with highly vulnerable moments, some in which I chose to protect myself and some in which, even in face of my weaknesses, I allowed God to give me the strength (as I held on to Him for dear life) to offer an *'I Love You Anyhow'* kind of love. I have learned that the blessings of the latter far outweigh the former. I would not choose to return to a life of missing out on loving those whom He wants to love through me for anything this world has to offer! If only for my precious Godchildren, I thank God for His faithfulness!

No one is perfect, thus if perfection is required for our relationships, they will last only as long as it takes for the next imperfection to manifest itself. Relationships will be very short lived if they are based solely on a commitment to one another – not a marital one, not a parent/child one, not a friend to friend one. For our relationships to thrive, there must be not only a commitment to one another, but they must also be brought to the altar and released to the Holy Spirit of God, allowing Jesus to take ownership of them. If we insist on maintaining ownership of them, our relationships will only ever be as good as we are. It is so easy to become selfish and possessive of those we love. That isn't love. We must release those we love. The greatest love we can show someone is to love that which they love, and those whom they love, with the same passion with which they love them. To release a relationship to God's ownership is to give Him the right to direct it in His way, holding back no portion of it for our own selfish desires.

Sometimes the Task is Daunting But We are Not Alone

These Biblical concepts on how to handle our relationships may seem a bit scary and overwhelming, particularly if you are accustomed to being in control. I couldn't agree more! Giving up control requires a great vulnerability. Remember, the God to whom we relinquish control of our precious relationships is the author of vulnerability. He understands. And He gave His all in order that we might invite Him to come walk with us and become our strength....

"I can do all things through Christ, who strengthens me." Philippians 4:13

When we trust Christ as our Savior, our very existence is with God. As Jesus walked this earth He gave us example after example of our co-existence with Him. In Jesus' last days on earth, He cried out to the Father to help us understand what this intimate connection looks like. Listen to His plea recorded in the book of John, 17th chapter....

"My prayer is not for them alone [the disciples] I pray also for those who will believe in me through their message, that all of them may be one, Father, just as you are in me and I am in you.

When He is in us and we are in Him, and thus through Christ we are in each other, we are so intricately connected that we can do nothing, feel nothing, be nothing, without affecting one another. As Christians, with Jesus living within us, we have all of the Trinity within us empowering us with authority over every other authority. This guarantees us that we will never run out of the resources we need to love and forgive! We have only to recognize and avail ourselves of the presence of the Godhead within us.

It's hard to fathom that though God gives His all to have this kind of intimate relationship with us, mankind continues to live self-serving 'me first' lives that destroy one another. Why? Why do we continue to believe the lie that the pain we feel due to hurtful circumstances has so much control that we can no longer deal with the pressures of life? No, we can't on our own! But when we boldly claim the spiritual resources that were deposited within us when Jesus came to live in our hearts, we are enabled for victory over our circumstances! We are not an island unto ourselves.

God lives in us and He hurts when we hurt. When we refuse to offer others the gift of "I Love You Anyhow," thwarting His very purpose for our lives, God laments, *"Even as you do this to the least of mine you are doing it unto me."* He feels our selfishness, our anger, and our judgment as much as those whom we lash out against with our unkind words and deeds.

Conveying Judgment Hurts God and Others

It is so easy to give off an air of judgment, without ever saying a word - a roll of our eyes, a shrug of our shoulders, a frown, or a shake of the head, they all scream 'rejection' to their intended recipient, without ever opening our mouths. Somehow we've gotten the idea that even though we aren't willing to take responsibility for speaking out our disapproval; perhaps our negative body language will serve to 'set others straight,' causing them enough sense of guilt to change their offensive behavior. And all the while, we believe that we can get by with it without being accountable for our judgmental attitudes, since we didn't 'say' anything negative. Thus, if confronted about our reactions, we can always refuse to accept responsibility for the judgment that others claim to have seen. But they know better, and so do we. And certainly, so does God!

As we discussed in the 'Beginning' section, somehow we have gotten the erroneous idea that we need to help God change people into what He wants them to be. It is worth repeating; 'He does not need nor want us to do that!' His Word and His Holy Spirit are sufficient to do the job. Otherwise, His commandment to us would have been, 'go out and change people so they become acceptable in my eyes.' Instead He has commanded, 'love others as I have loved you!' In doing so, we can help open doors for them to discover the love that was poured out for them on the cross. When we affirm others instead of judging them, they begin to trust us, becoming vulnerable enough to allow us to help them discover God's love and instruction. In doing so, they learn that He is willing and able to help them become all He desires for them to be.

They learn that no matter what baggage they may have, God loves them anyhow!

We are a Part of God's Plan for Reconciliation

God desperately wants the world reconciled to Him and for us to be reconciled to each other. He sent Jesus to make this possible and He clearly states that His plan for us, as Christians, is that we participate in carrying out this ministry of reconciliation. This commission demands a willingness on our part, to yield to the principles of affirmation and vulnerability! When through vulnerability and affirmation we begin to reconcile ourselves to God, and to each other, a Holy Spirit empowered change takes place that fulfills God's plan. Take a look at God's instruction regarding this process.....

> *"For if when we were God's enemies, we were reconciled to him through the death of his Son, how much more, having been reconciled, shall we be saved through his life! Not only is this so, but we rejoice in God through our Lord Jesus Christ, through whom we have now received reconciliation."* Romans 5:10-11

> *"All this is from God, who reconciled us to himself through Christ and gave us the ministry of reconciliation: That God was reconciling the world to himself in Christ, not counting men's sins against them. And he has committed to us the message of reconciliation. We are therefore Christ's ambassadors, as though God were making his appeal through us. We implore you on Christ's behalf; be reconciled to God."* II Corinthians 5:18-20

What vulnerability on God's part! Imagine Him trusting us – mere mortals – with the ministry of reconciliation 'as though He were reconciling the world to Himself <u>through</u> us!' It begs the question; *"What are you doing about this assignment? What am I?'* We have a huge calling, to be vulnerable enough to love those around us in a way that helps bring reconciliation between them and their Savior and between them and us! It doesn't matter what gender, or religion, or ethnic group, or belief they come from – our command is to love them! We will visit this scripture again in later chapters, as it relates to our Christian growth and assignment to pay forward all of the love we have received from the Lord.

Clearly 'affirmation' and 'vulnerability' go hand in hand. One without the other is virtually unobtainable. As Jesus - fully human yet fully God - hung vulnerably on the cross, He was powerfully affirming His love for <u>all</u> mankind, because *"It is not his desire that anyone should perish."*

God's Reconciliation is for All Eternity

God is not satisfied with a temporary 'fix,' giving us security and pleasure only for this world, but rather He seeks eternal reconciliation. Jesus makes this so clear during His travels, when He encounters a Samaritan woman drawing water at a well. She is one with whom no 'righteous' man of His day would have even spoken. [Jews did not associate with Samaritans, and she was not only a Samaritan but a prostitute.] Intentionally meeting her right where she is spiritually, He casually sits down to chat with her, with her eternal well-being in mind. Well aware of all her sins, He steers the conversation to openly discuss the unacceptability of her poor choices, while making it very clear to her that He loves her anyway. He vulnerably connects with her, risking the scorn of His peers for doing so, thus demonstrating His willingness to affirm her BEFORE her repentance and restoration. [Love comes first!] He gives her reason to believe that she can turn her life around, and directs her to 'go and sin no more.' But forgiving her and healing her from her current pain isn't enough for Jesus. As if to seal the eternal nature of her healing, He gives her a vision of her future place in the Kingdom. Knowing by her response that she is willing to allow the Holy Spirit to lead her as He has directed, He shares with her the good news of her eternal reconciliation to Him and her home in the Kingdom. Look carefully at their exchange....

> *"Sir," the woman said, "I can see that you are a prophet. Our fathers worshiped on this mountain, but you Jews claim that the place where we must worship is in Jerusalem." Jesus declared, "Believe me woman; a time is coming when you will worship the Father neither on this mountain nor in Jerusalem. You Samaritans worship what you do not know; we worship what we do know, for salvation is from the Jews. Yet a time is coming and has now come when the true worshipers will worship the Father in spirit and truth, for they are the kind of worshipers the Father seeks. God is spirit and his worshipers must worship in spirit and in truth." The woman said, "I know that Messiah" [called Christ] is coming. When he comes, he will explain everything to us." Then Jesus declared, "I who speak to you am he."* John 4:19-26

He loved her 'first.' He loved her 'anyhow.' He loved her eternally! He so believed in her and her willingness to turn her life around that, while they spoke He gave her a vision of how she would be worshipping Him in eternity. He touched her soul with such great love and affirmation that it resulted in her acceptance of His forgiveness and healing, giving her the desire to change her life. She ran back to her village and vulnerably began to tell everyone who would listen about this Savior who accepted her right where she was, loving and healing her, and inviting her to share eternity with Him! The Bible says that many in the village chose to get to know and follow Jesus because of her testimony.

Through this story we also see Jesus' willingness to meet us in the midst of our own failures. He meets us as He met her, to call out our sin and offer forgiveness and eternal healing. Oh that we would follow His example and vulnerably participate with Him in the ministry of reconciling the world to Him, being willing to love people in the midst of their ugliness, introducing them to Jesus and His unconditional love, that they might also repent and have the assurance of His forgiveness and eternal life! What would this world look like if we did? What would our churches look like? What would our families look like? We can only imagine!

We Are All Frogs

Like the woman at the well, we are all acutely aware of our shortcomings. We all know we aren't yet what we want to be…what He wants us to be. We are a work in progress.

There is an age-old story, less Biblical than the woman at the well, but a good mind picture just the same. It is a picture of the healing power of unconditional love. We are all like the character within this story….the story of the infamous frog and the beautiful maiden who loved him. You remember the fairytale. As the frog [probably a toad to be honest] sits upon a lily pad, ugly, alone and dejected, along comes a lovely maiden who scoops him up, lifts him to her warm lips, and gently kisses him. Suddenly the prince of her dreams emerges from the ugly frog. The kiss of the maiden sets the frog free from the spell of the wicked one, and a handsome and grateful prince falls at her feet and praises her for her unselfish act.

Friends, we are under the spell of the wicked one whom the Bible says is roaming this earth, 'looking for whom he may devour.' When successful, he disguises us as ugly frogs – convincing us and others around us that we are unworthy of anyone's loving touch. We desperately need the affirmation of one who cares. If we are to carry out God's commission to love others – to be an example of His reconciliation power - I have a question; how many of us are willing to kiss a frog – an unsightly 'extra grace required' one? And how many of us desperately need to have the handsome prince [or princess] from within set free, so that we can become what God created us to be instead of the ugly frogs we feel we are? If only we could be released from the spell of the master of all liars who brainwashes us with the idea that we are not worthy! Whose kiss will God use to set us free from this lie? He sent Jesus. And Jesus sends us. He asks us to be His representatives – His hands – His feet – His love here on earth, to reconcile all the frogs to Him. We are all frogs at one time or another. Have we also all been willing to become the gracious sire or maiden that God can use for His purpose, to set other frogs free?

From time to time each of us is given opportunities for divine appointments. Sometimes we fail to recognize them as such. Our own agendas take precedent over His. Whenever we allow Him to speak through us, to hug through us, to love through us, He wins and perhaps a prince or princess emerges! So where is God leading you? Who are those in your life that are struggling with attacks from this world, and don't know where to turn for help – those who are feeling like frogs? Can God count on you to reach out and touch them with the truth of how much He loves them - anyhow?

My Journal Reveals My Failure to Yield

We are all vulnerable to this world's pulls. We all need each other's compassion and forgiveness. Though we may be able to help someone else through his/her life's traumas, we aren't always able to work so smoothly through our own. I share from my own experience. Many times when I have felt the most down and discouraged – the most like a frog, instead of sharing my discouragement with someone who may be able to help, I have distanced myself, reasoning that they will probably think I'm dumb for feeling the way I do. What if they give me some kind of advice for my dilemma that I don't want to take? I don't want to feel obligated to listen. Worse yet, what if they stand in judgment of my failures? I couldn't stand that. What if they ask too many questions that I don't want to answer? I'm not quick to be transparent. I know many times I have protected myself from being too vulnerable, even from my own husband. Did I feel he wouldn't 'love me anyhow?' I believe when we are not willing to open up and share our hurts and our needs with those with whom we are the closest, it's because we want to protect ourselves from being too vulnerable. After all, they are the most important people in our lives. We fear that letting them know how we really feel about those 'private' things going on in our head and our heart may cause them to love us less or to think less of us, and it keeps us quiet! We reason that being too vulnerable to our significant others will cost too much. Thus, we clam up. We justify. And in an attempt to protect our own sense of well-being, we judge them, creating a self-fulfilling prophecy. Case in point .....

Personal Reflection
It was about 4:30 and my husband would be coming home from work any time. I had not managed my time well that day and thus not only did I not live up to his expectations [house picked up and dinner ready] but neither my own [getting my son to practice on time]. Thus with an already embedded sense of guilt, harried and frustrated, I was flying out the door to take our son to baseball practice when he arrived. Reading my frustrated expression and observing the condition of the house, he gave me a questioning [or as I read it 'judgmental'] look. My insecurities overtook God's desire for me to be vulnerable, so instead of greeting my husband with a loving hug and asking him to excuse the chaos, I flew out the door exclaiming, "Just don't get all bent out of shape, I'm going to run our son to practice and I'll be home in a minute!"

Sometimes the unexpected confounds things even more. When we arrived at the baseball field the coach was not yet there. Not being one to leave our children without adult supervision, I stayed. Then, while waiting for the coach to arrive, a friend came along and a conversation started. Again not managing my time well, after we had visited for well over a half an hour my husband appeared, frustrated and concerned about my whereabouts. Needless to say I became defensive. My thoughts? "I had a right to talk to a friend, didn't I?" "Who did he think he was, anyway?" "For heaven's sake, He doesn't own me!" We both exchanged a few heated words and stormed off in our separate cars to head for home – a very silent home. The 'silent treatment' was often our way of coping with that which we were afraid to confront. Self-righteously I fixed supper – in total silence. We ate supper – in total silence. The air was thick and communications nonexistent. We were acting out the 'silent treatment' scene referred to in "The Beginning" chapter of this book, from Reuben Welch's, "We Really Do Need Each Other." This was far from the first time that 'unfulfilled expectations' had plummeted us into this state, threatening to drive us further and further apart. But this time something different happened.

God's love crept into a tiny crack of vulnerability in my heart and I listened. I didn't always. But this time for some reason I did. His words pierced by soul, "You know you have the power to turn this thing around, don't you?" "What happened to all this studying you've been doing – to the 'vulnerability' and 'affirmation' thing? What about, saying, "I Love You Anyhow?" Though I was unable to respond, I tucked His words into my heart to ponder them and went about my business - silently.

I found that, though I wanted to respond to His plea, I just couldn't open my mouth and admit to any culpability in the matter – thinking doing so would surely indicate, 'I was wrong and my husband was right – yet again.' And that would most certainly say to him, 'You can treat me this way anytime you want to.' My spirit was so conflicted that as soon as I could get supper cleared away, I went out on the porch and wept bitterly. What was happening? This wasn't the end of the world for heaven's sake. Then why did it feel like it was? I was so tired of seeing judgmental looks and being confronted with what I saw as a 'holier than thou' attitude! I deserved better, didn't I? As I sat there, I decided I was just done - done subjecting myself to this. Oh, he had assured me time and time again that he wasn't judging me, but then why did it always feel that way? I just wanted to get in the car and leave, at least for awhile. I remembered how many times my mother had threatened to leave and how it cut me to the core to think of her going. And I knew that leaving too often becomes the easy way out, and that it would also be running away from a truth that God was trying to reveal in my heart in order to bring healing. And I knew that no matter where we might run to, we can't run away from ourselves. I pondered on His principle that 'the best is always yet to come' and knew that leaving would steal that opportunity from us. As I sat there mentally beating up on myself, I began to think: Perhaps it's all me. Perhaps all these kind of issues come out of my own programmed background screaming at me, "you're not okay – never were – never will be!"

Though it certainly didn't feel like it at that moment – God was at work. I do not ascribe to the theory that these times are of God's doing. He is not the author of hateful attitudes, or jealousy or judgment. Yet we are told that He uses these tough times of our own creation to get our attention, and if we will let Him, He will use them to bring about healing and restoration. And so He did on this occasion.

God had been at work in my husband's heart as well. He walked out on the porch to join me, sat down and silently put his arm around my shoulder. His gentle touch defused my anger and before he could say anything, the Holy Spirit opened up my mouth and spoke. The apology was simple and clear, void of my oft accusatory tone. It was like an out-of-body experience because it certainly wasn't like me to open up and offer such a confession and apology. My dear husband was taken back. Quite frankly, so was I.

We held each other and we cried. We actually entered into a discussion about these repeated times of distress, and what was causing them, and what we might be able to do to help eliminate them. We prayed together – for the first time in our married life. Though we were individually devoted to personal time, and though we had advocated the importance of shared prayer to others, it had not been a reality in our own relationship, until that moment.

When we are willing to be vulnerable and open up to God's leading, we invite Him into our circumstances. When we allow Him into the midst of the muck and the mire within us, He reveals His plan. 'Inviting' Him in is the key.

Though by this time each of us had invited Jesus to come into our individual lives, we had never thought to invite Him to come into the 'one' life that, according to the Bible, was created at the time of our marriage. God clearly states that when husband and wife are joined together, they become 'one.' How does that 'one' new life become fully committed to a life in Christ, a life that is supposed to come under submission to His laws of relationships? We decided that, just as we had as individuals, we would now together invite Jesus to become the Lord of our 'one' united life. We've often reflected since, that taking that step that night may likely be the key reason why we are still together fifty-two+ years later, and continue wholly committed to live out our promise *'until death us do part.'* Unfortunately frustrations similar to that night have too often been repeated, because we are forgiven, not perfect. But God is faithful and learning to live out an, *"I Love You Anyhow"* kind of relationship becomes more and more doable every day. We praise Him for His faithfulness and thank Him for His continued forgiveness! Human life is complicated, too complicated to grasp the fullness of it all. Though in this world we see through a glass dimly, we know that one day we shall put on His nature, and then see all things clearly!

Hate the Sin Not the Sinner

One of the hardest lessons learned in my Christian walk has been trying to understand how to balance *loving the sinner* [including myself] while *rejecting the sin*. What I have observed is though we have the admirable goal of not 'compromising' our principles so as to not fall into the current practice of 'embracing the sin,' we often come dangerously close to swinging the pendulum too far and condemning the sinners for whom Jesus gave His very life. As we look for the right balance, we need to be constantly reminded that we are commissioned to love and reconcile the world to Jesus, 'teaching others all that He has taught us,' and while doing so, 'to be holy even as He is holy.' Thus, we need to continually and diligently ask the Holy Spirit to protect us from engaging in the sin, while at the same time fully loving the sinner for the sake of Jesus. When loving others for Christ, let's be bold in our honesty about their involvement in a lifestyle that robs them of God's greatest blessings, but let's do it in the name and with the love of Christ, assuring them that while we in no way condone the sin, we love them 'anyhow.'

There is a dear young man with whom I had the privilege of sharing the Lord one day. I bowed with him in prayer as he clearly opened his heart to Jesus. He is smart, handsome, and charming. Now, later in his life, he has chosen to live with a partner, engaging in the homosexual lifestyle. I have never stopped praying for God to give him the desire, strength, and discipline to instead choose a lifestyle upon which God is free to pour out His fullest blessings. While traveling on a business trip to the state in which he lives, I chose to visit their home. I was received with a warm genuine love, the same kind of love I had chosen to offer them. Keeping a loving connection with him has kept the doors of communication open, and while he knows I love him with the love of Christ, it has allowed me to share with him that his chosen lifestyle saddens God and prevents Him from being free to bestow the very best of His blessings on him. When last together, as we hugged goodbye he whispered in my ear; *"Don't stop praying for me."* I believe he truly wants to break the bondage of this lifestyle that is robbing him of God's very best. And when he does, I will be there to support him and rejoice with him as he makes the transition!

It takes an open vulnerability and an unselfish commitment to be willing to find a way to affirm those whose choices are clearly contrary to God's Word. For a choice to be unacceptable according to God's Word is for it to be unacceptable to His people. There is no grey area here. But remember, though we don't agree with one's life style, we must agree with God that they are precious to Him....period. In fact, they are so precious to Him that He affirms them in the midst of their sin, by sending His Holy Spirit [perhaps through you] to help convict them of that sin and reconcile them to Jesus Christ.

How are we doing at being the vessels through which He can plant seeds of love and conviction? When we grow inward, protecting ourselves from being vulnerable, God's principle of sowing and reaping becomes a negative reality in our lives. He tells us that 'when we sow sparingly, we also reap sparingly, but when we sow generously we also will reap generously.' What kind of victories are you reaping right now? Perhaps if we are not receiving the generous amount of affirmation for which we long, it is because we are holding back on sowing seeds of affirmation in the lives of others. As we vulnerably affirm God's love for those around us, He is able to break the chains of bondage and free them [and us] from a life of mediocre existence.

Though we are commissioned to reach out and affirm others, we must be careful to do so with the goal in mind of helping them turn to Christ, and not to us, to get in touch with God's love and forgiveness for them. Otherwise there is a danger that they will establish a misplaced allegiance to us instead of to Him. In doing so, we risk making their circumstances worse than they were before. Love others sincerely, and remember that the source of love and forgiveness we share is <u>only</u> <u>ever</u> God. He is the source, we are simply His vessel.

It Is All For Christ

Just as we are given the assignment to reach out in the Lord's name to affirm others, we all need someone to come alongside of us in the traumas of our lives. Things happen to us all that just don't seem fair. We can choose our response. We can become victims, sulking in our desperate need for affirmation, or we can seek God's love and healing, reconciling ourselves to Him and His purposes. He is the ultimate healer. And though He works through people, ultimately we must learn to go to Him and seek His fulfillment and purpose for our lives. While it is God's commission that we love and affirm one another, if we become too dependent on people to fill our 'emotional tank' with enough affirmation to make us feel 'okay,' we will be disappointed. It takes a delicate balance to give and receive a vulnerable/affirmative love, while remembering it is all for Christ. If it is not for Him, we run the risk of establishing an unhealthy human co-dependency, both for us and for those we love. When we do so, we are setting ourselves up for disappointment. I know. I've fallen into this trap and thank God, as He always does, He met me on my growing edge and turned my eyes towards Him for my sense of well-being. The story went like this:

> **Personal Reflection**
> *I had worked for a ministry company for dozens of years. Money was not plentiful. My 'office' space was frequently shifted from corner to corner. I had helped the founder to develop this company from its birth. I idolized him and his ministry and he invested huge amounts of time mentoring me. At one point, we decided to hire a director over one of the areas of our operation. He came aboard and we were*

delighted to have his help. It was my assignment to train him and report back to the company president as to his progress. It was back in the day when a 'woman' in the work force just wasn't seen on the same level as her male counterparts. Though our new director was given a salary much higher than mine and a spacious private office, my secretary and I continued to share an area of operation in a very small corner. Because that's just the way it was back then, I thought I was okay with it. Together we oversaw a growing international operation, with clients in fifty-three countries. In order to adequately carry out this assignment, there were so many things I needed, but couldn't get due to the 'tight budget.' It made the work difficult but I kept telling myself it was just the way it was and that someday [when we had more resources] I would be able to get a decent typewriter and maybe even a private corner in which to conduct all the president's communications for which I had been given charge. As I look back I knew I was subconsciously struggling with the seeming 'unfairness' of the situation. Then one day our new director called me to come to his office, saying he would like to show me something and get my opinion. When I arrived he had several catalogues scattered across his desk from which he ascertained whether I thought he should choose the 'walnut' or 'cherry wood' furniture ensemble, stating that he had been given the 'ok' to select whatever he liked. My mind and my spirit went blank. Anger, hurt, jealousy, and a total sense of worthlessness overtook my soul. Where was any fairness in this? Where was the affirmation I so longed for from our company leadership, the one whom I considered the dearest of friends? My need for more space and more equipment had been totally ignored, while it seemed to be flowing freely in the direction of our new director. I had to leave. I quietly picked up my things, got in the car, and started to drive – and drive – and drive. For miles and miles and miles I drove [my chosen method of therapy at the time]. And as I drove, I cried and cried and cried. Then, when it seemed I had emptied myself of every possible tear – still driving – God began to speak, gently challenging me: "You want a title....I have called you my child – a child of God! You want your own space?....I am building you a mansion, here with me! You want more income?....Have I not always supplied you with anything you have ever really needed?" My heart melted. My spirit began to yield and to heal. Now the tears were those of gratitude, as I checked into a hotel in the middle of nowhere and spent the next 12 hours lying across the bed, pouring out all the anger that had built up, and seeking His peace. He truly had offered me all the affirmation and supply I ever really needed, while I had been seeking it all from human affirmation and circumstances that never really could. I returned to the office the next day and for 18 productive years thereafter, determined to never again allow myself to seek affirmation from anyone or anything outside of what was already mine in the Lord. As a result God allowed me the blessing of being a part of a ministry through which He has brought thousands to Christ. I am forever grateful to God for meeting me right where I was with His direction, compassion, love, and healing, and restoring me so I could continue serving Him!

Vulnerability Births Honesty

We all have a special someone, or if we are extra blessed perhaps several 'someones' in our lives from which we desire love and affirmation. And I believe that's a blessing. But when we expect from human beings that which is only God's to give, we open ourselves and our relationships to a lot of pain and failure. We can become so dependent on human approval that we fear being transparent and sometimes even honest, lest they won't like what they see or hear. We protect ourselves so much that we end up with only very shallow relationships.

Ask yourself: How do I think I am doing in this area? What if my spouse, child, or dear friend is totally honest with me, telling me something that shocks me and rocks me to the core? Have I made a commitment, for the Lord's sake, that I will not 'react' in shock, no matter what they may tell me? Have I determined that instead of 'reacting' out of my own emotions I will instead 'act' upon God's principles of relationships?

When we can sincerely determine to do this, others will sense that they can be honest with us, while having the assurance that we will love them anyhow. This doesn't mean we will accept and approve everything they say or do. Likely, we will not. But it does mean that we are committed to working through the issues with them. We cannot encourage someone regarding the reality of their life's dilemmas, if we never encounter the truth of their inner existence. God can never use us to help bring healing into the life of a troubled soul, if our judgment prevents them from honestly sharing their inside pain with us. This was a tough lesson learned by Pastor and author Bruce Larsen, regarding his relationship with his son, as recorded in his book, *"No Longer Strangers."* Check out his moving account of this story later, in the Communications chapter.

Do you have people in your life who, when they don't react to you in a way that somehow affirms you, you quickly entertain thoughts of judgment? Your mind whirls, *"What's wrong with them anyway?" "Who put a chip on their shoulder?"* Ask yourself, *"What would happen if I were able to have the kind of relationship with them that allowed authenticity? What would happen if they knew that they could let me know their very inner being and I would, 'love them anyhow?' What would happen if the two of us were able to have an up-front agreement that there is 'nothing' either of us could ever say or do, that would ever destroy our love for one another?"* It is possible. When we truly realize how fully we are loved by our creator [even though He knows EVERYTHING about us] we can risk loving that radically. When we are sincerely willing to make an 'I will always love you anyhow' commitment to one another, we are able to risk vulnerably laying our souls out there in the space between one another. That's the kind of action that allows the deepest relationship possible.

Also in Bruce Larsen's book, 'No Longer Strangers," he shares a poem by Earnest L. Stech that grips my soul with the very reality of its claim. In sharing this poem with workshop attendees around the world, I have found that it resonates with everyone who hears it. Could it be that, at one time or another, we all could have been its author? As you read it, ask yourself, "Have I ever been vulnerable enough to put my soul out there? What happened when I did? How do I treat the souls of others laid before me?"

THAT'S MY SOUL

That's my soul lying there.
You don't know what a soul is?
You think it's some kind of ghostly sheet like
thing you can see through and it floats in the air?
Well, that's my soul lying there.

Remember when my hand shook because I was
nervous in the group?
Remember the night I goofed and argued too much
and got mad and couldn't get out of the whole mess?
I was putting my soul on the line.

Another time I said that someone once told me
something about herself that she didn't have to.
I said that she told me something that could have hurt her.
And I guess I was asking you to do the same.
I was asking you to let me know you.
That's part of my soul too.

When I told you that my mother didn't love my dad
and I knew it as a kid.
When I said that my eyes water when I get hurt
even though I'm thirty-four and too much a man to cry,
I was putting my soul out there in the space between you and me.
Yeah, that's my soul lying there.

I've never met God.
I mean I've never met that old man who sits on a
cloud with a crown and a staff and knows everything.
But I've met you.

Is that God in your face?
Is that God in your soul lying there?

Well, that's my soul lying there.
I'll let you pick it up.
That's why I put it there.

It'll bruise and turn rancid like an old banana
if you want to ignore it.

But if you want to put your soul there beside it
There may be love.
There may even be God!

How many times has it been your soul lying there – yearning for love and acceptance? How many of us have put our soul out there between us and a friend only to have it 'manhandled' until it turned rancid like an old banana? And we've come away vowing – never again! So we go on silently crying out for connection that counts – time and time again, grasping at the world's very poor, short range, counterfeit substitutes for the love we seek – believing that the next friend, or significant other, or spouse, or promotion will fill the void inside. It won't. We are commanded to treat one another's souls with gentleness and love so that in the process, there may be true reconciliation with God. God awaits patiently for the day when we wake up and realize that if we are willing to put our souls out there on the line for Him, they will be safe in His hands!

As you continue to read you will hear of many more accounts of lives that have been touched when souls were laid out there on the line - some victorious - some not so much. Just a reminder...the personal reflections as well as other stories that are penned are true, but the names of those involved are not, so as to protect the dear ones involved.

The stories shared in this book are told for the purpose of giving testimony to God's faithful and unconditional love. Revealing that He brings restoration and healing in spite of our human inadequacies. You will read of how relationships are both torn down and built up as a result of our actions in the midst of circumstances such as:

- communications breakdown
- using the 'silent treatment' to try and manipulate
- playing the 'if' game
- realizing that though we fail, we are not a failure
- finding a way to affirm the unlovely and to be vulnerable enough to let others in
- relational role reversals
- identifying the *real* 'strings of stress' that are tearing our relationships apart – as opposed to the symptoms they create
- applying the dynamics of forgiveness rather that the disaster of retaliation
- connecting with God's empowerment to grow and pay forward His blessings

"*Precious Jesus, we want to put our souls out there for your sake. Help us do that. We come to you naked from the clothes of pretense. You know us right where we are, and yet you demonstrate your love for us anyhow. Thank you! You know our insecurities and our needs even before we do. You are willing to guide and protect us as we try to love as you have loved us. Help us not to fear open, honest relationships. You have said that 'perfect love' casts out fear. God we no longer want to fear being vulnerable enough to affirm those around us. We want to be willing to vulnerably put our souls out there and to gently respect the souls of others, as they are revealed to us. We ask you to come into the midst of our relationships and strengthen and heal them. Teach us, Lord, how to be vulnerable enough to affirm others in such a way that those to whom you send us will clearly hear us proclaim, I Love You Anyhow! Thank you!* Amen"

Personal Application

TRUTH:

God has a plan for our lives and gifts us to live out His purpose for us. When we keep our eyes on Christ, rather than the people and circumstances around us, it allows the Holy Spirit access to empower us with a vulnerability to affirm others, even in the face of unfulfilled expectations.

1. Jeremiah declares that God has a plan for our lives [Jeremiah 29:11-13]. What does Proverbs 3:5-6 and Romans 8:28 tell us about how we might seek out that plan?

2. Do you have a relationship[s] that takes precedent over your relationship with God? Take a minute now to confess your need to set your priorities straight and ask God to help you allow Him to take His rightful place in them.

3. What does it mean to you personally when you ponder God's offer, "*Here take mine?*"

4. Think back on your relationships…can you think of incidents when instead of participating with God in the ministry of reconciliation, you chose to play the blame game? How would you handle those incidents differently now?

5. In reflecting back over your life, note times when you absolutely felt like a frog. Think of times when someone was willing to embrace you in your *frogly* state. How did that make you feel? Times when you were willing to embrace a frog. What did you do? In your current acquaintances are there those to whom you believe God may be calling you to affirm them in their *frogly* state? Note who they are and write down a plan as to what action steps you will take to help reconcile them to God and to others.

Journal Entry
— — CC Hays 5/1969

He sits in his own private shell
Where the interruptive noises of
the world outside
can be stilled,
and the inner thoughts and
outer hell
can conflict and war in serenity.

He wrestles with foes he cannot see,
and hurts from wounds that do not bleed.
To take a stand, to fight
or flee
is his temptation.
Superimposed upon him by integrity
is the notion that he must succeed,
and failure causes his frustration.

From within the dark cavern of his soul
there come cries for help,
and most of all for understanding.
With whispers as loud as thunder he
makes his bold
and pitiable plea for acceptance
that often sounds demanding.

Alas, his cries go on unheeded.
Feeling unneeded
and unwanted by a too busy world,
he is driven further into the darkness
of selfishness
until the last glow of communication
is snuffed out by apathy
and he is alone.

"A misfit" the world says, as
he takes his private walks
and gathers private hammer and nail
to construct further barriers
to involvement.
Can no one see that by his talk
he wants to mention
that his empty life could be transformed from
Hell to Happiness
if someone would pay attention?

Journal Entry: ***You and I and God Are One***
God is Spirit
And we are one
And with that....
A thought, well begun
But, only just begun.

In the depth of a soul
In an outstretched hand
In an anguished cry
From a dying man....

With a tear stained face,
And a hurt inside
That knaws and aches
With the loss of pride...

God completed this thought
This idea begun...
When He exposed His heart,
His beloved Son.

Can we do less
Than He has done?

As "One with Him"
So "One with His"
One in hurt, in pain, in love
One in Spirit – in Reality

"One"...where indifference cannot belong
Where God Himself keeps the bonds so strong
That, as we daily walk and talk and live,
Our 'Oneness' grows in the bond of love

The cement that bonds us "one-to-one"
The blood of Christ,
In a work well done.

There are but few who will carry on
Expose their heart, and share His Son
To those who do, the ultimate comes
In a beautiful work – well begun

The Truth that's felt in reality
That you and I and God are One!

CHAPTER THREE
COMMUNICATIONS

When has two-way communication really happened? When you have spoken? Or when someone else has really heard what you've said? Or when the person you have spoken to actually responds to what you have said?

What are the unseen elements that damage and destroy our communications? We each have our own communication style, and while some of that style comes to us as a result of the elements of our inheritance, much of our communication style is the result of learned relational behaviors. The effectiveness of our communications – good or bad - is often the axis around which our relationships live or die.

As we touched on in the first chapter we all communicate, verbally with our words, and non-verbally with our body language – often louder than our words. Too often the meaning of our words is lost because of the manner in which they are spoken, allowing attitude to get in the way of intent. Remember too that communication is two-way. If we are to have effective communications with our families, friends, and with the Lord, it takes commitment not only to speaking but also to listening. Reflect for a moment on your listening style. Do you give eye contact to one who is speaking to you? What is your body language saying while others are telling you something? Do you interrupt; perhaps stop listening altogether, while your mind wonders on to something else? Do you practice 'active listening,' giving feedback in the form of questions that help clarify what one is saying to you? If we just talk and never listen, we are missing out on the heart of what others, including the Lord, want to say to us. When we pour out our hearts in prayer, abruptly ending with "*Amen*," it's like hanging up the phone on a friend before they've ever gotten a chance to respond. If we don't discipline ourselves to sit quietly and listen for God's response, how do we ever know what direction He might have given us in addressing our spoken requests? Remember, effective communication is presenting a clear sincere message and then listening for a response with an open heart and both ears!

So what are some of the ways we can practice better communication? And most important, what Biblical communication principles can we adopt that will help bring healing to our relationships? What were Jesus' communication techniques in drawing people to Himself, the rich and the poor, the educated and the illiterate, the religious and the heathen? He was the ultimate communicator, even to the children who flocked to Him and were not forbade from doing so, because he directed those who tried to stop them, "let the little children come to me." In this chapter we will investigate the golden nuggets of truth revealed throughout the Bible, regarding Godly communications. So, let's start unpacking some of the basic elements of effective, Godly communications.

Speak Softly [but don't carry a big stick]

When working with a group of children or even an adult group, have you ever begun speaking very softly, almost in a whisper, as opposed to using your bold outside voice? Have you noticed how quickly your audience quiets down and listens? I have. As a pre-school director and teacher of young people for 10 years, I have often used this communication technique to reach a rowdy group and/or a screaming and distraught child. In mentoring our teaching staff to do the same, we were blessed to see that the children would nearly always stop and listen whenever those of us teaching would start whispering, instead of attempting to 'out-yell' them.

We live in a loud and consistently noisy world. All of our electronics keep dialogue pouring into our ears to a degree that 'quiet time' is nearly non-existent. Because we've become so acclimated to this constant noisiness, it seems the louder an appeal the more chance it has of getting attention. All too often we find ourselves yelling, or at least elevating our voices beyond what is necessary to make our point. But the truth is, whenever we are able to keep our communications calm, instead of allowing them to escalate into a panic mode [especially in the midst of difficult situations] we will help bring about a sense of calmness around us. This often results in reducing a potentially explosive situation to a much more reasonable, perhaps even loving one. Jesus was not a yeller, save for one recorded account describing His reaction to the corruption in the temple courts. Jesus showed us by the turning over of tables in the temple, that there is a time for righteous anger. However, we see very little of that kind of reaction from Him. Instead we read of numerous very difficult situations in which Jesus calmly brought about the needed understanding, answers, and healing to those around Him.

For example, the last night with His disciples Jesus' accusers come to arrest Him. In anger, Peter jumps up and cuts off the ear of a servant to the high priest. In contrast, as Jesus rebukes Peter from such violent reaction, He instead calmly replaces the soldier's ear, and then obediently moves on with those who have come to arrest Him.

This is very different from today's society, where our communications seem to present a high level of accusatory anger much of the time. Again we look at Jesus' response. When asked repeatedly to defend himself in front of His accusers, He simply and calmly stated who He was. He knew He didn't have to defend Himself – neither before God nor before the Sanhedrin.

We are not on our own to defend ourselves when we are falsely accused. We don't have to raise our voice in anger. We can rest in the fact that the Bible clearly states that the Holy Spirit will intercede on our behalf, before the throne of God! He is our advocate. He knows the source of our inner struggles even better than we do. In Romans 8:26 He pleads before God on our behalf.

> *"In the same way, the Spirit helps us in our weakness. We do not know what we ought to pray for, but the spirit himself intercedes for us with groans that words cannot express."*

Go to the Lord and pour out your petitions, allowing His Spirit to advocate for you, instead of thinking the louder and more unreasonable you become, the better chance you will get what you want. And yes, yelling may get us what we <u>want</u>, but will it get us what we <u>need</u>? Will it get us the very best that God has prepared for us in the end?

Short-Sighted Communication vs Communication for a Higher Purpose

Our understanding of a given situation is limited; our point of reference encompasses only what is immediately visible. Unfortunately, we often don't take the time to consider how the impact of a current situation will affect our future. We speak and act out of a survival mode, with a 'fast food' mentality that demands immediate satisfaction. Jesus, on the other hand, used His communications to lay the ground work for a higher purpose. He often spoke in parables, so His disciples would see the bigger picture of what he was trying to communicate. He was in no hurry and didn't panic even when, from a human point of view, situations seemed to demand it. Consider this story ….

> *"After leaving them [the disciples], he [Jesus] went into the hills to pray. When evening came, the boat was in the middle of the lake, and he was alone on land.*

He saw the disciples straining at the oars, because the wind was against them. About the fourth watch of the night he went out to them, walking on the lake. He was about to pass by them, but when they saw him walking on the lake, they thought he was a ghost. They cried out, because they all saw him and they were terrified. Immediately he spoke to them and said, "Take courage! It is I. Don't be afraid." Then he climbed into the boat with them, and the wind died down. They were completely amazed..." Mark 6:46-51a

What a calm, effective example of an 'in control' response! Imagine, Jesus calmly walked across a stormy sea, climbed into the boat, and said, "*It's all right. Don't be afraid.*" That was no normal feat! And yet it doesn't appear from the Biblical recording of the incident that there was much fanfare or drama to it. He could have just stood on the shore and calmed the sea, after all He and his Father are in charge of the elements. He must have had an additional message that He wanted the disciples [and us] to learn from His response. Perhaps it is to 'trust' that He is in charge of the scary situations that happen in our lives. He is there to get in the boat with us. He is not only able, but also willing to calm the storms in our lives. Trusting Him to do so will enable our reactions to a given trauma to be calmer.

You may be reasoning, of course He could calm the storm because He is Jesus, right? But likewise, the power of the Holy Spirit that comes to live in our lives when we decide to trust Jesus' [see Colossians 1:5 and Ephesians 1:18-20] will help calm the storms in our lives. When we allow the Holy Spirit within us to have control, He will give us the same assured calmness. What do you suppose would have been the disciple's reactions had Jesus begun yelling at them, "Where's your faith? Grow up and quit screaming!" We are given many opportunities to respond to the trauma in the lives of those around us with a Christ-like calmness, re-assuring them that God is there for them, willing to calm the storms in their lives.

Body Language vs Verbal Language

In addition to Jesus' words, let us observe His actions. He not only said, "*It is all right – don't be afraid*" He also calmly climbed into the boat and sat down with them. By doing so, He showed His belief that He believed what He said….it was truly going to be all right. Are we willing to climb into the boat with those around us who are battling the fears, failures and storms of their lives? And when we do, are we willing and able to allow God to speak calmly through us? He asks us to be.

By getting in the boat and calmly sitting with the disciples in the midst of the storm, Jesus demonstrates a critical truth about communications: they are not always just verbal. In fact, I would venture to say more often than not, our body language speaks much louder than our words. Jesus' body language supported His words, *'It's alright. Don't be afraid."*

When a person's actions display *"you exasperate me"* but their words say, *"no nothing's wrong,"* which are you going to be quicker to believe, the words? Or the actions? You've heard the claim, *"I can't hear you – your actions are speaking louder than your words!"* So true! Some people are much more sensitive to facial expressions and body language than others. I realize I am one of those people. But I think most of us pick up on such responses, and react almost automatically to the roll of the eyes, or a frown, or a deep breath of exasperation, taken at just the right moment to get a point across, without words. We need to accept the challenge to be extremely aware of our body language, asking the Lord for His calmness in the midst of our storms.

To help us get a mind picture of this principle, consider the task of an animal trainer. His subjects are conditioned to respond to the tone of their trainer's voice and the manner in which commands are given. It is inherent in the animal's nature. So if the trainer angrily bellers *'GOOD BOY'* with a scowl and a gruff voice, the animal learns to shy away – not from the words but 'how' they were spoken. Likewise, *'BAD BOY'* with a smile and a pat on the head will get a lick of appreciation. Our body language truly does make a huge difference – most especially to insightful and/or sensitive people.

Remember though words reflect our external communications, our tone and actions often reflect attitudes that come from deep within. Who sets on the throne of your communications – self or Jesus? One clue in determining the answer is to examine who is taking charge of your communications in the midst of difficult situations. Is it the calmness of Jesus? Or is it the frustrations and insecurities of 'self?'

Take Charge of Your Own Response

God does not accept the excuse, "But look how they treat me" or "Well when they start acting like a Christian, I'll treat them like one." We cannot control how others treat us. But we must control how we respond to them. Again let's revisit this important truth in Romans:

> *"Bless those who persecute you; bless and do not curse…Do not repay anyone evil for evil…If it is possible, as far as it depends on you, live at peace with everyone."* Romans 12:14,17,18

What better way to communicate *"I Love You Anyhow"* than with a God-sent smile, loving eyes, or a gentle touch, when a punch in the nose seems like a more natural response! This God-given ability to respond in love is a gift that just keeps on giving – take it and pay it forward! The more you do the more natural it will become. Quit allowing the way others treat you to control how you respond, thus stealing your joy and ultimately your intimate walk with Jesus!

Inherited Reactions

It's commonly accepted that our human DNA influences our reactions to situations. It would not be wise to ignore that. However, the inheritance of our human makeup is never stronger than our spiritual inheritance – for we have been created in our Heavenly Father's image. Not to recognize that is a tragedy! Thus, the spiritual family traits that you and I have inherited far outweigh our ancestral family traits. Let us be aware of and claim the true source of our communication traits!

> *"So God created man in his own image, in the image of God he created him; male and female he created them."* Genesis 1:27

The way that you and I respond in our communications needs to be driven by our spiritual inheritance, just as Jesus' words reflected the love and kindness of His Father and the truth and empowerment of the Holy Spirit. We have been made in His image and likeness, and when He lives within us, the same Holy Spirit that empowered Jesus' actions, lives in us. When life's storms come, instead of responding in anger, hate, and judgment, we have the power and inheritance to act upon God's command to love one another 'anyhow!'

The Child - The Adult - and The Parent Within

Helpful in understanding the impetus behind our communications is to understand that within each of us we harbor a *'child,'* an *'adult,'* and a *'parent.'* It is from this complex of people that our reactions and thus our communications stem, different ones on different occasions. Sometimes a spontaneous reaction from our *'child'* can be delightful, a giggle, a hug, a show of unabashed affection. Other times childish reactions can be disastrous! The *'adult'* in us will sometimes choose to be appropriately mature while other times appear too controlling. Sometimes the *'parent'* in us can tend to come across as 'lording over' those with whom we are attempting to have a positive influence, especially when we are feeling strained or backed into a corner. Often, as each of these complexities respond [sometimes perceived to be in a negative way] it isn't how we really mean to come across, but our words have come spontaneously tumbling out spawned by our insecure feelings.

It was the *'child'* expressing itself from within the crowds that surrounded Jesus, jeering, belittling, and ridiculing Him before Pilot. So, what was His reaction to them all? It had to be so hurtful. These were the people He came to redeem, those for whom He would ultimately give His life. Yet He offered silence and Grace, even to the point of asking mercy on their souls when on the cross he uttered, *"Father forgive them for they know not what they do."* Incredible…a true communication of, *"I Love You Anyhow!"* Instead when we are put into a situation of defending ourselves, the child in us strikes out to hurt those who are causing us hurt. And it really does not help!

Remember; in any given situation Satan is always ready to call up whichever person in us that he can most destructively use to suit his purpose. Be on your guard. Be aware. Think before you speak and daily ask the Lord to guide your communications so that they will be made in such a manner as to build up and not tear down.

The Tongue

What kind of priority does God put on how we verbalize our communications?

God spoke and creations happened.
God spoke through the prophets and His plan for the future was revealed.
Jesus spoke and demons fled, people were healed, the storm was calmed.
The Angels spoke and the pregnancy of a virgin was revealed, one who would bear God's Son.

Words are powerful. Our ability to communicate is a gift, a God-given gift. Use this gift in such a manner that those with whom you communicate will be drawn closer to Him and never pushed further away. Consider your voice inflections, so they won't reveal a different meaning than your words intended, making it easy for your intentions to be misinterpreted. Remember, in some cases the voice inflection gives away how we really feel more than our spoken words. Try the little speaking exercise below and see how this principle plays out. As you speak each of the sentences, put emphasis on the word in bold letters. For instance: *I didn't say you took the money.* As your voice emphasizes the word 'I,' can you see how that infers that, though someone accused the listener of stealing some money, it certainly wasn't the current speaker? Now, speak aloud the same sentence, each time putting the emphasis on a different bolded word….

I didn't say you took the money.
*I **didn't** say you took the money.*
*I didn't **say** you took the money.*
*I didn't say **you** took the money.*
*I didn't say you **took** the money.*
*I didn't say you took **the** money.*
*I didn't say you took the **money**.*

Interesting isn't it, how our voice inflection drastically changes the intention of the sentence. Honestly? I think sometimes we do this on purpose to redirect the true meaning behind our words, without our having to take responsibility for them. I actually don't think we have a clue most of the time how powerfully our words are used – either by God or by Satan. Our tongues are cunning tools, used effectively to either build up or tear down. Remember to ask God to take control of your tongue. And do it in the morning, before it's too late to claim the day for Jesus.

Take a look at Biblical accounts of God's instructions as to the results of how we use our tongues. He makes it impeccably clear that the misuse of our tongues reaps painful consequences for everyone concerned. Tongues were given to us for the express purpose of praising God and declaring His glorious name. As you will see in the scriptures following, when we use our tongues to criticize, judge, and condemn, it deeply saddens and angers Him. And as it is written, the negative consequences we reap are huge!

Though the list is really much longer, the following reveals just a few of the scriptures we find related to the tongue. I encourage you to take the time to camp on them for awhile, examining your heart as to how they address the manner in which you have been using your tongue. Let's first check out the clue we get in Psalms 139.

*"Before a word is on my **tongue** you know it completely, O LORD."*

This would indicate to us communication begins in our minds, starting with our thoughts before they are on our tongues. Thus, we would do well to hold our thoughts in check, before they take the form of words that spill out on others and destroy our relationships. On the other hand, when our words are God-driven, they will lift up and encourage and heal. Let's take a look at some of the consequences of our words....

*"May the LORD cut off all flattering lips and every boastful **tongue**."* Psalm 12:3

*".... We will triumph with our **tongues**; we own our lips — who is our master?"* Psalm 12:4

*"Keep your **tongue** from evil and your lips from speaking lies."* Psalm 34:13

*"The mouth of the righteous man utters wisdom, and his **tongue** speaks what is just."* Psalm 37:30

*"You love every harmful word, O you deceitful **tongue**!"* Psalm 52:4

*"When words are many, sin is not absent, but he who holds his **tongue** is wise."* Proverbs 10:19

"A man who lacks judgment derides his neighbor, but a man of understanding holds his tongue." Proverbs 11:12

"Reckless words pierce like a sword, but the tongue of the wise brings healing." Proverbs 12:18

"Truthful lips endure forever, but a lying tongue lasts only a moment." Proverbs 12:19

"The tongue of the wise commends knowledge, but the mouth of the fool gushes folly." Proverbs 15:2

"The tongue that brings healing is a tree of life, but a deceitful tongue crushes the spirit." Proverbs 15:4

"A wicked man listens to evil lips; a liar pays attention to a malicious tongue." Proverbs 17:4

"A man of perverse heart does not prosper; he whose tongue is deceitful falls into trouble." Proverbs 17:20

"Even a fool is thought wise if he keeps silent, and discerning if he holds his tongue." Proverbs 17:28

"The tongue has the power of life and death, and those who love it will eat its fruit." Proverbs 18:21

"A fortune made by a lying tongue is a fleeting vapor and a deadly snare." Proverbs 21:6

"He who guards his mouth and his tongue keeps himself from calamity." Proverbs 21:23

"As a north wind brings rain, so a sly tongue brings angry looks." Proverbs 25:23

"A lying tongue hates those it hurts, and a flattering mouth works ruin." Proverbs 26:28

"My lips will not speak wickedness, and my tongue will utter no deceit." Job 27:4

"Their tongue is a deadly arrow; it speaks with deceit. With his mouth each speaks cordially to his neighbor, but in his heart he sets a trap for him." Jeremiah 9:8

"Their throats are open graves; their tongues practice deceit. The poison of vipers is on their lips." Romans 3:13

*"If anyone considers himself religious and yet does not keep a tight rein on his **tongue**, he deceives himself and his religion is worthless."* James 1:26

*"The **tongue** also is a fire, a world of evil among the parts of the body. It corrupts the whole person, sets the whole course of his life on fire, and is itself set on fire by hell."* James 3:6

*"With the **tongue** we praise our Lord and Father, and with it we curse men, who have been made in God's likeness."* James 3:9

*"....Whoever would love life and see good days must keep his **tongue** from evil and his lips from deceitful speech."* I Peter 3:10

Our ability to communicate was given to us for Godly purposes. God is the author of communications. He wants us to communicate but He wants our communication to be driven by His desire for us to love those He places in our lives. Unfortunately, we often use our gift of communication to 'react' harmfully to the emotions of others.

Are You an *'Actor'* or a *'Reactor?'*

Our communications can become positive and used of the Lord when our goal is to become an *'actor'* instead of a *'reactor.'* Instead of 'reacting' to situations around you with words that you later wish you could take back, make it your goal to intentionally choose to 'act' on the truths of God's Word, claiming the presence and power of the Holy Spirit. It never helps a situation when we allow our words [or our body language] to 'react' to the emotions of another's dilemma. When we do we allow the other person or situation to come camp in our minds, controlling us and our well-being. Instead we can choose to stay calm and 'act' on God's principles of communications, out of a desire to express His love. When we do, it gives Him control instead. He is the only one that deserves control over our lives, and the only one that can and will use that control for <u>everyone's</u> good! Let us make it our communications goal to become 'actors' instead of 'reactors.'

We would do well to keep in mind one of the main purposes for which God gave us the gift of words. Take a look at one additional scripture......

"Let every tongue confess that Jesus Christ is Lord, to the glory of God the Father." Philippians 2:11

Pent Up Feelings – The Punish and Pout Scenario

When we hold pent up feelings that send us into a 'punish and pout' mode, it sends up a 'red flag' regarding our communication style. Though we don't want our communication to be harsh or harmful to others, we need to be cautious about holding 'pent up' feelings that need to be appropriately expressed, simply because we are concerned about not 'upsetting the apple cart.' What we don't realize when we do this, is that when those thoughts truly hold importance in a relationship, just having them has already upset the applecart anyway. Those unspoken frustrations will often inadvertently drive us into a 'pout and punish' mode with those for whom we harbor them. Thus unresolved anger and resentment build up. When this happens we often adopt a 'passive-aggressive' attitude, risking an explosive situation, where one day it will all just get to be too much, leaving everyone involved wondering what happened!

My experience in helping many others with relational issues has revealed time and time again a disclosure of this kind of circumstance within troubled relationships. On the surface, when inquiring from each party as to the quality of their communication, their response is *"great – no problem as far as I can see."* However, during further evaluation of the base of the relationship's difficulties, sooner or later it comes out that there have been unspoken issues – maybe for years – that have built up huge walls between them. While we don't want to just demonstratively blurt out inappropriate comments on sensitive issues, we must be careful not to 'bury' feelings that need to be appropriately discussed. When we do, we end up harboring unspoken blame toward one another, due to unmet expectations. History has proven that this practice of a 'pout and punish' mentality is not a gender nor position driven condition – men do it and women do it – parents do it and kids do it – friends do it to friends – employees and supervisors do it to each other. When not uncovered and set right, it becomes like an emotional cancer within otherwise healthy relationships, which destroys and metastasizes because we are not islands unto ourselves, and we tend to share our frustrations with others instead of the one with whom we are frustrated.

Allow Honest Openness

If our desire is to have healthy relationships, *openness* and *honesty* is a must. Instead of taking what appears at the time to be the easy way out, it requires the hard work of honest, humble and vulnerable communications. Holding in feelings of disappointment and stress creates bitterness and breeds disaster. It eventually erodes the relationship, one day becoming the impetus to the inevitable 'straw that broke the camel's back' scenario, before anyone saw it coming.

Help protect your relationships from this kind of disaster by practicing the skill and humility of allowing others to say whatever they feel they need to, without risking a judgmental, shocked, 'I can't believe it' reaction from you. If those with whom we relate are not allowed to be honest with us, we don't permit them the opportunity to find out that they can count on an *'I Love You*

Anyhow' attitude from us. Thus we miss the opportunity for God to use us in His healing process.

A caution here: I am not suggesting that everything one may reveal to us will always be that of an *'ok'* or *'appropriate'* attitude or behavior, or that we must react as though it is. But our immediate reaction to anything that is revealed must be one of interest and concern for a person who is valued in God's eyes. This gives us an opportunity to let God work through us to help others see how their behavior affects the whole picture, as it relates to maintaining a healthy relationship with God, and with their loved ones. How can we have the opportunity to be a Godly influence in the lives of those whom we befriend if they fear sharing honestly with us about the things in their lives with which they struggle, and for which they may desperately need prayer?

As a pastor, Bruce Larson naturally offered effective relational counseling. This created an atmosphere of expectation on the part of his church members, that his family would have their relational act together. However, in his book, *"No Longer Strangers,"* Bruce divulges that, though he was able to help so many others with their broken relationships, He was wrestling with a very difficult emotional separation from his own teen-age son. His son had grown distant, rejecting his family and their faith and friends. He seemed particularly estranged from his father. His actions became an embarrassment to the family. Bruce's response, like most of ours might be, was one of frustration and criticism. As a result, they grew further and further apart, his son becoming a total recluse, holding up in his room most of the time. With little open honest communication between them, Bruce really had no idea of the debilitating conflict going on inside of his son, until one day while alone in his son room he found and read a poem lying on the desk, which he later learned his son had written. Consider this heart wrenching writing that, though it pained Bruce terribly, opened his heart to realize his son's desperate need....

Hello out there, world;
It's me in here
What? You're having trouble hearing me?

But, I'm in here.
Yes, that's right.
Inside where?
Inside myself, of course.

The outside shell is very thick;
I'm having trouble getting out.
Who am I? You say I don't sound like myself?
That's because you've never heard me.

This other guy: Oh, he's the shell I told you about.
You say that's me?
No, I'm in here.
He's just my protection.

Protection from what?
From you, the world.
I can't be hurt here.
You see, my shell keeps you away.

You, the world, are pain.
I'm safe in here;
I'll never be laughed at.
The shell? Oh, he doesn't mind laughter.

Come to think of it
I'm comfortable in here
Why should I leave:
Hello, world, still listening?

What's that, world?
I thought for a minute you said something.
It was a faint voice;
It sounded human – real – I thought.
I thought it was answering me.

Maybe not.
I can't hear too well inside this shell
Well, I feel funny – sleepy
And it's so comfortable in here,
Goodbye, world.

What an outpouring of the heart and soul of one who is hurting! Bruce shares that as he read this heart wrenching poem written by his son it was like a knife was driven through his heart. He now realized that this boy of his with whom he had been having so much trouble relating, and whom he had been relentlessly criticizing about his attitude and withdrawal from the family, was really a man very much like himself - a man who was very lonesome and often misunderstood.

This writing was an expression of the inner soul, looking for understanding and help from someone with whom it might trust its deepest secrets. Are your communications such that those whom you know, who are hurting, know that you are willing to be that person for them?

In order to be this vulnerable yet strong in our horizontal communications, we first must make every effort to have a consistent vertical communication with the Lord. Without receiving the Godly strength and instruction we need from the source of all proper communications, we will fall flat on our faces when we try to address the tough issues. Talk to God first - others after!

Vertical Communications

In order to avoid shallow protective horizontal communications, we must be diligent in our *vertical* communications – those between ourselves and our Savior. Humanly, we do not have the where-with-all to empower our horizontal communications with an attitude that fosters, *"I Love You Anyhow"* relationships. Only the power of the Holy Spirit within us will enable our communications to put other's needs and well-being ahead of our own.

Mankind had to learn this the hard way, with a huge penalty as the consequence. In the very beginning communication problems devastated the course of creation. Consider with me a message from the book of Genesis. God created and placed Adam and Eve, the first two humans, in the Garden of Eden. He gave them the full run of the garden to enjoy, save one tree.

> *"The Lord God took the man and put him in the Garden of Eden to work it and take care of it. And the Lord God commanded the man, 'you are free to eat from any tree in the garden; but you must not eat from the tree of the knowledge of good and evil, for when you eat of it you will surely die."* Genesis 2:15-17

That's all – just one tree was off limits. He could enjoy everything else. Not too tough an assignment. Adam was given Eve to be a suitable partner with whom he could spend his life. And as we read on, we see that together they made a conscious decision to ignore God's communication to them, not taking His instruction to heart. When they encounter the serpent [the devil] lurking around the garden, he begins to communicate his evil ways to Eve, and Eve listens. Then she decides to communicate the serpent's message to Adam, and Adam responds to it – all without any communication about the situation at all, with God.

Once they finally take responsibility for going against God's instruction, their eyes are opened to their vulnerability [nakedness] before God, and so they run and hide from Him, thinking they can avoid the consequences. They cannot – nor can we! And soon they hear the voice of God calling to them, and Adam responds…

> *"I heard you in the garden, and I was afraid because I was naked; so I hid. And he [God] said, who told you that you were naked? Have you eaten from the tree that I commanded you not to eat from?"* Genesis 3:10-11

As a result of neither Adam nor Eve first seeking vertical communications with God about the serpent's story before acting upon it, their horizontal line of communication with each other was immediately jeopardized! Take a look at Adam's excuse in response to God's question.

"The woman you put here with me – she gave me some fruit from the tree, and I ate it."

We see here that Adam immediately begins to play the blame game,,,it was the woman's fault! And Eve follows suite....

"Then the Lord God said to the woman, 'What is this you have done?' The woman said, 'The serpent deceived me, and I ate." Genesis 3:13

Adam blamed Eve and Eve blamed Satan. Their failure to practice the very basic principle of seeking a vertical line of communication with God before engaging in a horizontal line of communication with one another got them in trouble, immediately alienating them from one another and from God, and resulting in an eternity of disaster for millions. Their communications reveal that they were so busy blaming someone else for their poor choices that they neglected to consider their own culpability in the situation. Thus, no confession and no repentance! Sadly, we continue to make the same mistake!

Oh how often we all get caught up in a similar kind of scenario of blaming one another, and God, for our circumstances! And just as Adam blamed Eve, and Eve blamed the serpent [and ultimately God for putting him there], we tend to blame everyone else instead of determining what our responsibility is in difficult situations. Where were the apologies for the mess they had created? We have no record that there was any attempt on their parts to say *"I'm sorry – I blew it"* nor *"I Love You Anyhow,"* neither to each other nor to God. Thus their actions were not followed by repentance, restoration, or reconciliation. Instead their lives became riddled with the pain and emptiness of loss and want.

Adam and Eve's disobedience brought about a sin that has been passed down to all mankind ever since, and without the provision of Jesus' death on the cross for our sins, we would all suffer from an eternal separation from God.

It is written that we have inherited Adam and Eve's sin....

"For all have sinned and fallen short of the glory of God" Romans 3:20

The results are devastating:

"But your iniquities have separated you from your God; your sins have hidden his face from you so that he will not hear." Isaiah 59: 2

You see, though God desires us to spend eternity in Heaven with Him, His nature will not allow sin to enter into Heaven. So how is it that He continues to declare *"I Love You anyhow?"* God gives us the opportunity to trust His Son's act of Grace upon the cross – taking the world's sins upon Himself. When we do, He clearly communicates His intention for our restitution....

> *"The Lord is compassionate and gracious; slow to anger, abounding in love. He will not accuse, nor will he harbor his anger forever; he does not treat us as our sins deserve or repay us according to our iniquities. For as high as the heavens are above the earth, so great is his love for those who fear him; as far as the east is from the west, so far has he removed our transgressions from us."* Psalm 103:8-12

> *"Consequently, just as the result of one trespass was condemnation for all men, so also the result of one act of righteousness was justification that brings life for all men. For just as through the disobedience of the one man the many were made sinners, so also through the obedience of the one man the many will be made righteous."* Romans 5:18-19

> *"The wages of sin is death, but the free gift of God is eternal life in Christ Jesus."* Romans 6:23

It was never God's desire to be separated from us. So, He sent Jesus to bring us vertical reconciliation so that we could once again fellowship with Him in the garden of our hearts, for all eternity. He tells us if we will believe in Him and receive the hand He offers us through Christ, trusting that His presence and forgiveness restores us, He will declare us a part of His family again.

> *"Yet to all who received him, to those who believed in his name, he gave the right to become children of God – children born not of natural descent, nor of human decision or a husband's will, but born of God."* John 1: 12-13

Will we listen to this incredible vertical communications from Him and respond, or will we, like Adam and Eve, just keep on blaming Him and each other for our unhappiness, justifying our actions and living outside of His desires for us? Will we continue to draw into our personal shells and talk to no one, too reclusive to share our hurts and fears, because we have believed the serpent's lie that no one else, including God, cares anyway? When we allow this kind of erosion in our communications, we suffer alienation from each other and from God. Yet we strive to understand why it is that God would let us get into such predicaments, while in fact we really need to stay open and listen to His instructions about our situations - <u>before</u> they result in such dilemmas.

We would do well to go to God first thing in the morning and engage in a dialogue with Him regarding our intentions for the day. Remember a dialogue includes both talking and listening. Share your heart and listen patiently for

His input. Note the insights into the practice and power of listening to God that are shared in this book, in the Prayer section within the chapter on Commitment and Growth.

Just as the Holy Spirit will gives us insights into God's Will, when we listen for it, He also communicates with us through scriptures. The Bible is a living Word from God. Each time you read it – even when it's the same scripture that you may have read many times - God will bring new meaning for you, communicating His message that will meet that day's specific needs. Do these things to shore up your vertical communications, BEFORE you attempt to deal with your horizontal communications each day!

When the opportunity presents itself, if at all possible go to prayer and share the Word together with those special people in your life. When we go together in prayer, vulnerably sharing our concerns with the Lord [and thus which each other] it opens up opportunities to also honestly address those concerns with each other after our prayer time. This gives God the opportunity to speak through you to one another, and with His guidance the serpent is short circuited! It is very difficult, if not impossible, to be mad at someone for whom and with whom you are praying.

There are times when things escalate so much that there appears to be no human answer to the trauma we face. But don't give up. The key word here is that there *'appears'* to be no answer. The road to reconciliation? Go to God **FIRST**. Seek His understanding, forgiveness, and guidance. Once you are on solid ground in your openness and honesty with Him, having the assurance of His presence in the situation, then go to one another. Be humbly honest with each other, while together seeking answers based on His instruction. If you find that with a certain situation or person it is just not possible to go to God together, you still do your part and persistently ask God to bring the other person into the circle. The serpent can paint a pretty dismal picture of any hopes to reconcile, but *"nothing is impossible to God!"* Listen to one such case where, when His divine intervention was sought and followed by everyone concerned, as always God's faithfulness overruled human frailty....

Personal Reflection
Tina and her husband are our good friends – the best kind - friends that we missed terribly when they moved away. They didn't go far, but far enough that our paths no longer crossed as often as we had enjoyed in the past. When Tina and I finally did get an opportunity to meet for coffee one day, I sensed that something was terribly wrong. What? I had no idea. I just knew something was not the same. After letting it go for a few days, while praying for God's insights, I decided it was time to try and get involved enough to see if I could help. I made several attempts to set up another meeting time. She was never available. Over the next couple

of weeks I kept trying, but her response continued the same, she was not available. I kept praying about it and one day God prompted me to go sit in my car outside her place of work, and when she came out, to just simply ask her if she would be willing to go for a ride with me. I don't think she was happy about my presence there, but she got in the car anyway and we began to drive. After a bit I asked her what was wrong. She began to cry as she blurted out, "What's the worst possible thing you can think of?" The first words that came to my mind to say [they had to be God's words] was, "Tina, the worst thing I can think of is that you don't believe that God loves you." She sobbed even harder. After awhile, through her sobs, she was able to get out her dilemma. She was pregnant and the baby was not her husband's – couldn't be. They had been going through rocky times and communications between them were nearly non-existent. She had been so lonesome and had been feeling like the proverbial frog for so long. She is a lovely and kind woman, and as the world would have it, someone else had noticed these great qualities. His attentions towards her were like cool water offered to one alone, dehydrated, and lost in the dessert. But she and her husband already had school age children who were precious to them, and this would destroy their entire family. Her body racked with sobs as she kept repeating, "What have I done! What have I done!"

I felt a bit like a robin caught in a snowstorm, not having the slightest idea what to do. As I continued to drive around, stunned and without words, I began to wonder why on earth I had continued to pursue my friend's condition. What do you say? How does one give hope in such a hopeless case? After a few blocks of driving and silent prayer, I remembered God's promise to Peter, "don't worry about what to say, for I will give you the words to say at the time." I claimed it, parked, took a deep breath and a huge leap of faith. I took her hand, and encouraged her that we needed to spend the next few days praying about what God would have her to do, seeking His guidance. I told her that though she and I both knew that she had gone against God's instructions, He still loved her 'right where she was.' I tried to encourage her that no matter what mistakes we make, when we acknowledge them and turn to Him, He stands with arms wide open, ready to forgive us and receive our broken hearts, our broken promises, and our devastated spirits. He accepts our repentance and awaits our acknowledgment that, because of Jesus, we have forgiveness awaiting us <u>whenever</u> we turn to Him. I assured her that God's promises to her were still intact. That He loves her and has a plan for her life…a plan for good and not for harm – for hope and a future. I knew I could say these things with assurance because they are His promises, not mine, and they are clearly recorded in His Word for everyone who will turn to Him.

After awhile I dropped Tina off at her car with my promise that we would meet again the next day, after which I agonized all the way home as to whether I had done the right thing – said the right thing – given false hope – misspoke what God's intentions were toward her? Sometimes the spirit is willing but the flesh is weak and though we step out in faith, our humanness cringes under our weakness. But God meets us on our growing edge and like Thomas, I cried out, "God I believe, help thou my unbelief!"

I said nothing to anyone – except God – about what I had learned. It wasn't my story to tell. I had no idea where to go from there with her. I knew, though her husband was really a good guy, he had a volatile temper. What might he do when he learned of the situation? What might any man do! After meeting with Tina for a few minutes every day for awhile, listening and sharing her pain, and praying with her, I clarified that I had no idea what to advise her, except that God has the power to bring clarity and healing to her life, and that He sent Jesus to bring her forgiveness and restoration. As we prayed together, she invited Jesus to be her Savior and guide her steps. And I cried. I knew that with that invitation, according to the Word, we could claim that she had just received 'all of the God head bodily, and that together they have authority over every other authority.' Together they had her back! She was no longer drawing from only her own wisdom and strength, but from all the wisdom and strength of the Trinity.

Eventually with God's help, I convinced her that it would be a good thing to invite another Christian to join us in our search for an answer. She hesitantly agreed to include my husband in the story and invite him to pray with us for direction. After the three of us had met and prayed together a number of times, she came to me one day and said that after a lot of prayer she had come to a conclusion as to what she was supposed to do. She handed me an envelope addressed to her husband, calmly stating that God had told her to write down her feelings and her plight and ask me to deliver it to him. Whoa! I don't think so! Sure didn't seem like the answer I was thinking God might send her! But, alas it appeared to be. So shortly after, I drove to their new home city and with a rock in my stomach, sat in the driveway awaiting Tim's arrival home. How was I going to approach him? I had no clue. But I knew that my husband, who had followed me in his car, was sitting a few blocks away praying for me. And I knew that where God guides He provides. And believe me when I say that I reminded Him as I sat there waiting that I was counting on Him doing so! As Tim pulled in the driveway, my heart was pumping out of my chest.

We greeted one another. It was obvious by his expression that he was puzzled as to why I was there, as we hadn't seen one another for quite some time. I told him immediately that I had a message for him from Tina. He gave me an intensely curious look, but invited me in. I didn't waste any time handing him the letter, telling him that Tina had asked me to personally deliver it to him. As he read it, I sat quietly, pleading with the Lord for His presence. After finishing the lengthy letter Tim looked up and asked, "Where is Tina now?" I told him that she was nearby and would like to come home if he would let her. As a Christian counselor later stated to me, "His response was surely not Tim. In fact it was not even human!" It was not 'normal' coming from a husband who had just had a ton of bricks unloaded on his heart. But without a doubt, it surely was God, as he exclaimed, "Of course she can come home, this is her home isn't it." I called her. She came. I called my husband and he joined us as well. We all cried together. We encouraged Tim, as we had Tina that though in our humanness there was no answer to their dilemma, God could bring forgiveness and healing and hope where there was none. We assured him, as we had Tina, that He had already determined up front that He loved them both anyhow, no matter what culpability each may have had in what had happened. I shared with Tim that we had been praying with Tina for several weeks, for God's solution, and that she was doing everything she knew to do to turn the situation over to Jesus. We invited him to also trust Jesus with his life and seek God for answers. As Tim prayed, he asked Jesus to take over his life and to help him with his anger management issues, and to help them know what to do next. Again, I cried. God is so faithful and I am so grateful!

The ensuing few weeks were extremely difficult....tough decisions to be made and a huge uncertainty about the future. But God is faithful and as always He was willing to meet them on their growing edge. Thus, even as baby Christians, through much pain and prayer they were able to work through their issues, moving on with their lives and searching for God's 'new normals' that would govern their individual lives and their marriage.

So what about the many years since? Tim and Tina have been humbly obedient to God's principles of forgiveness presented herein, in the Forgiveness chapter. As a result, they have enjoyed a new level of communications, keeping their family together and devoting much of their lives to a ministry of reconciliation, communicating their story to other couples across the country, within the setting of marriage retreats. As they share their story and God's faithfulness, they challenge their listeners with a plea to seek vertical communications with God daily, and to open up their lives and marriages to Christ, seeking God's protection from this world and the evil one that lurks within, looking for whom he may devour. Many have, and God wins all the way around!

As Tina and Tim have been willing to be scripted into God's story, their powerful testimony of the relational destruction of broken communications and the willingness of God to heal, has been used to help dozens of broken relationships to also heal. When we seek to restore our *horizontal* communications by first seeking proper *vertical* communications with Him, He will turn our stumbling blocks into stepping stones for His purposes.

The Healing Power of the Word – God's Letters Written to Us

No matter who we are, since Adam and Eve we have been vulnerable to the human instincts to ignore God's warnings. The fact is that no human is sufficient to run his/her own life's matters victoriously, without successful communications [both vertical and horizontal]. We are exhorted to be diligent in our efforts to communicate with Him, by spending time studying His letters to us, recorded in the Bible. If we are willing to learn from Adam and Eve and follow what we hear from God, we will save ourselves a ton of grief. If we know where to go in the Bible to find the promises and directions that address specific needs, those golden nuggets of truth will be like healing medications to our bodies and our souls. God caused these truths to be recorded for us as a way of empowering us to live a victorious life. Learn them. Know where to find them. Claim them loud and clear, and apply them to your life's situations. Make it your commitment to know the scriptures so well that you are able to help communicate their truths to those whom He desires to heal!

The Bible tells us that the evil one is right there at all times, 'going to and fro throughout the earth seeking whom he may devour.' Thus, don't ever be lulled into thinking that you are immune to temptations and traumas in your own life. Each of us will face situation that only life-giving communications with God will empower us to survive. As you maintain those special relationships in your life, make Godly communication a high priority. We need His instruction to know what to say on a dark day when everything is going awry. Like putting toothpaste back into the tube once it's already been squeezed out, words are so easily said and so hard to take back. Once they are out, they are out to stay! Hide God's Word in your heart. Give thought to your words before you open your mouth. As you take time to ponder what you should say, you will be giving God time to speak to your heart about the matter. He cautions us about taking time to think first, before we speak....

> *"My dear brothers, take note of this: Everyone should be quick to listen, slow to speak and slow to become angry, for man's anger does not bring about the righteous life that God desires."* James 1:19-20

The Bible tells us that when we belong to Jesus we have an advocate that will help us communicate the way God wants us to. That advocate is the Holy Spirit, who comes to live in us when we invite Jesus into our hearts. He is the conveyor of Truth, enabling us to know and do as God Wills us. God cautions us to be careful how we live, as our actions can cause the Holy Spirit sorrow. In order to communicate with others the way God would have us, we need to know His desire for us regarding how we live and interact with others. Consider the following instructions.....

> *"...... do not grieve the Holy Spirit of God, with whom you were sealed for the day of redemption."* Ephesians 4:30

> *"For you were once darkness, but now you are light in the Lord. Live as children of light."* Ephesians 5:8

Having commanded that we treat others in a manner that does not grieve the Holy Spirit, God clarifies some of the areas in which we tend to mess up in the way that we communicate with and treat one another...

"Therefore each of you must put off falsehood and speak truthfully to his neighbor, for we are all members of one body. In your anger do not sin. Do not let the sun go down while you are still angry, and do not give the devil a foothold....Do not let any unwholesome talk come out of your mouths, but only what is helpful for building others up according to their needs, that it may benefit those who listen...Get rid of all bitterness, rage, and anger, brawling and slander, along with every form of malice. Be kind and compassionate to one another, forgiving each other, just as in Christ God forgave you." Excerpts from Ephesians 4: 25-32

Are you building strong Godly relationships by following these important guidelines? Or is your communication style leading you in the opposite direction? Is it any wonder we have relational problems when our horizontal communications are conducted so far outside of the way that God instructs us! Unfortunately, even within the church community, and sometimes most especially within the church community, we have not grasped the importance of appropriate Godly communications and how the lack of them can drive people away from a relationship with us and with Christ.

Since we are told in the book of Romans, *"In as much as it is possible for you to do so, be at peace with everyone."* it clearly puts the responsibility on each of us to do what we can to make a difference. If we sincerely want to improve our relationships, it is clear that we need to examine our communication style and determine what adjustments are needed in order to align them with God's instruction, and then commit to actively taking ownership in making those adjustments. When we do, God promises it will make a difference in our broken relationships. Let's continue to examine more of His instructions as to Godly communications......

"Have nothing to do with godless myths and old wives' tales; rather, train yourself to be godly." I Timothy 4:7

"A fool shows his annoyance at once, but a prudent man overlooks an insult." Proverbs 12:16

[so which are you?]

"Reckless words pierce like a sword, but the tongue of the wise brings healing" Proverbs 12:18

"Pride only brings quarrels, but wisdom is found in those who take advice." Proverbs 13:10

For those in leadership positions...moms, dads, teachers:

"Keep reminding them of these things. Warn them before God against quarreling about words; it is of no value, and only ruins those who listen." II Timothy 2:14

Are your vertical communications with the Lord, through prayer and Bible study, consistent enough that these instructions are kept in the forefront of your mind when you are tempted to allow horizontal communications to go awry? Reviewing and committing God's instructions regarding appropriate communications will be time well spent!

Another caution here: though our goal is Godly communications, we need not '*play God*' in the process. **Let God be God**. He is able to direct people as He desires. Encourage your loved ones in His truths but be careful not to become arrogant and demanding in your attempts to 'help' or 'change' them. Remember, it is God who is at work in their lives making them into what He wants them to be.

"*Who are you to judge someone else's servant? To his own master he stands or falls. And he will stand, for the Lord is able to make him stand.*" Romans 14:4

When we allow our egos and insecurities to contaminate our communications, hurting those with whom we are communicating, we reap the results in great measure. Again…this Biblical principle….

"*Do not be deceived: God cannot be mocked. A man reaps what he sows.*" Galatians 6:7

At the beginning of the day, have you ever had what seemed like just a tiny little disagreement resulting in unkind or negative words [or even words of indifference] and then later that day experienced the results of that tiny seed? Often that bitsy seed has blossomed into a bushel of trouble….a seemingly insurmountable barrier! The analogy Jesus used here to explain this Biblical principle is: when we sow tiny seeds of corn they come back at harvest time in bushels. What seeds of communication are you planting? Will they yield a bushel of love and affirmation at the end of the day? Or will they come back yielding a bushel of brokenness and pain?

In a powerful book on relationships, written by Howard Hendricks and entitled, "We Really Do Need Each Other," he shares the following observation:

"*The idea of employing words to transmit our thoughts seems elementary, like taking an automobile trip. We've done it often; it's become a familiar habit. But certain pre-requisites must be met. We take for granted that, in order to drive from here to there, we first of all need a worthy car in good repair. There must be an adequate road. We must allow sufficient time. The weather must be cooperative. There must be sufficient fuel available. Having met all these requirements the trip is a simple matter. Similarly, communication is facilitated with the right words, in the right direction, supported with the understanding that guides the words aright."*

In other words, good communication doesn't just happen! It takes proactive commitment to the task. When that commitment is there, communication is a beautiful thing.

"Dear Lord,
Thank you for your precious Word, powerfully communicating your love to us. Thank you for sending Jesus to redeem our souls, and with Him, the Holy Spirit to help us restore our broken communications, with you and with others. Thank you that with Jesus as our Savior, the Trinity lives within us to instruct and empower our communications to become what you command them to be. God help us to begin each day talking with you. And remind us to take the time to listen to what you have to say. Help us to hide your Word in our hearts. Thank you, Lord, that you empower us to help draw others to you through lovingly and effectively communicating your message to them. Let them see and hear the Jesus within us, for your sake. Amen"

Personal Application

TRUTH:

The art of communication started with God, and so it is that God has designed appropriate communications to bring restoration, healing and joy into our relationships. *Vertical* communications, through prayer and the reading His Word, gives us His instructions and empowers us in effective *horizontal* communication with our loved ones.

1. What part does *'body language'* play in your communications?

2. Note action steps you will take to improve your *vertical* communications.

3. Would you say your communication style is a reflection more of an *'actor'* or a *'reactor?'*

4. Recall the many principles of communication in this chapter and note the top three that you will personalize to help bring your communications more in line with God's instructions. Will it be becoming an *actor* instead of a *reactor*? Ceasing to play the blame game? Stopping the manipulation of the *silent treatment?*' Or the manipulation of a *punish and pout* style? Learning to speak in a low tone? Not using inappropriate body language? These are only a few. Take time to consider them all before answering.

5. Recall the insights we see in Jesus' communications with His disciples. What communication style does He reveal in the midst of trauma? Is this your style in the midst of trauma? If not, list the principles you have learned in this chapter that will help you better align with Jesus' methods of communication in the face of adversity.

Journal Entry: **Communicating With God**

Your eyes are so warm and tender.
Your face overflows with compassion.
And, as I sit and study your picture, Lord,
It so clearly says.... 'I understand.'
Thank God you understand!
No one else really does you know!

Your arms are strong and warm...I'm sure
Power and strength, and humbleness and love
Would pour from you to me through their touch,
If only you could hold me...this I know, cause
The words in your book tell me so.

But now – suddenly, I almost feel them, Lord!
Their warmth and strength, and tenderness!
They don't drain my being – nor ask anything of my tomorrows,
Nor demand anything of my today.
They're just there – around me – securely holding me
And helping to turn the world away.

Thank you for this precious completeness!
Now I can face the world again.
But Lord, one more thing before I do....
Through this day, along the way,
If someone else is struggling too,
It matters not with what,
Help me - with meaning - to be able to say,
'I love you'- enough to hold you till the storm passes by
Without draining anything from you,
Nor expecting anything from your tomorrows,
Nor demanding anything from your today.

But just to be there with you,
To help the Lord take His place in your soul
As He holds you in His arms,
And you look upon His face,
And for you too - He makes the world go away!

Thanks for your 'I Love You Anyhow' kind of love,
A most precious undeserved gift from above,
Now I know what it means to truly love and be loved!

CHAPTER FOUR
FORGIVENESS

Forgiveness Was Always God's Plan

In chapter three, on Communications, we read of Adam and Eve's miserable failure to listen and follow God's command. We were reminded that their sin has infected all of mankind thereafter. Thus a devastating dilemma for mankind, because the Bible makes it quite clear that sin cannot co-exist with God. Yet God's deep desire, even after the fall in the garden, has always been to have eternal fellowship with His creation. So, instead of having to endure eternal separation from us, He determined to provide a way, where there was no way...

> *"If we confess our sins, He is faithful and just and will forgive us our sins and purify us from all unrighteousness."* I John 1:9

Forgiveness was always the plan, as the Trinity [Father, Jesus, and Holy Spirit] created the world, making man and woman after God's own image and placing them in the garden.

> *"In the beginning was the Word [Jesus], and the Word was with God, and the Word was God. He was with God in the beginning. Through him all things were made; without him nothing was made that has been made. In him was life, and that life was the light of men. The light shines in the darkness, but the darkness has not understood it."* John 1:1-5

Even as God created the world and placed humankind in it, He knew that one day, in order for their sin to be forgiven once and for all, Jesus would have to leave His glory in Heaven, come to earth, die a horrible sacrificial death, and descend into hell taking all of humankind's sins with Him. But that was not the end of the story, because He once again victoriously ascended into Heaven, and now awaits His forgiven children to join Him for all eternity! That we are counted worthy of this kind of sacrifice and forgiveness on the part of almighty God is more than astounding!

Could God have created us as puppets, with no choice but to obey? Yes. But He did not. He gave us the freedom to choose. He foreknew that there would be times when we would choose to sin. Thus, He made a conscious choice upfront that Jesus would have to come to earth to make provision for our eternal forgiveness. Willingly, Jesus became the sacrificial lamb, once and for all. Those who accept this truth, claiming it for themselves, find freedom and reconciliation with God, through Jesus Christ.

The Psalmist David so trusted that God's forgiveness was available to him that, even after he had fallen into unthinkable sin, this truth released him to continue to serve as one of God's most powerful servants. He knew when he went to God and confessed his sin, God's forgiveness awaited him. He records his unwavering trust in God's forgiveness ...

> *"If you, O Lord, kept a record of sins, O Lord, who could stand? But with you there is forgiveness; therefore you are feared."* Psalm 130:3-4

Let's unpack the dynamics of this scripture.
1. David recognizes that, were God unable to forgive, we would all be so doomed that even praying would be futile.
2. He expresses total confidence, without reservation, that not only is God *able*, but He is also *willing* to forgive.
3. By praising God for that forgiveness, David confirms that he knows the incredible dynamics of what really happens when God forgives.

God's forgiveness is full of 'action-steps'....*Mercy* [withholding a deserved punishment], *Grace*, [offering an underserved gift – the gift of forgiveness], and Love [the outward expression of an internal compassion and acceptance]. He commands us to do the same.

With this in mind, reflect on your own relationships and ask yourself, *"How's that going for me? Am I offering mercy and grace to those with whom I relate? Or does it sometimes seem like I might be giving up too much control if I would truly release another, by fully forgiving them?"*

Satan plants the thought in our minds that perhaps holding a little unforgiveness over someone's head will keep our expectations in the forefront of a compromised relationship, causing that other person to 'perform' more the way we want them to. We reason that reminding someone of their offense will result in them trying harder to become more of what we need from that relationship, ultimately changing them into more of what God wants them to be. It doesn't seem to work that way. Instead, it just diminishes our relationships. Another important reality resulting from an unforgiving attitude, it births an ongoing grudge against those for whom we withhold forgiveness. This allows that person to take up residence in our mind, control our response, and often foster within us a misplaced responsibility to change their future behavior, as earlier mentioned. God doesn't see it that way. Take another look.....

"For who are you to judge someone else's servant? To his own master he stands or falls. And he will stand, for the Lord is able to make him stand" Romans 14:4

Judgment Clouds Transparency

None of us want to be judged by others. Have you ever wondered [like I have] *"What if I was to be fully transparent, revealing the really stupid things I have done or dumb thoughts I entertain? Would there be forgiveness forthcoming from those special people in my life?"* If we are convinced that one with whom we desire a good relationship would never truly accept and forgive us if they knew everything about us, we will never fully reveal our true selves to them. Thus we may remain so guarded that we have no hope of effectively praying for one another's true needs, or being used of God to help each other. We are left with only shallow acquaintances.

Having said this, it is also important to be discrete about what we share. Discretion is wisdom, least we disclose unnecessary things that are not helpful to anyone and actually may lead to hurting someone else. Make no mistake; the dynamics of forgiveness God's way are essential to experiencing intimate relationships – both vertical [with God] and horizontal [with each other].

Is All Sin Forgivable?

I can find no reference in God's Word that would give us reason to believe that we are allowed to pick and choose which sins we will forgive and which ones we will hold in our hearts. God clearly commands that we must forgive all of our transgressors.

Regarding God's forgiveness towards mankind, however, He cautions us of one unforgivable sin. Jesus clarifies that this one and only 'unforgivable' sin has to do with mankind's refusal to respond to the Holy Spirit's call regarding the truth about who Jesus Christ is and what His purpose is for having come to this earth. The scriptures clearly define that the Holy Spirit is sent to convict souls that Jesus Christ is who He says He is, and that we are called to trust Jesus to be our one and only Savior. When Jesus was about to leave this earth to ascend back to Heaven, He introduced His disciples to the ministry and purpose of the Holy Spirit...

"Unless I go away, the Counselor [Holy Spirit] will not come to you; but if I go, I will send him to you. When he comes, he will convict the world of guilt in regard to sin and righteousness and judgment; in regard to sin, because men do not believe in me; in regard to righteousness, because I am going to the Father, where you can see me no longer; and in regard to judgment, because the prince of this world [Satan] now stands condemned."
John 16: 7b-11

If we reject His claim, when the Holy Spirit speaks to our hearts about Jesus - thus rejecting Jesus - we have no forgiveness and no access to Heaven. Once we have truly heard of Jesus' sacrifice for us, it is unforgivable to reject Him as the Son of God who came to die for us.

Once again, in Jesus' own words recorded in Mark 3:28, 29, He clarifies...

"I tell you the truth, all the sins and blasphemies of men will be forgiven them. But whoever blasphemes against the Holy Spirit will never be forgiven; he is guilty of eternal sin."

The scripture goes on to clarify that when Jesus said this, it was because those to whom He was speaking were rejecting the Holy Spirit's conviction that Jesus is the Son of God, and were instead claiming "He was an evil spirit."

It is not a matter of God's unwillingness to forgive us, but rather our unwillingness to accept the free gift of forgiveness and salvation, as God offers it to us, through the sacrificial death of Jesus Christ. I would be remiss at this point not to ask you, *"Have you personally accepted Jesus' forgiveness?"* It's a *free gift!* It's an essential step to receiving the forgiveness and freedom God offers you!

When we fully understand and accept the forgiveness Jesus provides for us, it radically changes our response to Him and to others. It empowers us to get back up and be restored to Him after our failures, releasing us to offer the gift of forgiveness to others as well.

An Unforgiving Heart Interferes With our Relationship with God

Jesus taught us to pray, *"Forgive us our trespasses as we forgive those who trespass against us."* This divine principle reveals a critical truth! Somehow our receiving forgiveness is intricately dependent upon our willingness to forgive others, a complicated concept, but Biblically confirmed over and over again. Check out the scripture following the Lord's Prayer, in Matthew 6: 14...

"For if you forgive men when they sin against you, your heavenly Father will forgive you. But if you do not forgive men their sins, your Father will not forgive your sins."

Ouch! This appears to leave no room for misunderstanding about, or justification for an unforgiving attitude regarding this principle. Do we sincerely want God's forgiveness and healing? Then according to His Word, we must be open to forgiving our offenders! Again in Mark 11:25 we find:

"And when you stand praying, if you hold anything against anyone, forgive him, so that your Father in heaven may forgive you your sins."

Once again, in Colossians 3:13

"Bear with each other and forgive whatever grievances you may have against one another. Forgive as the Lord forgave you."

The Seemingly Impossible Is Possible!

We've clearly seen throughout the Bible that God's instruction leaves no question concerning His command that we must forgive, and He is well aware of our difficulty in doing so. He knows our weaknesses and is keenly aware that forgiveness is not an easy task, especially when dealing with someone who has hurt and betrayed us – maybe over and over again. He also knows that it often is impossible to forgive and forget the offense without the Holy Spirit working through us. Take heart, what is impossible for us is possible through Him. He will always empower us to do that which He commands us to do, never leading us where He cannot keep us!

"Jesus looked at them and said; "With man this is impossible, but not with God; All things are possible with God." Mark 10:27

Unload the burden of unforgiven instances at the altar of God. Remember, in order for Him to take our burdens from us, we have to let go of them. When we do, He faithfully takes them. As you leave your offenses at the cross and walk away, be aware that Satan will try to resurrect old hurts and transgressions. When he does, do as Peter did when he firmly declared, *"Get thee behind me Satan."* The scriptures show us that there is mighty healing power in just uttering His name! Boldly declare your command in the name of Jesus!

Relinquishing Ownership Precedes and Enables Forgiveness

Such an important truth! Your loved ones do not belong to you! Whether children, spouse, siblings, friends, or whomever "they" may be, they belong to God. He has only loaned them to us to love and to take care of - for Him. Whenever we take misplaced responsibility for their actions, we assume inappropriate ownership. That wrongly assigned ownership becomes a heavy burden regarding our sense of responsibility for one who is willfully turning away from God. Sometimes our tendency to hold on too tight and not truly forgive is spawned by fear that we may lose our perceived control, thus our ability to change the one for whom we are troubled. It works just the opposite. God instructs us to love with all our hearts, but in doing so He doesn't give us the right to take over His job in our loved ones lives. It is He who has the authority to bring about a change of heart. If we try to usurp His job, we actually get in the way of what He is trying to do. As we forgive and relinquish ownership of our relationships to the Lord, we are released to let go and trust Him to do the work that in faith we believe He can do. Only then are we able to declare that even though we may not support the behavior of our love one, we indeed 'love them anyhow.'

Personal Reflection:

A very dark time in a family's life…devastating and scary…a young teenager who succumbed to the pull of her peers, attending a questionable party and drinking a drink that, unbeknown to her, had been spiked with drugs. She became hopelessly addicted. Following were months of unacceptable behavior and continued drug abuse. Periodic hope turned to disappointment and despair. It was a challenge for her family to forgive and believe for her healing. The longer it continued, the more they became determined to somehow force a behavioral change. It didn't work. They had come to a dead-end and all but given up, not knowing where to turn and not really having the means to get sufficient treatment to address her needs.

But the young lady's mom had not given up. Her unwavering love for her daughter remained so strong that she was given the strength and wisdom to do what most of us would have determined unthinkable. After much prayer, she decided to sign papers making her precious daughter a ward of the state, in order to help facilitate her entry into a lock-down treatment facility. A devastating move! But one that she was determined to make. The rest of the family was not happy! But due to her willingness to forgive her daughter and act on her desire for the very best for her, she let go of attempts to control her daughter, relinquishing ownership to the Lord, and believing that through this professional treatment program He could do what the rest of the family could not. The wisdom she'd gained about such situations as a psyche nurse compelled her that being willing to take this step was critical to the survival of her daughter. She had to let go and trust that God loved her daughter more than anyone else. And that given a chance, He had a plan for her healing.

And a plan He did have! He was there for this precious young lady in so many ways, through the facility staff, through the continual support and visits from her family, and by providing perspective for her daily well-being and ultimate healing. She became a modern day miracle. The facility staff declared that, due to her kind of addictions, her healing was absolutely nothing short of that – a miracle! Walking away from all addictions, giving her life to Christ, and becoming one of the most beautiful children of God, wife, and now mother of four, that anyone could imagine! Now as she lives out her life as a loving disciple of Christ, doing the best she knows how to raise her children in the ways of the Lord, others look on and learn from her example of God's victory and faithful Christian living.

God is faithful to heal our loved ones as we offer forgiveness and release them to Him. He truly does love our loved ones even more than we do, and with a far deeper divine understanding of what they need! Don't hold on to a misplaced ownership of your loved ones. Make a conscious effort to forgive and let go, giving God a chance to work miracles in their lives!

Author, Merlin Carothers has written many powerful books about the victory and power of relinquishing ownership and instead determining to praise God for all things. A couple of my favorites are: *"Prison to Praise,"* and *"Power in Praise."* His stories are full of victory as people believe God for healing to their dilemmas. He tells the story of a woman who for 20 years desperately tried to change her husband's smoking habits, while at the same time relentlessly trying to bring him to the Lord. She continually complained about his smoking habit, pointing out the damages it was causing to his health, and how it did not please God to see him smoke. Daily she assumed the role of taking her husband's sins to the Lord, asking for forgiveness on his behalf, and continually pointing out to her husband that she was doing so. In other words, she nagged him continually and then used her own righteousness to excuse her nagging. He successfully ignored her criticism and judgment and continued to smoke.

Completely exasperated and worn out from all her unsuccessful efforts, she sought counsel as to what more she could do to help him. The counselor, Merlin Corothers, encouraged her to let go, and stop trying to force the change she desired, praising God for her husband, and turning his habits over to God, believing that He could and would affect the change that they both wanted for this man. Finally in desperation, she gave up trying to change her husband and began to consistently approach the Lord with a plea something like this:

"Lord, because I know you love him, for twenty years I have tried to change him, while pleading with you to forgive him. I'm tired, exhausted, and don't know what else to try. From now on I'm giving him up to you. Instead of me trying to change him I'm determined to do the best I can just to love him, and to trust you to change him into whatever you want him to be."

Merlin Corothers goes on to recount that miraculously, God changed them both. In sight of six months her husband not only came to know the Lord as his Savior but he had also quit smoking, without his wife even noticing. She had become so determined to let go and put all of her focus on loving him [refraining from judging and trying to change him] that it wasn't until one day when her husband said to her that he was surprised she hadn't mentioned the fact that he wasn't smoking anymore, that she even realized he'd stopped! That is truly forgiving, letting go of control, and giving the Lord charge. Because she was so focused on praising God for her husband that she willingly stepped out of the way and let God do His work, the way was cleared for him to be reached by the only one who could truly help him change

Don't bear the burden in matters of forgiveness related to your loved ones issues with the Lord. While praying for them and lovingly encouraging them to draw close to the Lord, make it your commitment to keep your communications about these matters free from judgment and misplaced ownership. God will mold them into what He wants them to be…in His time.

Forgiveness/Praise/Relinquishing Ownership Go Hand-in-Hand

Most of us can identify with this woman's story. As spouses, siblings, or friends, we often feel as though we aren't doing our 'job' if we aren't spending nearly every moment trying to push our loved ones into the mold we think God wants them to assume. Perhaps the hardest relationships for us to relinquish to the Lord are our relationships with our children. As parents we feel a huge weight of responsibility to encourage our children [and sometimes even manipulate them] to do and be everything we believe God wants them to do and be. We believe we are 'helping.' Often we are not. We mistakenly believe the task of maturing our children depends on us. It seems we need to be reminded time and time again to give them back to God who maintains ownership of them. They have only been loaned to us to love and train in the ways of the Lord, calling them to accountability on His behalf. When they make mistakes or poor choices, God is able to convict them with the foolishness of their actions. Understanding this releases us from the sense of responsibility that we need to make them grovel before us and offer all kinds of promises about their intentions for changed behavior, before we are willing to give forgiveness and a restoration of our blessings. Don't get me wrong; however misguided we may be, our intentions are good. We are called to speak God's truth to our kids and God expects us to carry out His assignment with diligence and commitment as we train them up in the way that they should go, but the outcome is between our children and God.

He gives us some insight in His Word as to how He desires for us to handle these tough times. In the 15th chapter of Luke we read the story of the Prodigal Son, a parable told by Jesus. The parable is of a son who, after having hassled his father for his premature inheritance, goes off into the world and foolishly squanders his ill-gotten fortune. Having made one poor decision after another, spending everything and finding himself with nowhere else to go, he returns home. In an attempt to make sure he has learned his lesson, His father does not drag his son through all the ugliness of his disobedience, rehearsing dead issues that can no longer be changed. He doesn't tell him how stupid he has been, nor does he even demand an apology along with a promise to never do such things again. No. Instead, he praises God for the return of his son, and upon the first sight of him coming up the path toward home he summons his servants to 'bring him the finest robe, kill the fattest calf, and prepare a welcome home celebration.'

We can almost see him dancing as he declares, "My son who was lost has come home at last!" The eldest son, who had stayed home and attended to his father's wishes, was a bit chagrined at his father's jubilation. Perhaps he thought that the younger son should be rejected, or at least made to pay a high price for his disobedience. Perhaps he thought the party should have instead been held in his honor. After all, he was the eldest and obedient son. But that is not how God reveals the story.

What can we learn from this parable? The main purpose of the parable is neither the story of a rebellious son turned repentant, nor of an obedient son turned jealous. The lesson to be learned is one of a father who puts love, forgiveness, and reconciliation above all else. He loves both sons equally and he doesn't require that any love be stolen from one son in order to honor the other.

That's the kind of forgiveness our Heavenly Father has for us. Because of Jesus, it is a forgiveness that offers unconditional love, calling for a celebration when we come home to Him. In fact, because the blood of Jesus <u>totally</u> covers <u>all</u> of our sins, the Bible tells us that when we appear at Heaven's gate, we appear as white as snow, sins removed as far as the east is from the west. And heaven throws a party! All of Heaven's Angels break into a praise song when even just one forgiven sinner comes to Jesus.

> *"In the same way I tell you there is rejoicing in the presence of the Angels of God over one sinner who repents."* Luke 15:10

God loves and forgives beyond what we can fathom. He asks us to do likewise. When our loved ones who have made poor choices determine to come back to Him, He wants us to join Him in receiving them with love, forgiveness, and encouragement. Who are we to rub their faces in their mistakes when God doesn't? God does not give us that permission. Rather He commands us to love them through all things. When we don't, we alienate ourselves from our loved ones and from God.

Sin Is NOT Okay

With all of the above in mind, let me be quite clear. God's Word declares that we must be careful not to justify sin in the process of loving the sinner. It is clear throughout the Bible, and clearly evident in life, that there are and should be consequences as a result of our actions. We cannot condone sin. God doesn't. Yet we must not withhold our love from the sinner. God never stops loving His children. This takes an Agape Love and a divine forgiveness that only God enables us to offer. It's complicated. Human forgiveness doesn't forget the offense, nor does it desire the best for the offender. Holy Spirit forgiveness leaves no room for judgment nor for holding grudges. When you allow the Holy Spirit in to enable you to forgive others, it is finished.

Divine Forgiveness vs Human Forgiveness

To offer Biblically based forgiveness, it must come from the heart, out of our desire to please God. Too often we *claim* we have forgiven, but all we've actually done is to *bury* our hurt. On the surface all seems fine, but the anger lay lurking for the opportunity to be resurrected again. There are common tell-tale behaviors present when this happens. They play out something like this:

1. In order to cover up our hurt we make light of the offense, perhaps making snide and sarcastic jokes about it with our offender and others, subconsciously hoping to make our offender look bad. The hurt continues to fester within the relationship, ultimately turning into bitterness and resentment.

2. In order to 'punish' our offender without taking the responsibility for having done so, we become passive aggressive, using all kinds of unrelated reasons to carry out our 'punish' and 'pout' routine. Our words and body language defy one another as to what is truly in our hearts.

3. Instead of forgiving God's way, without keeping score, we record the offense so as to keep a tally of who owes whom what apologies!

    *"Love is patient, love is kind. It does not envy, it does not boast, it is not proud. It is not rude, it is not self-seeking, it is not easily angered, **IT KEEPS NO RECORD OF WRONGS.**" I Corinthians 13:4-5*

4. We try to sweep the offense under the carpet. We think a little pile of hurt and dirt under our emotional rug won't matter. But next week or next month or next year, as offenses continue to pile up, one day we emotionally trip over this huge pile of garbage and lay destroyed, looking up from a slain position asking, *"What happened? Everything was alright and then all of the sudden..."* But don't kid yourself. It wasn't *all of a sudden*. It may have been accumulating for years, because we just didn't want to talk about things, and we thought we were handling it okay by ourselves. Without true Biblically based

forgiveness, this just doesn't work! God's example of divine forgiveness calls for '*forgetting*' not '*burying*' our offenses.

Blot it Out

Satan is never at rest. The Bible tells us that he is always roaming around the earth looking for whom he may devour. He is especially interested in destroying the relationships of those who belong to Christ, because in doing so he not only brings a negative effect in their lives, but can also discourage those with whom they have a ministry. Don't bury skeletons of unforgiveness in your closet, giving him an opportunity to dig them out at your most vulnerable moments.

If you have truly forgiven [to a point of forgetting the pain] you won't find yourself requiring others to continually recall, pay for, or justify their past failures. God says when it's over, it's over. When offenses have been confessed and forgiven, it is time to heal and love, praying for God's best for one another.

> *"Their sins and lawless acts I will remember no more. And where these have been forgiven, there is no longer any sacrifice for sin. Therefore brother, since we have confidence to enter the Most Holy Place by the blood of Jesus, by a new and living way opened for us through the curtain, that is, his body, and since we have a great priest over the house of God, let us draw near to God with a sincere heart in full assurance of faith, having our hearts sprinkled to cleanse us from a guilty conscience, and having our bodies washed with pure water. Let us hold unswervingly to the hope we profess, for he who promised is faithful. And let us consider how we may spur one another on toward love and good deeds."* Hebrews 10:17-24

Like a permanent marker blots out a word, divine forgiveness obliterates the offense, preventing one sin from piling upon another, not allowing an insurmountable mountain of junk to build up!

Personal Reflection
It was a joy-filled day and evening. I had just completed helping with the administration of a fund raising house party for one of my favorite political candidates. I knew my cell had been buzzing with a message, but ignored it until after the event. As soon as I climbed into the car and headed for home, I decided to sit for a minute so I could listen to my message. I sat stunned in disbelief.

The message, full of expletives and condemnation, left me numb. It was given in response to an earlier conversation between an especially dear Christian sister and me, in which we had entertained differing opinions on a matter. And the crazy thing was that the subject about which we were discussing didn't really matter at all! Why such a violent response to such an insignificant issue? As I sat there trying to put things into perspective, I needed to remember that Satan is alive and well, always seeking whom he may devour, and He was having a hay day with us!

It was earlier that morning when our breakfast group shared differing opinions about the operation of a particular public service entity – I suggested that this service was now entirely privately operated, while others believed it was still fully operated and controlled by the government. Being wired in such a way as to automatically do factual research when I'm not sure about something, I decided to look it up on the internet when I returned home. Finding that actually both positions were valid, I cut and pasted my findings into an E-mail to my friends, primarily to clarify that I had been wrong about my presumption that it was now privately owned. I noted that, though the service is now privately operated, it is still under the management of the federal government, as they had believed it to be.

For one friend the email had been very offensive, believing that my motivation in sending it was to somehow declare that I was right. That was unacceptable to her, as she had very adamantly declared in her message, saying that she was tired of my always thinking I was right! Did I? I didn't realize I did. For sure it is not my intention; and certainly not in this case. I couldn't believe the depth of her anger and disappointment in me. My mind raced and my human instincts to defend myself ran ramped. I truly needed to examine my heart and motives, but at that moment my shock and gut wrenching disbelief wouldn't allow me to do anything but hatefully and determinedly declare that I was just done – done with any attempts at rebuilding this relationship. I started driving home, sobbing as I drove, and knowing this would be devastating to my husband as well, since we had become close friends as couples and would sorely miss our social and spiritual interaction with them!

I decided to pull over and call my friend and try to clarify my intentions. I found she had not actually read my email but rather been given the message verbally through her husband. Perhaps the verbal interpretation had created some of the issue. Her judgment, anger and cursing flooded out. She was very explosive about the situation and not at all open to reconciliation, and I was not pushing for it - uncharacteristic of either one of us. We coldly ended our conversation and hung up.

Following were days of prayer, repentance, and begging God for an understanding of what my culpability was in the situation. He gave me the desire and strength to forgive. He must have done so for her too, because we have never spoken of the incident again. Our relationship has resumed and God's grace abounds. We love each other, support each other, pray for each other's family, and cherish each other as Christian sisters. Biblically-based forgiveness allows God to heal and do that which we are totally unable to do for ourselves. Thank God for His faithfulness!

Whatsoever God commands of us, let us willingly obey. What is right in God's eyes is a forgiveness that leads to expressing 'I Love You Anyhow.' Since God knew from the beginning that the fall of Adam and Eve would pass on all sorts sinful desires, He determined ahead of time to provide a way for those sins to be washed away.

> *"You, however, are controlled not by the sinful nature but by the Spirit, if the Spirit of God lives in you. And if anyone does not have the Spirit of Christ, he does not belong to Christ. But if Christ is in you, your body is dead because of sin, yet your spirit is alive because of righteousness."* Romans 8:9-10

Notice how in this scripture He doesn't say we have no charges against us. On the contrary, He declares that we do have a sinful nature, but when we have the Spirit of Christ living in us, we are not controlled by that nature. The miraculous thing is that <u>He</u> <u>chooses</u> to blot out all our sins with the blood of Christ!

How Many Times Must We Offer Forgiveness?

In coping with someone's continual offenses, do you ever ask yourself, as I have, "Just how long is this going to go on, and how many times must I forgive the same offense?" Surely there is a limit. It happened last week and the week before that, and the week before that. We cry out, 'God, must I keep forgiving the same thing over and over again?' His answer is "yes."

When the Apostle Peter was confronted with this issue, He sought the Lord's direction. Though God knows the frailness of our human condition, He made it very clear to Peter that his source of forgiveness never runs out, because God Himself is the source. That message is for us as well....

> *"Then Peter came to him and asked, 'Lord, how many times shall I forgive my brother when he sins against me? Up to seven times? Jesus answered, 'I tell you, not seven times, but seventy-seven times."* Matthew 18:21-22

In other words...on into infinity. Impossible? No - because *'all things are possible, through Christ who strengthens us.'* (Philippians 4:13) God knows that we do not have it within us to forgive as He forgives so He sent us a helper, the Holy Spirit. Unless we call upon the Holy Spirit within us to empower us to forgive for Jesus' sake, forgiveness God's way is unattainable.

Who is Responsible to Take the Offense to the Cross?

Jesus' actions clearly show us that it is the offended who must take the offense to the cross. Yet when we are offended, how often do we wait and insist that our offender come to us and ask for forgiveness first, before we are willing to let go of the offense? It is right and good for them to do so, but Jesus' example?

He went to the cross while His accusers were still persecuting Him [even though He was free of sin and all the accusations being hurled at Him]. His actions declared loud and clear that it is the responsibility of the offended to go to God [just as He did] crying out, *"Father forgive them for they know not what they do!"* He expects us to do likewise.

What if we would do so? What if we would take all of the offenses hurled at us to the cross and leave them there, as Jesus did? What if we would forget about what 'other people think' and just radically forgive? If so, perhaps the channels would be opened up through which Jesus could heal our broken relationships.

In Wayne Jacobsen's book, *"He Loves Me, He Loves Me Not,"* he challenges us, *"When you are willing to take the plunge to love outside the lines you are choosing to give up serving your reputation and trust it to God!"* He follows that challenge with an unbelievable story of one such woman. Take a look at an overview of this incredible story.....

It seems this woman's husband told her one day, after a number of years of marriage, that he preferred the gay lifestyle, adding that he had been in a gay relationship for some time and had decided to move out from his home with her and into a place with his gay partner. Of course she was devastated, and she turned to her relationship with the Lord to help seek healing. Some time later she learned that her, then x-husband, was suffering from aids. His partner was unable to take care of him, so she moved in with them and took care of him until his dying day. During this time she talked with him about the love and forgiveness of Jesus. He gave his life to Christ. Later when she learned that her late husband's gay partner also had aids, again she moved back in to take care of him in his dying days. He also gave his life to Christ. Word spread of her love, compassion, and forgiveness, and over the next years she continued to take care of dozens of dying aids patients. They all received Jesus Christ as their Lord and Savior!

This Godly woman could have basked in self pity, remorse, and unforgiveness, instead of risking her reputation to vulnerably serve God's purpose, giving of herself in the name of Jesus. She sowed seeds of forgiveness and love that the Holy Spirit used to bring dozens of souls into Heaven. And through her selfless ministry we have to believe that she reaped even more than she sowed, because the Bible promises us that.

Are we willing to do so great a thing? Or do we find ourselves enjoying our own little 'pity party,' not feeling like anyone appreciates us? And certainly not willing to forgive those who hurt us, let alone committing ourselves to serving them.

So how do we turn the devastation of sin into victory? What happens between sin and forgiveness? It takes dying to self and being filled with the gift of God's

Grace. When the power of the One who was sent to 'overcome' is allowed to direct our relationships, we are released to forgive and love. Scriptures give us insight to this dynamic process.

> *"But the gift is not like the trespass. For if the many died by the trespass of the one man [Adam], how much more did God's grace and the gift that came by the grace of the one man, Jesus Christ, overflow to the many! Again, the gift of God is not like the result of the one man's sin: The judgment followed one sin and brought condemnation, but the gift followed many trespasses and brought justification. For if, by the trespass of the one man, death reigned through that one man, how much more will those who receive God's abundant provision of grace and of the gift of righteousness reign in life through the one man, Jesus Christ. Consequently, just as the result of one trespass was condemnation for all men, so also the result of one act of righteousness was justification that brings life for all men. For just as through the disobedience of the one man the many were made sinners, so also through the obedience of the one man the many will be made righteous.* Romans 5:15-19

A Divine Implant Enables Radical Love

We've clearly seen that it is through Jesus and Jesus alone that sin is forgiven. In and of ourselves we are incapable of forgiving the way Jesus does. We can hardly imagine dying for someone, let alone someone who doesn't even love us, but rather cries out for our crucifixion. God knows us and He fulfills His promise that *'wherever He guides He also provides.'* He makes provision to enable us to do as He commands. Just like no loving earthly father would ever command their child to do something that he knew ahead of time was impossible for them to do, God provides a way for us to do what He asks us to do. So how has He provided for us to enable us to forgive like Christ does? We have been given a *divine implant* that enables us to do so. Take a look.

> *"God made him who had no sin to be sin for us, so that in him we might become the righteousness of God."* II Corinthians 5:21

God poured our sin into Jesus and through His death and resurrection, poured His righteousness into us, giving us the capacity to love and forgive. So it becomes our choice, doesn't it? Our seeming inability to forgive isn't because we can't; it's because we don't want to. Our unwillingness to forgive becomes like a cancer that permeates our emotions and kills our relationships. We can either let the cancer take over or we can recognize our culpability in a situation, relinquishing our 'rights' to a higher power who can and will fill and heal us with enough love to declare "I Love You Anyhow," right in the middle of the battle. Sometimes I have chosen to do so. Sometimes I have failed miserably, foolishly holding out because of unfulfilled expectations.

Personal Reflection

Journal Entry — Unfulfilled Expectations....

We arrived here about 5PM yesterday. Our first long awaited "snowbird" trip to the warmth of the south – out of the winter snows of the Midwest – a dream come true! The condo is so beautiful, beyond our wildest dreams. Right from our deck – a full view of the glittering waters of the ocean for as far as one can see in every direction - white sugary sand beaches, warm breeze, palm trees, and each other. Retirement – that time in life when all the happiness we've looked forward to can now be ours! Yet tonight a heavy sadness hangs in the air.

No time to walk the beach yet – tomorrow. Slept in this morning – sat on the deck with my coffee [all alone] taking in the breathtaking view – we cleaned up about noon and went to the Waffle House for brunch – little to no conversation. Went grocery shopping – good to have cupboards full. Fixed broiled pork loin, baked potatoes and salad for supper. Cleaned up the kitchen while he went in to watch TV – basketball – not especially a highlight for me.

I guess I could get more enthused about the game if I weren't resisting the idea. After yesterday's proclamation during our trip down here I don't even want to like it! I still can't accept his comment. Following one of my too exuberant exclamations of how excited I was to be arriving here and how wonderful the prospects of a month on the beach with him were to me, I fell from ecstasy to agony! When will I learn not to make everything about me, instead of letting it just be what it is! If I would admit it, I know I probably baited him with my questions. As the conversation went, I could have re-directed it. Looking back, I realize I was wrongly seeking human affirmation instead of looking to God for His affirmation. So I baited....
"Are you excited?"

"Ya, but probably not as excited as you are."

"So then tell me, what is it in life that ever gets you really excited?"

I quietly but anxiously awaited his answer, fearing that we were not on the same page in this conversation. After a very long pause....

"I guess what comes to my mind is that long winning shot that Ptacek sank in the last minute of that High School game in our senior year. Wow, what a game!"

Are you kidding me! Oh the pain of the truth that he actually got more excited thinking about a basketball game experience 40 years ago than spending a month on the beach with me. And what a shame, because other than that 'very low' moment, the trip was really great – nice weather, good roads, pleasant overnight on the way at our nephew's, and a wonderful two nights seeing some great talent in Nashville. So why do I keep letting these down moments rob me of the pleasures of the good ones?

Why do I allow myself to feel so alone and crushed, allowing my emotions to be controlled by unfulfilled expectations? Will I never learn that I cannot look to him [or anyone else for that matter] nor whatever our life style brings us – nor any current circumstance, to give me true fulfillment and joy? I'm so grateful, God, that you don't give up on me. Thank you for loving me 'anyhow' and helping me through these selfish disappointing times. To be honest, right now I don't want to forgive him for the hurt...maybe tomorrow. Goodnight.

As I look back over this journal page, I realize that the whole time I was reacting to this incident & allowing it to control my actions, I knew better. I was choosing not to be forgiving because I wanted my husband to hurt like I was. I knew better. I knew he meant no harm to me by his comments. I knew when I married him that he wasn't a romantic like me, but I chose not to allow that truth to excuse him. I was disappointed and making a *conscious choice* not to say *"I Love You Anyhow."* That saddens God's heart!

Whenever we allow our emotions to be governed by our unfulfilled expectations, we open ourselves up to 'reacting' to disappointments, rather than 'acting' upon God's promise to be our fulfillment. God asks us to let Him be the object or our affections. I knew the truth about what God wanted of me in the area of forgiveness. But 'knowing' it wasn't enough. He wanted me to 'act' upon it. I have heard it said that one cannot sincerely pray for someone while at the same time being unwilling to forgive them. I believe this to be true. When we truly forgive, we want the best for the one whom we have forgiven. The sincerity of our forgiveness should be reflected in our actions toward the forgiven.

When Jesus walked this earth, by His actions He gave us undeniable proof of His willingness and authority to forgive.

"Which is easier: to say, 'your sins are forgiven,' or to say, 'Get up and walk'? But so that you may know that the Son of Man has authority on earth to forgive sins....Get up, take your mat and go home." Matthew 9:5-6

He pleads with us to do the same. Are we showing our love and willingness to forgive by our actions?

"Dear children let us not love with word or tongue but with actions and with truth." I John 3:18

When we forgive, <u>healing</u> results. When we don't, <u>God</u> <u>hold's</u> <u>us</u> <u>accountable</u>.

"We love because he first loved us. If anyone says, "I love God," yet hates his brother, he is a liar. For anyone who does not love his brother, whom he has seen,

cannot love God, whom he has not seen. And he has given us this command: Whoever loves God must also love his brother." I John 4:19

I praise God that He loves you and me with an Agape love that compels Him to forgive us in our trespasses and heal us from our selfishness. It is because of this love, and in response for what He has done for us, that we are equipped and empowered to forgive every offense that comes our way. We do it for His sake, because He commands it.

"Dear God,
Thank you for sending Jesus Christ to demonstrate the kind of Agape love that forgives. Thank you for your willingness to forgive our trespasses through Jesus Christ, who took them to the cross, erasing them for all eternity. We accept the truth that forgiveness is a matter of divine principle, inherent in those who belong to Christ. Today we accept the responsibility of forgiving anything we may still be holding against another. God we not only want to forgive the offense, but we truly want to forget it, so much so that we are willing to offer the radical love of Jesus Christ to those for whom we offer forgiveness. Help us to fully forgive so that we can be released to effectively pray for those whom you have placed in our lives to love for you. Thank you for the power of the Holy Spirit who brings us the truth, and empowers us to act upon it. Amen"

Personal Application

TRUTH:

God fully forgives. Offering forgiveness is not an option. The empowerment to sincerely forgive comes from God, through His Holy Spirit living within.

1. In your own words define the kind of *"mercy"* and *'grace'* God offers to us and asks us to offer them to others.

2. Holding back issues for which we are unwilling to forgive alienates us from God. Recall a time when you have chosen not to forgive. How did it affect your sense of well-being? With others? With God? How did you resolve the issue?

3. Considering the scriptures regarding the unforgiveable sin [refusing to accept the Holy Spirit's ministry regarding Jesus' life and purpose] what has been your response to the claims of Christ?

4. When we truly accept the truth that others belong to God, it releases us from a sense of responsibility for their behavior. How did the prodigal son's father demonstrate this principle?

5. What are the results of shallow human attempts at forgiveness? How is Holy Spirit driven forgiveness different? Recall instances in your life when you personally struggled with attempts at human forgiveness? How would you handle those incidents differently now?

6. What has been your response to the unfulfilled expectations in your life? What insights shared within this chapter will you apply to help you offer a more Godly response in these circumstances?

7. Jesus demonstrated that it is the offender's response to take the offenses to the cross. Examine your heart for any unforgiven offenses. Take time right now to meet with God and give those offenses over to Him.

Journal Entry: **You Forgive Me....You Are There**

When I feel like nothing is right in my life
    Yet nothing is really wrong,
When I feel like just shutting the world out,
    And singing a private, quiet song;
Lord, You forgive me...You are there.

When I'm all shook up about some little thing,
    Yet I really don't know why,
When I just want to let the tears poor out,
    But all I can do is quietly sigh,
You forgive me...You are there.

When people sometimes seem ruffled and mad
    And they seem to take it out on me,
When I'm crying inside for someone to care,
    Yet no one but you can hear my plea;
You forgive me....You are there.

When the thunder roars endlessly loud,
    And the rain falls day and night,
When it seems like the rainbow will never come,
    And darkness overcomes the light;
You forgive me....You are there.

When love is nowhere to be found
    And gratefulness is far from my lips
When emptiness is all around
    And my heart yearns to feel you near
You forgive me....You are there.

When guilt floods in and my heart is heavy
    And I know I've blown it once again
And the knawing ache of disappointment and
    Self-condemnation comes creeping in
You forgive me...You are there.

When I turn to you and confess my sin
    I can survive - the victory is mine,
Cause you poured out your love,
    Hung on a cross, and died for me,
Lord, You forgave me....You are here!

CHAPTER FIVE
LIVING OUT LIFE'S ROLES

God has designed each of us for His purpose, and in doing so He has gifted each of us for the role for which He has designed us. He was there in our very formation as He delicately designed and equipped each of us to carry out His purpose.

> *"For you created my inmost being; you knit me together in my mother's womb. I praise you because I am fearfully and wonderfully made; your works are wonderful, I know that full well. My frame was not hidden from you when I was made in the secret place. When I was woven together in the depths of the earth, your eyes saw my unformed body. All the days ordained for me were written in your book before one of them came to be."* Psalm 139:13-16

It is critical for each of us to get in touch with our true self; the "self" God fashioned in our mother's womb. You will never find true peace of mind until you find a way to set aside some time in your busy schedule to get to know the true 'you' that God created you to be.

There is an insightful book which I have found to be of great help in understanding how to more effectively minister to my own personal needs, helping me to get in touch with my true identity. The book, *"Real Moments,"* written by Dr. Barbara DeAngelo, explores the damage done when we allow ourselves to be continually pulled in all directions, while attempting to meet the demands of the various roles we serve. Too often we unwisely save no time for ourselves, thus no time to establish our own secure base in which we spend time with God, searching our souls, and just *'being'* instead of always *'doing.'*

We have become a driven people, a society quite accomplished at '*doing*.' But most of us are really lousy at just '*being*.' And since we have forgotten how to just 'be' from time to time, we have robbed ourselves of the 'real moments' that bring our lives clarity and peace. This condition leaves us out of touch with what God created us to be, even in our mother's womb. On many occasions when teaching seminars and retreats, I challenge participants to write down a statement describing 'who' they are. Inevitably the descriptions are about '*whose*' they are, instead of '*who*' they are. Answers like, I am someone's husband or wife, or I am so and so's mom or dad or child, or I belong to such and such church, or am employed by.....

The first role we must correctly assume is that of the person God created us to be in the womb. Do you know who you really are? What opinions are truly yours? What likes and dislikes are your own? Most of us don't even know. We have become such a combination of response to the expectations of others, choosing a lifestyle that pleases others and making choices that we would not make on our own, that we have lost touch with our personal convictions and with what would truly make us happy. We have lost our individuality. Instead, we define ourselves by our various titles of, Mom, Dad, Child, Grandparent, Teacher, Friend, Boss, or Employee. Who are you aside from all these roles you play? When we lose our own sense of purpose and direction, the ability to live life by our own values and beliefs, we lose the power of '*real moments*' in our lives. Dr. DeAngelo writes....

> "*We have been hurled out of balance by the state of emotional and spiritual crisis our world has brought us to. We have more material comforts than any previous civilization, and yet we also show more evidence of personal unhappiness. We know that the world is not the safe and hopeful place we wish it could be. And often we turn away from the fears and sadness this truth brings and develop a protective layer of numbness that makes it difficult for us to experience the 'real moments' that we need now more than ever. Moments of compassion toward our fellow human beings...moments of connections with those we love and those who need love...moments of centering and healing for ourselves.*" Excerpts from pgs 30-31

So what are '*real moments*?' How do we know when we are allowing ourselves the real moments we need in order to be in touch with ourselves and those around us? Take a look at an overview of Dr. DeAngelo's suggestion that there are three elements of experience that must be present in order to truly experience real moments...[and be sure to get her book for much more]

- *Consciousness*
  Only when you are consciously and completely experiencing where you are, what you are doing, and how you are feeling.

- *Connection*
  Moments in which you have made an emotional connection with another person. They are moments in which the usual boundaries and barriers are penetrated, and in that connection, a kind of magic occurs.
- *Surrender*
  Real Moments happen when you totally surrender into whatever you are experiencing, and let go of trying to be in control. You are 100% engaged in what you are doing, whether it is taking a walk, making love, baking bread, or watching children play – you are fully embracing the moment, rather than trying to control the experience.

For me, this means no diversion by any outside element can be present or the real moment becomes diluted. So, when was the last time you had a '*real moment*' with God, praying with your whole being, laying your soul out there for Him to heal? When was the last time you had a 'real moment' with yourself, searching your heart for your true feelings and coming to grips with the reality of your sub-conscious as well as your conscious reactions to life? I believe that in taking time to reflect properly on these moments that God puts before us, we will find His peace.

> *"Finally brothers, whatever is true, whatever is noble, whatever is right, whatever is pure, whatever is lovely, whatever is admirable - if anything is excellent or praiseworthy - think about such things.* Philippians 4:8

Reflect on your lifestyle. Do you have any real moments in your life in which you can focus on what is true, noble, right, pure, lovely, and admirable? Are you experiencing any real moments with yourself? With your loved ones? Or is life just dragging you through, leaving you with only the wherewithal to 'react' instead of the forethought to 'act' upon those real moments?

I am thankful to Dr. DeAngelo, for pointing out some tell-tale signs of the lack of real moments:

- *You find yourself needing to constantly be doing something*
- *You have an addiction to something or someone*
- *You are cynical, pessimistic, or sarcastic*
- *You live your life through others*
- *You are judgmental*
- *You are too busy or distracted to ever truly give undivided attention*
- *You avoid 'real moments' because you are afraid of them*
- *You put boundaries between yourself and others*

How do we begin to take back the power to experience real moments? We start by rediscovering our own truth – our own values and choices, and living them every day. In the process, we become who God means us to be. This process restores our true sense of integrity and gives us the freedom to say 'no' when 'no' is appropriate. As long as we live we will move in and out of crises and adversity, and our joys will live alongside sorrows. When we know who we are and turn to God for help in embracing the inevitable changes life throws at us, we will be victorious in the roles in which we serve, and be able to offer a love that goes beyond our human resources. We will be able to pour out a divine "*I Love You Anyhow*' kind of love.

As we continue to examine glimpses of truth regarding our God-given roles, let's keep this concept of 'real moments' in mind. Many of the relational difficulties we experience are likely spawned by the lack of 'real moments,' real moments with God, with ourselves, and with others.

Though each of us are individually designed to carry out His specific purpose, we are also divinely intertwined with one another for God's purpose in helping each other in our roles as husbands, wives, children, family members, co-workers, and friends. Take a look at how God has designed each of us to function, individually and as a whole.....

> "*The body is a unit, though it is made up of many parts; and though all its parts are many, they form one body. So it is with Christ....If the foot should say, 'Because I am not a hand, I do not belong to the body,' it would not for that reason cease to be part of the body. And if the ear should say, "Because I am not an eye, I do not belong to the body,' it would not for that reason cease to be part of the body. If the whole body were an eye, where would the sense of smell be? But in fact God has arranged the parts in the body, every one of them, just as he wanted them to be. If they were all one part, where would the body be? As it is, there are many parts, but one body. The eye cannot say to the hand, 'I don't need you!' And the head cannot say to the feet, 'I don't need you!' On the contrary, those parts of the body that seem to be weaker are indispensable, and the parts that we think are less honorable we treat with special honor.....But God has combined the members of the body and has given greater honor to the parts that lacked it, so that there should be no division in the body, but that its parts should have equal concern for each other. If one part suffers, every part suffers with it; if one part is honored, every part rejoices with it.*" I Corinthians 12:12-26 [excerpts]

This *golden nugget of truth* is huge! It is foundational to the success of the Christian family, both individual families and the greater family of God. It clearly gives us a glimpse of the individual purposes for our existence as well as our collective interactions with one another. When we can fully grasp that we are critically important as individuals and as a vital part of the success of the whole, it gives us insights and incentive for victoriously living out an '*I Love You Anyhow*' kind of love.

Considering Our Roles with One Another

All of these Biblical nuggets of truth are recorded for the well-being of our interactions between one another, within the family of God, and within our earthly families. It is God's desire for His Holy Spirit to indwell each and every marriage. When we choose a marriage partner who belongs to Christ, we choose His covering of protection over that relationship. As Christians we are not only called to honor and uplift one another, but we are each spiritually empowered to do so. When we are 'equally yoked' God has open access to our hearts, individually and collectively.

God warns us of His concern if we should choose to yoke ourselves with a non-believer, putting ourselves in the very vulnerable position of our partner lacking the guidance and empowerment of the Holy Spirit who comes into our heart when we receive Christ.

> *"Do not be yoked together with unbelievers. For what do righteousness and wickedness have in common? Or what fellowship can light have with darkness? What harmony is there between Christ and Belial? What does a believer have in common with an unbeliever? What agreement is there between the temple of God and idols?* 2 Corinthians 6:14-16a

Being in an *'unequally yoked'* relationship opens us up to difficult relational issues. Having said this, it is important to keep in mind that God is always with us helping guide us in our relationships, whether those relationships are with believers or non-believers. If you are one of the many who find yourself in a situation where you are already married to, working for, or in close relationship with nonbelievers, remember that God has given you a ministry of helping reconcile non-believers to Him. This is your highest calling! When one partner is not a believer, whether husband or wife, God encourages a believer to stick with the non-believer and win them over to Jesus by their loving actions....

> *"Wives, in the same way be submissive to your husbands so that, if any of them do not believe the word, they may be won over without talk, by the behavior of their wives, when they see the purity and reverence of your lives...Husbands, in the same way be considerate as you live with your wives, and treat them with respect as the weaker partner and as heirs with you of the gracious gift of life, so that nothing will hinder your prayers."* I Peter 3:1-2, 7

> *"How do you know, wife, whether you will save your husband? Or, how do you know, husband, whether you will save your wife?"* I Corinthians 7:16

We can clearly see in these instructions that God expects us to treat one another, believer or non-believer, with a great deal of love and respect, for these are the things that empower the ministry of reconciliation to which we are called. Therefore, as you seek to serve Him in the reconciliation process of these special loved ones, cling close to His truths and remember: when Christ came into your heart, He brought with Him all of the Trinity, and together they have authority over every other authority. [Colossians 2:9-10] Believe it. Claim it. And offer God's grace as you act upon it, becoming God's hands, feet and voice to those over whom you have influence! Never, never give up!

Throughout the rest of this chapter we will look more closely at God's defined roles within a family of believers in Christ.

Take a minute to reflect on the many roles in which you function – husband, wife, child, sibling. How are they going for you? Are you allowing God His rightful place in each of these relationships? It's a constant challenge and one for which success does not just happen! But we know that success is possible because of God's promise that; *"all things are possible through Christ who strengthens us."* Again, believe it and claim it for each of your relationships!

Let's unpack some of the most significant roles within our earthly families. What insights does His Word give us for functioning in these roles with the ability to offer an 'I Love You Anyhow' kind of love?

In this and the next chapter we will examine these roles, challenging ourselves to carry out God's Biblical design for each. In doing so, we will search out ways to better declare, 'I Love You Anyhow,' and show it by our actions - even in the midst of the toughest of times!

Role Reversals

As I have traveled worldwide I find that it doesn't seem to matter in which culture we exist, role reversals are as common as the air we breathe. All of us suffer from a lost sense of identity, at times taking neither pride in, nor making good, on our commitment to the roles for which God has equipped us.

Let us clarify up-front what this writing is not about. It is not about, 'Should a wife and mom stay home or is it okay for her to go to work?' Nor is it about, 'Should a husband stay home and mind the kids so his wife can follow her profession?' Rather, it is about the God-given giftedness we have to carry out our respective roles, interacting appropriately with one another, as God designs us to do.

In order to lift our relationships above the narcissistic existence that is all too common today, we must protect ourselves from Satan's attempts to confuse our relationships with role reversals through which he can and does capitalize, in his attempts to destroy them. As each of us live out our various chosen roles, it becomes a challenge to stay within character.

Having been involved in film production for over 30 years, I learned that one of the most essential elements of an effective and successful dramatic film is the proper development of the characters. The films we produced are great human stories, dramatically portrayed on the screen with the intent to bring a response towards the things of God. As these dramatic films continue to be shown world-wide, viewers can identify with at least one of the characters within the story [some true to their roles – some not so much] because they are so true to real life. When audiences are given the opportunity to respond to Christ after the film, the response continues to be phenomenal! People all over the world are looking for answers about how they can get their lives in order and find peace in their relationships. The Bible has those answers!

As you and I are faithful to our chosen roles we allow God to work in a positive way in our relationships. But when we allow ourselves to participate in 'role reversals' within our relationships, we become vulnerable to Satan's cunning influence. As those professionals who evaluate problematic relationships are observing, role reversals are becoming more and more prevalent in today's society. It happens between family members, where very often the roles of husband, wife, mother, father, child, disciplinarian, and wage earner, become so jumbled that there is little or no clarity. Role reversals also happen at work, when an employee forgets who owns the company and decides to do an end run to push their agenda as if the business were their own. They happen in churches where church leadership forgets who it is that God has chosen to shepherd the membership and determines to go their own way, splitting the membership. For every person involved in a relationship, God's word offers instruction as to the proper management of their given role. Ignored, there exists a potential role reversal scenario every time.

Perhaps the most disturbing role reversal is one we discussed at length in earlier chapters, that of taking on God's role as Savior and Judge. As stated earlier, it just doesn't work!

One key area of role reversals is that of society's ever-growing tendency toward mixed up roles within the family, and it sorely saddens God's heart. In the Garden, in the very beginning, He established the family unit for the purpose of both serving Him and serving one another. It is God's intention that proper interaction within our human families will give us a glimpse of the joy and interaction of our Heavenly family – those united in Christ with whom we will spend eternity. But often our family roles are so messed up that we have become narcissistic individuals, without allegiance or compassion either for Him or our own family members.

He planned that we would find fulfillment, trust, compassion, joy, peace, and a sense of belonging within our families. Why then are so many families desperately alienated from one another? Family counselors have determined that one driving force in these alienations is the practice of role reversal. Instead of cheerfully assuming the roles for which God has designed us, we covet someone else's role and determine to usurp it for ourselves.

Jesus used parables in His teachings to help give insights to His principles. I would like to do the same here as we look in on a dramatic production of a typical family struggling to put it all together. We'll call them the Bradley family. As in film production each of the cast is carefully selected for their appropriateness to their character, and each carefully studies their specific scripted roles, preparing to play out their assigned character. The characters in our drama: Mom – Carol, Dad – Mike, daughter – Jody, sons – Josh, Jason & Jeremy. Let the cameras role…..

The Bradley Family Self-Destructs

The drama starts out well. All is orderly, and everyone plays their parts stunningly. But by the second act Carol becomes weary of her role, deciding, if only she could live Mike's role she would be happy. She is unaware that entertaining thoughts of 'if only' often opens the door to a discontent that Satan will quickly capitalize upon. She reflects, 'if only' I could get out more, 'if only' I could meet more people, have more friends. She still mechanically performs her functions as a wife and mother, but her heart is no longer in it. Nurturing her family has become boring and she's decides it would be more exciting to take over Mike's roll.

About this same time Mike becomes disenchanted with being the spiritual leader of his family. Work has grown tedious, and his wife irritable. He envies, 'if only' I could have the freedom and social friendships Josh has, I could forget all these responsibilities and go out with my buddies and have some fun. He subconsciously begins assuming the role of his 17 yr. old son, Josh. He still gets up every morning and goes to work, mechanically performing the only real function he retains as a husband and father image. But his top priority is to play, thus he is rarely home.

Carol is also more and more absent from the home scene, presuming the kids are old enough to look after themselves, forgetting that though they can meet their own physical needs, there are still spiritual, emotional, and psychological needs that are being sadly ignored. Mike is gone way too much and when he is at home, his mind is otherwise occupied. So Carol has decided she will need to find companionship to fill her needs outside the home. And after all, he doesn't care anyway. No one seems to talk much anymore, and evening meals where the family used to gather to share the day's events, have long since gone by the wayside.

Being the oldest, Jody begins to feel the need to take over mom's role in the care and discipline of her two younger siblings, Jason and Jeremy, who have become a bit obnoxious and rebellious. Carol's older sibling, Josh, has started not coming home from school until late in the evening, and resents Jody's constant inquisitions. Mom and dad aren't around enough to observe this change in his behavior, and she becomes more and more concerned that someone needs to know where he is and what he is doing, so her prying for this information intensifies.

And Satan, who has been patiently waiting on the sidelines for the right groundwork to be laid that will allow him to move in and do his relationally destructive work, now jumps in and takes over. What began as good and right, a family who cared for and nurtured each other, has become a playground of destruction, so full of role reversals that no one seems to any longer know who they really are.

This scenario resonates with so many families with whom I have prayed for solutions to the relational brokenness in their homes. Unfortunately, it is all too familiar throughout every society today. Now as I look back upon my childhood, I believe to some degree it may have played a destructive role in our home. Though my mom and dad were generally around, I believe [as wonderful as my dad was] his hesitation to take the role of the spiritual leader and disciplinarian in our home took its toll, perhaps even contributing to some of my mom's insecurities.

Are you content to play the roles, at home, at work, within the church and with your friends, for which God has designed you? This doesn't mean that one should not be aware and responsive to new possibilities of serving in whatever new roles God may direct. We are all a work in progress, and as we grow in our talents, abilities, and spiritual lives, we will successfully undertake new adventures, calling for us to seek God's wisdom in how to serve in the new roles we will assume. The key is our willingness to invite God into our circumstances, allowing Him to direct and bless as a result of consulting Him and finding scriptural support for whatever roles we choose to pursue.

Most of the chaos experienced by the Bradley family [and many like them] would not have happened if all the characters would have stayed true to their given roles. Mom could have worked and Dad could have played while still keeping their focus appropriately fixed on the priorities God outlined for them within the roles they served, and consulting Him and each other as to the struggles they were experiencing, instead of allowing 'if' to creep in and playing the blame game.

A long time ago the stage was set for another family scenario. There was the moon and the stars, the trees and beautiful flowers, birds and animals, and man. God set the stage, created the characters, and then said: *"It is not good for man to be alone. Let us make a companion for him, a helper suited to his needs."*

Thus 'family' was created. And in doing so, God determined not to make His people puppets, having no choice in the matters of life, but rather He allowed each of us to choose how we will live. His desire is for us to respond to His wishes because we *'choose'* to, not because we *'have'* to. He set down guidelines for us to follow as we live out our roles with one another, not just for His pleasure, but also for our well being. He made man and woman in His image [Genesis 1:27, Acts 17:28] thus He knows best what will make us complete, fulfilled, and happy. Following Biblical guidelines for living out our roles in life not only pleases God, but it is the kindest thing we can possibly do for ourselves and those we love.

Individual roles assigned within the family are inescapable. When we read the development of the first man and woman in Genesis 2:18-24, we see that God planned for them to complement each other, helping meet each other's needs.

> *"The Lord God said, "It is not good for the man to be alone. I will make a helper suitable for him." Now the Lord God had formed out of the ground all the beasts of the field and all the birds of the air. He brought them to the man to see what he would name them, and whatever the man called each living creature, that was its name. So the man gave names to all the livestock, the birds of the air, and all the beasts of the field. But for Adam no suitable helper was found. So the Lord God caused the man to fall into a deep sleep; and while he was sleeping, he took one of the man's ribs and closed up the place with flesh. Then the Lord God made a woman from the rib he had taken out of the man, and he brought her to the man. The man said, 'This is bone of my bones and flesh of my flesh; she shall be called 'woman' for she was taken out of man.' For this reason a man will leave his father and mother and be united to his wife, and they will become one flesh."*

God created man and woman, each to function within their pre-designed purposes. Additionally, within our marriages God designed husbands and wives, though with separate purposes, to function together as one. Our rejection of these roles is a rejection of God's design. Refusing to be what God designed us to be results in sin that destroys us and our families. Contentment within our marriage depends upon how well we accept and conform to the design God set up for *'male' 'female'* and *'marriage.'* A woman is designed to be a partner to her husband, having a *'helping'* ministry within her home, however that plays out. A husband is called to be a spiritual leader, protector, and provider.

Submission within a marriage is a three-way commitment. First, it is essential that each marriage partner personally submit to Jesus Christ. Second, each marriage partner will be irrevocably submitted to their marriage. And third, the marital union [when the two are joined together they become one] will be submitted to Christ, and thus to God's plan and authority. This fundamental alignment of Godly submissions lays a solid foundation for a husband and wife to experience a secure joyful fulfillment in their marriage.

There are some great analogies that help illuminate the necessary alignment of partnership within a marriage. One such analogy comes to mind….Liken your marriage relationship to that of a strong oak tree - the husband being the root system, through which the entire tree is fed, kept growing and made strong against the winds that threaten to blow it down. The wife, represented by the flourishing and beautiful foliage, nurtures and protects those who seek their home within her branches. If the root system fails, it drains the life from the entire tree. When the foliage refuses to flourish, providing neither home nor protection for those who seek shelter within, God's intended function for the tree is entirely lost. In the next few pages we will take a look at the specific Biblical functions of a wife and a husband, as well as insights as to how we are to function together under God's designed plan.

The Biblical Role of a Wife

God is truly the author of the liberation of women. In Genesis 2:18-24, He explains that 'woman' was created to be a 'help-meet' for man, placing woman in the position of being a 'co-partner' to man, which He made in His image. How much more exalted can a woman be than to be considered a 'joint heir' with her husband in God's perfect creation! He considers women highly important in His declared assignment that we might partner with Him in reconciling the world to Christ! Women, if we are looking for significance – a high calling – a purpose for our lives, we need seek no further!

God spells out His expectations of the ministry to which wives are called, specifying a huge assignment for which He empowers them. Take a look…

"A wife of noble character who can find? She is worth far more than rubies. Her husband has full confidence in her and she lacks nothing of value. She brings him good, not harm, all the days of her life. She selects wool and flax and works with eager hands. She is like the merchant ships, bringing her food from afar. She gets up while it is still dark; she provides food for her family and portions for her servant girls. She considers a field and buys it; out of her earnings she plants a vineyard. She sets about her work vigorously; her arms are strong for her tasks. She sees that her trading is profitable, and her lamp does not go out at night. In her hand she holds the distaff and grasps the spindle with her fingers. She opens her arms to the poor and extends her hands to the needy. When it snows, she has no fear for her household; for all of them are clothed in scarlet. She makes covering for her bed; she is clothed in fine linen and purple. Her husband is respected at the city gate, where he takes his seat among the elders of the land. She makes linen garments and sells them, and supplies the merchants with sashes. She is clothed with strength and dignity; she can laugh at the days to come. She speaks with wisdom, and faithful instruction is on her tongue. She watches over the affairs of her household and does not eat the bread of idleness. Her children arise and call her blessed; her husband also, and he praises her: 'Many women do noble things, but you surpass

them all.' Charm is deceptive and beauty is fleeting; but a woman who fears the Lord is to be praised. Give her the reward she has earned, and let her works bring her praise at the city gate." Proverbs 31:10-31

This scripture makes one misconception very clear... for a woman to <u>richly satisfy</u> her husband's needs refers to <u>a whole lot more than sex!</u> This is critically important because it is where so many of us stumble over the whole idea of submissiveness. The minute someone says that a wife should be submissive to her husband, the immediate interpretation is all too often the act of satisfying him in bed. This is an important part of a marriage union – God makes that clear.

"The husband should fulfill his marital duty to his wife, and likewise the wife to her husband. The wife's body does not belong to her alone but also to her husband. In the same way, the husband's body does not belong to him alone but also to his wife." I Corinthian 7:3-4

Obviously God intends for us to take our marital vows to cherish one another seriously. However, <u>richly satisfying</u> one another other must start at the breakfast table and continue throughout the entire day.

But, back to Proverbs 31...take note of the myriads of important areas in which God expects a wife to function. The 'fields' that she is tasked to 'choose' are the key avenues of the family's, physical survival, and often much of their income. When we read, 'out of her earnings she plants a vineyard,' we see that she is encouraged to have some kind of earning capacity. She dresses beautifully. She is benevolent. She is positive and able to 'laugh at the days to come.' The whole community sees that she respects her husband. She literally takes the responsibility of putting clothes on her family's backs. Wow – what a woman! Oh that the women of today would see this scripture as God's calling to them regarding the importance of their position within the family and take great pride in living it out! And, oh that husbands of today would see their wives as women whom God honors and lifts to such a high calling!

As we humbly accept our roles within the family unit, we must seek the definition and purpose for those roles in God's Word. Concerning a faithful wife, God further says,

"Wives submit to your husbands, as to the Lord. For the husband is the head of the wife as Christ is the head of the church, his body, of which he is the Savior. Now as the church submits to Christ, so also wives should submit to their husbands in everything." Ephesians 5:22-24

The question then looms, "Wives [who are given to the Lord] would you find it difficult to be submissive to the Lord, were He standing before you with a request?" Likely not. Thus, in your role as a wife, whenever it becomes difficult to live out the submissiveness toward your husband that God asks of you, remember this verse. Wives, when you submit to your husband you are doing so, "as unto the Lord" and He is pleased with your submission!

Finding Fulfillment

Women, God has given us the talents and skills we have with the expectations of us using them for the betterment of our families, finding fulfillment in our daily tasks within the home. Instead we tend to seek our identity and value in everything and everyone outside of our homes, then wonder why we don't feel fulfilled. Listen to one writer's expression of such emptiness....

What is Life?
a station wagon, a house in the suburbs, four kids, a dog, and bridge on Wednesdays?

I hope not.

What is happiness?
a clean house, soap operas at two o'clock, P.T.A. on Tuesdays, the Avon lady with
a new fragrance?

I pray not.

What is fulfillment?
Ten cents off on Ajax, an improved home permanent, the end of the month sales, TV dinners on Thursdays?

I beg not.

What is joy?
A better enzyme detergent, a new vacuum cleaner, freshly starched aprons, a roast
for Sunday dinner?

I implore not.

If this is what my life is to be, I might as well not have lived at all.
Author, Judith May Fleischman

I couldn't agree more - if we look at the tasks she notes as an end unto themselves.

Whether man or woman, until we find our fulfillment in doing the things we do as a result of God's calling, we will never feel fulfilled in carrying out our everyday roles. Until we see the tasks we are called to do as fulfilling God's roles for our lives, we will always feel used.

Contrary to the despair heard in this 'What is Life?' poem, an author friend of mine, shared with me a note he had jotted down one day, expressing the joy and fulfillment he finds in a willingness to submit to the roles to which God has called him:

> *"My ambition is quite simply to be unreservedly available to God. I want to go where he leads, say what he prescribes, and serve where he invites!"* Calvin C Hays

To have a station wagon [or mini-van], a house in the suburbs, four kids, a dog, clean house, attend PTA, do laundry, and all that goes with running a household is okay and can either be fulfilling or totally exhausting. If we see our role as serving God's purpose, being unreservedly available to God, going where he leads, saying what He prescribes, and serving where He invites, we will soar with a sense of joy and fulfillment. That doesn't mean wives are limited to home tasks for their fulfillment, but we must be careful as we seek other areas of fulfillment not to discount God's first priorities for us. Wives, which are you? Bored and depressed? Or spiritually stimulated to do what you do and do it even better, for the sake of the Lord and your family – a Proverbs 31 woman?

The Biblical Role of a Husband

For you husbands who seek to please the Lord, how's it going for you at home? He cares! It is critical to your victorious relationship with Him to successfully live out your God defined role as a husband and father. Just as Proverbs 31 defines numerous tasks for your wife, He also gives you a critical definitive assignment for your role - an impossible assignment! Impossible that is if attempted by human will and resources alone. But since God has clearly declared that, "In Him all things are possible," and we know that where He guides, He also provides, it is with great confidence that you can respond to His assignment....

> *"Husbands, love your wives just as Christ loved the church and gave himself up for her...in this same way, husbands ought to love their wives as their own bodies. He who loves his wife loves himself....For this reason a man will leave his father and mother and be united to his wife, and the two will become one flesh...Each one of you must love his wife as he loves himself, and the wife must respect her husband."* Ephesians 5:25,28,31,33

Hear this loud and clear, husbands, *"Love your wives as Christ loves the church!"* That is a whole lot of love, compassion, and forgiveness! An 'I Love You Anyhow' kind of love - to the death! An impossible task? Certainly could be, but not when you are committed to Christ and relying on the Holy Spirit within you to supply you with the truth, strength, and power you will need to carry it out. Otherwise, it would be like trying to drive a car without any gas….it may be a beautiful car but it is worthless to serve its purpose when it is empty! Only with the help and authority of the Holy Spirit within you will you be able to love your wife with an 'Agape' love, with which Christ loves the church even when she is undeserving and unlovely. This love calls for *unconditional love*, respect, protection, support, sacrifice and an unwavering belief in the value of your wife – just as Jesus believes in His Church - so much so that He gave His life for her. Spend some extra time in the 13th chapter of Corinthians, often referred to as the 'love chapter.' Reviewing these scriptures will bring to mind helpful insights to 'manning up' to this high calling for your role as a husband!

We Are a Team

From the beginning of time the Biblical roles of a man and a woman have been inherently intertwined. They are distinctively different and independent from one another, yet to be successful, totally dependent on one another. The key to harmony in the midst of these roles is remembering the scriptural promise, *"But everything comes from God."* When God becomes the object of our affections – the last word in our choices – and the compassion in our relationships, those relationships are lifted to a higher level of respect and spiritual fulfillment than is ever possible otherwise.

> *"In the Lord, however, woman is not independent of man, nor is a man independent of woman. For as woman came from man, so also man is born from woman. But everything comes from God."* I Corinthians 11:11-12

Husbands, you hold the key to the flow of blessings from God to your wives and children. It is as if God hands down a big umbrella of protection to each Christian husband, to hold over his family. The handle is as the spout of a funnel whose flare at the top, opened to the heavens, through which God's Holy Spirit pours down blessings upon the family. As a husband holds his umbrella over his family, and his wife draws their children underneath, they are all recipients of the Holy Spirit's blessings, while at the same time they are all are covered over by a divine protection from the evil one.

> *"Now I want you to realize that the head of every man is Christ, and the head of every woman is man, and the head of Christ is God."* I Corinthians 11:3

Men and women of God please hear me. When a husband refuses to hold his God-given 'umbrella of spiritual leadership' over his family, and when a wife chooses to step out from under her husband's umbrella of protection, the entire family becomes vulnerable to hurts, jealousy, selfishness, and an unhealthy independence. And the saddest thing about it - they take their children with them, out from under their rightful God-given flow of blessings and protection, exposing them to the decays of this world!

Don't misunderstand; God never leaves nor removes His Holy Spirit from those whom Christ has redeemed. But when we walk away from God's perfect plan for our lives, exposing ourselves to the vulnerability of a 'plan B,' we jeopardize the wholeness, peace of mind, and joy that He intends for us. In His compassion and forgiveness, He stands by to say 'I Love You Anyhow,' even though we reap the consequences of having chosen not to follow the plan for which He designed us, as He declares in Jeremiah 29:11-14. Thank God He heals and restores us when we turn back to Him and allow Him to do so!

As husbands and wives we need to serve one another in a way that helps the other become all that God intends for him/her to become. In doing so, we have our own roles to fulfill, differing from day to day. One is not more important than the other, and neither is sustainable without the other.

Another Helpful Analogy.....

A marriage partnership functions like a conductor and his music stand. The stand holds the music that allows the conductor to successfully lead the orchestra, bringing about a harmony of notes. Together they make beautiful music. As wives we are commissioned to stand firm [as a music stand] holding up and supporting that which our husbands need from us, in order to carry out their role as the conductors of our families. If we pull the music stand out from under the conductor, allowing the music to flutter to the floor, he is rendered vulnerable and ineffective, and the sweet music of the symphony turns sour.

Still another analogy my husband presented to me on one very difficult night....

Personal Reflection:
Journal – October 1983
"I am leaving tomorrow for several weeks of ministry in India. Our kids are raised and this is my long looked forward to opportunity to follow God's calling to, 'go unto the nations and teach others all that God had taught me.' But this last night at home I am terribly frightened and upset about that to which I have committed – an arduous schedule in a strange land, away from my family for way too long! What if someone in my family gets really sick while I am gone? What if they really need me? I've pleaded with my husband to go along as one of our needed 3ʳᵈ ministry team

members [if for no more reason other than just to be with me]. I was so sure he would say, 'yes.' But he doesn't feel called to go. I know I am wrong to try to pressure him into going. As I look at the grueling schedule ahead and the conditions in which we will be ministering, I know that to survive this trip, one truly needs to know that they are there because God is 'calling' them to be there! In the middle of my last minute packing, I lay here on the bed crying, wondering, what if I get too homesick and can't come home. What will I do? I feel panic. What have I done! Though my husband is away on a business trip, I'll call and share my panic with him. He'll know what to say to help me cope.

Yes, I knew he would help. He always seems to know what to say. He loving challenged me...

"Look at it this way: Together we are effectively like two extension ladders, each able to reach heights we could neither one ever reach alone. With me as your base, you have gone places and done things you never could have otherwise. And this is just another one of those times. As you go, I will hold down the home front. And vice-a-versa, with you as my base all these years, I have extended myself into so many areas that God has called me to go, that I would never have been able to without your support. Together we can each separately extend ourselves as we are called – because the other faithfully holds our base strong and steady."

He was right. God helped me deal with my fears throughout the whole incredible trip. For too many weeks I missed home, my husband, the kids, warm water, my own bed, and food I could actually keep down! But I gained so much more. I was privileged to take part in training thousands of indigenous Christians to share their faith in Jesus Christ. And because of God's faithfulness through these dear people [some actually new Christians themselves, who vulnerably shared with seekers following dozens of Gospel centered film showings] thousands of men, women, and children came to receive Jesus Christ as their Savior! God is so good!

Since that trip, I was privileged to minister back in India once again, as well as several similar ministry trips to Ireland, teaching and sharing my faith in Jesus Christ. Such a huge blessing! In addition to these phenomenal trips abroad, God has also allowed me to travel throughout the United States, teaching and ministering by the empowerment of the Holy Spirit and in the name of Jesus. I thank God everyday for giving me a husband that is a strong foundation from which I can extend myself beyond myself, for God's sake!

As husbands and wives, we set the tone for our family's interactions with each other and with God. Our children will see by our role modeling, what it takes to be the kind of husbands, wives, moms and dads, and children of God, that He calls us all to be. They will watch us closely to see the reflection of just how 'real' God truly is within our relationships, especially during times of challenge and stress. When they see authentic Christianity in action at home, they will know it is not just a good story but a reality.

The Strings of Stress Multiply

Between a husband and wife there are numerous issues to work through, bringing multiple strings of stress to every marriage. It's complicated at best to orchestrate these strings of stress within a marriage, bringing about harmony rather than chaos. Recognizing what pulls on those strings and going to God for the answers as to how to get relief from the pressures they create, gives us hope and victory in the midst of the stress. Remember, peace is not the absence of stress, it is knowing the presence of God in the midst of it.

As we each seek to live out our roles as God would have us, with each child these relational strings of stress become more and more entangled and more and more difficult to manage. For Godly victory over the strings of stress within our families, we will do well to remember who holds the answers and turn to Him for our solutions - never, never, never, giving up on one another – God doesn't! In the next chapter we will unpack the reality of some of the difficult issues posed by these strings of stress and delve into some possible scriptural solutions of holding it all together as a family.

"Lord, be our guide, our strength, and our victory, as we live out our roles as you designed them to be. Help us find joy, contentment and fulfillment in victoriously living out the roles we serve. Bind Satan from our relationships and bring us to our knees in submission to your calling for our lives. As husbands and wives, help us each to be a supportive base for our partners, lifting them up to all they can become, for your sake. Bless our marriages with your peace and your presence, filling them with an Agape kind of love, and helping us to find the strength to say, "I Love You Anyhow" to one another. Amen"

Personal Application

TRUTH:

God has given each of us clear instruction as to how to live out our roles as He has designed them and has empowered us to do.

1. Explain in your own words how the application of I Corinthians 12:12-26 [describing the parts of the body] relates to you personally.

2. As you reflect on your relationships, how has the confusion of *'role reversals'* affected them? How have you sought solutions? In which relationships do you still need to seek solutions? What action steps will you take to do so?

3. Wives...review Proverbs 31 and note which tasks correlate to those which you serve and how those tasks are working out for you. In which of these tasks do you need more of God's help in order to accomplish them more cheerfully? Find a prayer partner to join you in lifting these areas before God.

4. Husbands...As you reflect over the command to love your wife as Christ loved the church, note areas in which you need help to comply with this command. Note action steps you will take to do so and find a prayer partner to join you in lifting these areas before the Lord.

Journal Entry:

"IF"

"IF" is a game that children play
But, when we are grown,
it should pass away
[At least that's what they say]

No more dreams of the might have been,
Or more dangerous yet...What still could be...
Face it friend...We're all grown up
We must live in the 'here and now'
[Or - At least that's what they say]

You've set your course
You dare not even share the slightest hint
That 'if' creeps in (just now and then)
And drains your soul
And strains the stability of the course you've set
And the life you're in.

But it's here and now
And your course IS set
And you dare not think...
Think what?
Well, you dare not think at all sometimes,
Or 'IF' creeps in and blinds today with
A tomorrow that will (or may) never be.

We must live in the here and now
Keep our focus on life today....
'IF' just cannot be – it must not be...
[Anyway....that's what they say.]

Does this mean my thoughts just dare not drift..
To ponder – to quiz – or just to dream?
'IF' that were true, what loss my mind would suffer.
What limited vision my future see!

Yet, time wasted in dreams of the 'If Onlys' of life
Steal away the blessings and sunshine of today,
Leaving us with but hazy memories our yesterdays,
Of opportunities missed – or met only half way
Or at least for me....it surely seems that way!

Journal Entry:

THE 'CHOICES' IN MY LIFE

Oh God, how have I faired in the 'choices'
I've made in my life?
Daily, hourly, moment by moment 'choices'?

My heart aches for the times I know my 'choices'
Were made knowingly against your Will
Forgive me!

And yet, I rejoice in other times
When I dare to think that, maybe
My 'choices' brought a smile to your face.

But, what about those times
I'm not so sure of, Lord?
What about those times
I've searched my heart and prayed,
Just how do I serve this role I play?
I've sought the guidance of Godly counsel
[or I must admit sometimes not so Godly counsel]
And then I made my 'choices'.....

To do....or not to do?
To say....or not to say?
Sometimes the choice even seemed to be,
To love....or not to love...
But not really - in reality – the 'choices'
Were more just *'how'* to live out your love...

To choose to be a friend but not a security blanket,
To not try to 'fix' what belongs to you only to fix,
To choose to be a loving mother, yet not an enabler,
To choose to be a devoted wife, yet not cripple my husband,
That he might dig deeper and grow more on his own,
To choose to meet the demands of a working day,
Yet fill the kitchen with tasty meals along the way.

To hug....or to let go....
To discipline...yet get out of the way,
allowing your discipline.....more needed than mine.

So many 'choices'!!

To love and to serve,
Yet not to cripple or smother,
To cling or to let go,
To satisfy my earthly desires,
Or to do as you say - to
Offer my body as a living sacrifice.

To spend my resources on a luxury
Or is it really a necessity?
Which it is gets so cloudy sometimes.

Lord, how have I faired in the 'choices'
I've made in my life?

One thing I know;
One thing I am certain of;
One choice I made put a smile on your face;
The time I murmured through my tears,
"I choose to follow Jesus!"

But, wait a minute....
Was that really my choice, Lord?
Or - was it yours?
Maybe yours - since your word says,
"You did not choose me, I chose you."

Oh Lord, I would that all of the 'choices'
Of my life be as much yours!
As I respond to the guidance and
Gentle wooing of your Holy Spirit,
As I live out the roles in which I serve
May I 'will' to allow your control
Over all the 'choices' of my life!

CHAPTER SIX

AS BLESSINGS INCREASE - SO ALSO THE STRINGS OF STRESS

While living out our roles within the family, many of us come upon that special day when we are blessed with a bouncing bubbly new family member or perhaps over the years several such family members. As each new child enters into the lives of already established families, joys are multiplied, and so are the strings of stress. Family member's lives are changed totally as they become wholly engaged in the lives of each new member. As parents, don't we love to cheer each child on at their ball games, or dance recitals, or school musicals! This principle is certainly applicable to the growth of the greater family as well: nieces, nephews, in-law children etc. Each relationship carries with it strings of attachments that must be dealt with.

As with every life issue, God has given us multiple insights as to how He Wills us to interact with others. These principles are given for the sake [and sanity] of all participants! It is His desire that we become rich with such deep relational understanding that in the most stressful of times, we will still be able to love each other - anyhow.

Take into consideration parenting. We start out with the conviction to follow God's principles and become the best parents we can possibly be; but alas, somewhere along the way many of us find ourselves at a total loss as to how to deal with the huge challenges of parenthood! Part of the challenge is to refrain from putting an over-the-top priority on the moods, joys, and perceived needs of our children. Children are precious to be sure. They must have a high priority in our lives. At the same time though in order to have God-balanced families, they and their multitude of activities cannot take priority over our commitment to God and His principles. Our time and communication with Him must come first.

Throughout this chapter we will attempt to unpack some of the complexities of family relationships, remembering that we will be speaking somewhat in generalities, since circumstances vary with the personalities and special needs within each family.

Let's begin by diagramming the complexities of our family interactions by drawing two circles, one representing a husband and one a wife. Then we will draw a string from one to the other, representing the connection between them. This connection, though good most of the time, is also a source of the challenges and stresses that are naturally created when two people put their separate lives together. It is often times necessary for them to compromise their differing personalities and opinions for the sake of the partnership. Once joined as husband and wife, everything each one does - emotional, spiritual or physical - affects the other. Thus, strings of stress….

Immediately upon the entrance of a child into a marriage, from the day of conception this new person affects every part of that marriage. In addition to the string connecting husband and wife, we now have a string flowing between the child and each parent. Additionally, there are strings from dad to the relationship between mom and child, and from mom to the relationship between dad and child. At each string's intersection we find potential stress points.

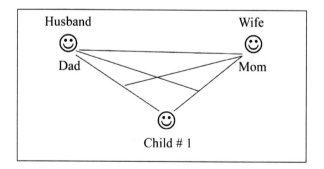

Every mom or dad has experienced that the relationship [good or bad] between them and their child can be dramatically affected by what's going on in that child's relationship with their other parent. Sometimes these stresses are caused by differing opinions related to parenting and sometimes just by trying to coordinate busy schedules. Sometimes these points of stress can be a result of manipulation. Children are wise enough to play one parent against another when it helps them to get the 'yes' they seek. i.e. a child goes to dad and asks permission to do something. Dad says, 'check and see what your mom thinks and come back and let me know.' Child goes to mom stating, *'Dad says it's okay ..... So is it okay with you?'* Dad did not say it was okay. He said to check and see what mom thinks and come back to him. Mom thought it would be okay for her daughter to now wear makeup, believing dad said it is okay. Dad really does not like the idea of makeup for now and is frustrated with mom for giving permission to do so. The results of scenarios such as this create on-going tensions. Thus the points where our 'strings of stress' intersect become more and more entangled.

Taking all of this into consideration, we begin to get a picture of the complexity of the stress points that affect all the relationships within our families. When those relational strings are vibrating with the joys and celebrations of one another's victories, and firm with support in the midst of one another's failures, it is incredibly wonderful. On the other hand, when the strings of stress are stretched to a breaking point as a result of anger, fear, failure, and unforgiveness, relational survival is an almost insurmountable challenge for everyone. As stated earlier, these principles definitely apply in the dynamics of the greater family as well as the immediate.

Now imagine our 'strings of stress' diagram with numbers of additional family member's strings. The stress points multiple hugely, including those intersecting between each new sibling and their parents, and connecting between each sibling and each of their other siblings, and between each parent and their spouse's relationship with each child. In our visual, we now have a mass of tangled strings for which only the presence and empowerment of God can ever keep us resonating with the relational love to which we all aspire. But don't despair, it can and does happen, because God is faithful to His promise to be with us in the thick of it all. We just need to be willing to acknowledge our need for Him and follow His guidance.

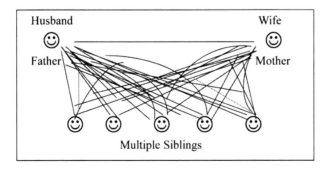

This analogy is not intended to give us a sense of hopelessness regarding the complex dynamics of family relationships. Its purpose is to alert us to a keen awareness of the commitment and focus it takes to experience family relationships free of painful brokenness. It doesn't just happen.

This analogy also strengthens our response to God's principle of choosing a marriage partner that has already decided to trust Christ as their Savior, equipping them with the power of the Holy Spirit to untangle the strings! As God guides us into Christian marriages and gifts us with children, He also keeps our families under the umbrella of His blessings and victory. Our part as Christian husbands and wives, fathers and mothers is to be committed to knowing and applying His principles of relationships, willingly to say *"I Love You Anyhow"* to one another, under all circumstances. And when we fail, if we invite Him, He will stand in the gap and help us repair the damage.

As you review this last 'strings of stress' diagram, can you see how when we as husbands and wives are constantly at odds with one another, we bring unmanageable stress upon the young folks in our families? It is obvious that since we are not perfect, we will have stress and we will have relational breakdowns from time-to-time. This is all the more reason why it is important that we and our children know where to turn at those times, and know in whom we can trust with our inner-most feelings of pain and insecurity. God promises, *'I will never leave you nor forsake you.'* [Hebrews 13:5] We can rest assured that in the toughest of times, He is there to listen, heal, and lift us above them.

Dr. Carol Barker, a Christian Psychologist, uses strings of stress illustrations to help families identify specific points that are causing relational breakdowns within the family. Likewise, I challenge you to diagram your family scenario and circle the spots where two strings come together with relational dynamics that pose extra stress. This exercise can be a first step in defining situations that need to be addressed to bring harmony back into the family, without subjective finger pointing. Have each family member note the areas presenting stress for them, related to specific cross points of your 'strings of stress' diagram. Depending on your family's size, identifying stress points can be complicated, but take heart....there is one more string that needs to be drawn....the one that makes all the difference....

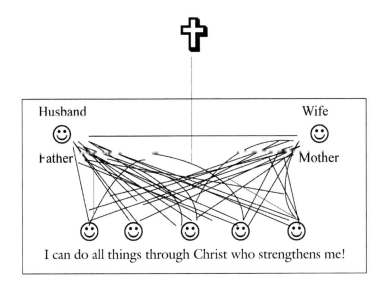

I can do all things through Christ who strengthens me!

....the string that leads to our Heavenly Father. This connection is the connection that empowers love to reign above it all! Even Jesus had moments when He called out to God in search of instruction and peace. When He called out to His Dad for help, He called, *"Abba"* meaning *"daddy daddy."* [Mark 14:36] In this, Jesus demonstrates for us that God's position as our 'father' is real and available! [Romans 8:15, Galatians 4:6] When we do the same, connecting with our Heavenly Father in our efforts to keep our families together and filled with the love He desires for us, as with Jesus, He stands ready to answer us. It is His desire to help empower us to untangle the strings of stress in our lives in such a manner as to have families that are full of love for one another and for Him. Unless we identify the stress points and turn them over to Him, this can't happen.

Throughout this chapter, as we concentrate primarily on Biblical principles that help untangle the strings of stress within your immediate family, I encourage you to broaden the scope of dynamics to include your 'greater' physical family, as well as your relationships within the Church – the greater family of God. The larger the family the more entangled the strings!

Obedience

Driven by His vast love for us, God demands obedience, knowing that anything less makes us vulnerable to the pains and harms of this world, and to Satan himself. He asks us to do the same for our children. Establishing an expectation of obedience greatly reduces unnecessary stresses caused by arguments resulting from uncertain expectations. In a world so lacking in absolutes, where everything seems to be negotiable, children are craving a sense of security. Establishing boundaries and giving logical consequences when those boundaries are crossed, strengthens their sense of security. Even without realizing it children are reaching out for the boundaries that will offer them security, all too often finding that there are none. Black and white seems to have faded into a washed out grayish mass that has no real definitive lines. Throughout the Bible God addresses this condition, pointing out a critical nugget of truth that rings just the opposite of what humanity suggests, that with obedience comes freedom, protection and security! We have a tendency to call it things like, lack of tolerance, insensitivity to other's views, even abuse. But God calls it wisdom. He speaks to parents and children alike about the commands and rewards of obedience that result in helping alleviate the strings of stress in our lives.

"Children obey your parents in the Lord, for this is right. Honor your father and mother – which is the first commandment with a promise – that it may go well with you and that you may enjoy long life on the earth." Ephesians 6:1-3

Fathers, do not exasperate your children; Instead, bring them up the training and instruction of the Lord." Ephesians 6:4

"Children obey your parents in everything, for this pleases the Lord. Fathers do not embitter your children, or they will become discouraged." Colossians 3:20-21

If we would choose to follow just these scriptures alone, among the many on this subject, they would be sufficient to guide our expectations within our families in such a manner as to loosen the strings of stress and empower us to declare, *"I Love You Anyhow"* in the toughest of times.

God surely believes in a system of punishments and rewards. He tells children that as a reward for honoring their parents they will enjoy a long life. What more incentive do we as parents need to help our kids follow His instructions? It is critical that we realize what a precarious position we put our children in when we don't live the kind of lives that give them reason to honor us. We lay ground work for a scenario in which they lose the covering of the promise of a long life! But what a wonderful promised reward, if we will but live and interact with our children in such a way that we give them a reason to honor us!

More and more these days, kids push back with, 'why should I obey you?' The answer is simple, because God tells them that in obeying their parents they are also obeying Him. On many occasions I have reminded my children that in not disciplining them, I would be putting myself in a position of having to answer to God for disobeying Him in my parental responsibilities.

Discipline

A misunderstanding of the purpose and process of Godly discipline is one huge cause of entangling the strings of stress. Appropriate Godly discipline is driven by love and compassion, not anger or a desire to shame or put down. Parents, when we exasperate our children by striking back at them personally, instead of calling out their inappropriate actions, we are disobeying God. The strings of stress draw tense and ultimately snap when we refuse to follow God's designed balance of grace and obedience. It is impossible to 'train up our children in the instruction of the Lord' if we have so exasperated them that they refuse to listen to us anymore. In His instruction, Jesus warns us that, 'if we cause even one of these little ones to fall, it is worse for us than having a mill stone tied around our neck and being thrown in the sea!' This leaves no question about His warning to be Godly in the way we exercise our authority. Parenthood is not for the week or faint hearted! There is no excuse for self-indulgent parenting where narcissistic egos drive one to become like emotionally-rot children ourselves in the process of disciplining those over which God has given us charge.

God makes it very clear that His correction is given out of love, with the intention of helping protect our future, and for our ultimate prosper. As we correct, our purpose needs to be likewise.

> *"When your days are over and you rest with your fathers, I will raise up your offspring to succeed you, who will come from your own body, and I will establish his kingdom. He is the one who will build a house for my name, and I will establish the throne of his kingdom forever. I will be his father, and he will be my son. When he does wrong, I will punish him with the rod of men, with floggings inflicted by men. But my love will never be taken away from him…"* II Samuel 7:12-15a

> *"If his sons forsake my law and do not follow my statutes, if they violate my decrees and fail to keep my commands, I will punish their sin with the rod, their iniquity with flogging, but I will not take my love from them."* Psalm 89:30-33

Interesting that though God foreknows our intentions to sin, in synch with His decision to give us a free will, He allows us to disobey. At the same time, He has pre-determined that He will redeem us through His discipline because He continues to love us so much!

Because of God's great love for His children and His unwavering faithfulness, He intentionally offers the kind of love that is best for us in the long-run. Our intentions regarding discipline and punishment must be the same, to ultimately protect and empower our children.

> *"Endure hardship as discipline; God is treating you as sons. For what son is not disciplined by his father? If you are not disciplined (and everyone undergoes*

discipline) then you are illegitimate children and not true sons. Moreover, we have all had human fathers who disciplined us and we respected them for it. How much more should we submit to the Father of our spirit and live! Our fathers disciplined us for a little while as they thought best; but God disciplines us for our good, that we may share in his holiness. No discipline seems pleasant at the time, but painful. Later on, however it produces a harvest of righteousness and peace for those who have been trained by it." Hebrews 12:7-11

Once again it is worth stressing that discipline is not the absence of love, but rather the presence of a love so great that it is willing to sacrifice immediate validation for ones future safety and victory in the Lord! Once understood, this truth allows us to see needed Godly discipline as a protector and reliever of the strings of stress in our lives.

Throughout the Bible, the word 'rod' is used as a term for God's correction in our lives. It is important that we find comfort in His rod, as a sign of His unconditional love for us and His plan to bring us into the Kingdom to spend eternity with Him. Notice how the Psalmist changes his communication from 3rd person to 'first person' as he reflects upon the guidance, correction, peace, and conditions of the eternal life that God has promised....

"The Lord is my shepherd. I shall lack nothing. He makes me lie down in green pastures, he leads me beside quiet waters, he restores my soul. He guides me in paths of righteousness for his name's sake. Even though I walk through the valley of the shadow of death, I will fear no evil, for you are with me; your rod and your staff, they comfort me. You prepare a table before me in the presence of my enemies. You anoint my head with oil; my cup overflows. Surely goodness and love will follow me all the days of my life, and I will dwell in the house of the Lord forever." Psalm 23

We see then, that God's love is a kind of 'tough love' poured out upon us because of His divine faithfulness to an ultimate plan for our good. Thus His rod and His staff are a comfort to us. He stresses that through this same kind of 'tough love' [bringing compassion, protection and correction to our children] He will ultimately save them for a heavenly future with Him. If we get in the way of God's correction in our children's lives, we stand in the way of God's ultimate protection and blessings for them. As parents, one of the hardest things for us to master is to trust that God's plan for our children is even better than our own. It's hard to stand by and watch our children hurt, trusting that it will always be better to allow God's disciplines in their lives than any protection we might offer by hovering over them in sympathy! Stand by them, yes. But don't excuse inappropriate behavior in the name of love. This creates nearly unbearable strings of stress, both in our children's lives and in the lives of all who must deal with them. God pleads with us to partner with

Him in the discipline process so that our children will be spared from future devastation.

> *"He who spares the rod hates his son, but he who loves him is careful to discipline him."* Proverbs 13:24

> *"The rod of correction imparts wisdom, but a child left to itself disgraces his mother."* Proverbs 29:15

> *"Discipline your son, for in that there is hope; do not be a willing party to his death."* Proverbs 19:18

> *"Do not withhold discipline from a child; if you punish him with the rod, he will not die. Punish him with the rod."* Proverbs 23:13-14

As we live in a way that earns our children's respect, disciplining them as God instructs, it will allow us a voice in their lives that God will use to help train them up in the things of the Spirit.

> *"Train up a child in the way he should go and when he is old he will not turn from it."* Proverbs 22:6

I have often talked with a distraught parent who feels they have done the very best they've known how to raise their child as God instructs, only to have them turn to disrespectful actions, harmful drug and alcohol use, and anything but a Godly life. My encouragement to them [directly from the Lord's instructions] is to continue loving them! Never, Never, Never give up on them! Thank God He never gives up on us! Be careful not to justify nor in any way support or condone inappropriate action, but let it be known loud and clear that you 'love them anyhow,' because God knows the end from the beginning. We do not.

In such circumstances, I encourage parents to take another careful look at Proverbs 22:6. It clearly promises, 'when they are old, they will not turn away from it.' Time and time again I have joyfully observed that, after a period of time of wandering, one day a life of disobedience gives way to the truths with which one has been raised, and that life then turns back to the Lord with great fervor. In reading the account of Franklin Graham, son of the great evangelist Billy Graham, we read of an epic example of this principle. His young life ran ramped with disobedience, pain, and disappointment. Later, through God's discipline, Franklin's life was miraculously redeemed to a point of committing his life to a vast international ministry, for the sake of the Gospel! There are hundreds of such stories. Never ever give up on the restoration of your child!

In our own family we have seen precious young people brought up in the ways of the Lord, who have chosen to walk away from Him, but who have eventually turned around and become fully devoted followers of Christ. We praise Him every day for fulfilling His promise in Proverbs 22:6, to restore our loved ones!

Remember though we may walk away from God, He never walks away from us. He is always waiting for those who have wondered away to turn around and come back to Him. Again, I can't stress enough the principle we are taught through the story of the prodigal son, don't ever give up on God's plan for your children! Keep loving them and advocating for them before the Lord. [This principle certainly also applies to any and all of our relationships.] When the day comes that we all turn to the Lord, we are restored to one another and heaven rejoices!

> *"When you and your children return to the Lord your God and obey him with all your heart and with all your soul according to everything I command you today, then the Lord your God will restore your fortunes and have compassion on you and gather you again...."* Deuteronomy 30:2-3a

He will loosen the strings of stress present in our family's relationships, as we persist in passing along to our children and grandchildren, all the truths He has revealed to us. Sometimes in the midst of our own life's traumas it isn't easy. But remember, just because we may find it difficult to live out God's commands during times of stress in our lives, it makes them no less true. Our loved ones need to hear us claim the validity of God's principles, even in the midst of our own personal struggles.

God's plan for the instruction of our families, thus the future of our civilization, rests with us. He has no plan 'B.' Take a look...

> *"Only be careful, and watch yourselves closely so that you do not forget the things your eyes have seen or let them slip from your heart as long as you live. Teach them to your children and to their children after them."* Deuteronomy 4:9

> *"Keep his decrees and commands, which I am giving you today, so that it may go well with you and your children after you and that you may live long in the land the Lord God gives you for all time."* Deuteronomy 4:40

> *"Walk in all the way that the Lord your God has commanded you, so that you may live and prosper and prolong your days in the land that you will possess. These are the commands, decrees and laws that the Lord your God directed me to teach you to observe in the land that you are crossing the Jordan to possess, so that you, your children and their children after them may fear the Lord your God as long as you live, by keeping all the decrees and commands that I give you, and so that you may enjoy long life."* Deuteronomy 5:33-6:2

"Love the Lord you God with all your heart and all your soul and with all your strength. These commandments I give you today are to be written upon your hearts. Impress them on your children. Talk about them when you sit at home and when you walk along the road, when you lie down and when you get up. Tie them as symbols on your hands and bind them on your foreheads. Write them on the door frames of your houses and on your gates." Deuteronomy 6:5-9

"Fix these words of mine in your hearts and minds; tie them as symbols on your hands and bind them on your foreheads. Teach them to your children, talking about them when you sit at home and when you walk along the road, when you lie down and when you get up. Write them on the door frames of your houses and on your gates, so that your days and the days of your children may be in the land that the Lord swore to give your forefathers, as many as the days that the heavens are above the earth." Deuteronomy 11:18-21

"I will open my mouth in parables, I will utter things hidden from of old, things we have heard and known, things our fathers have told us. We will not hide them from their children: we will tell the next generation the praiseworthy deeds of the Lord, his power and the wonders he has done. He decreed statutes from Jacob and established the law in Israel which he commanded our forefathers to teach their children, so the next generation would know them, even the children yet to be born, and they in turn would tell their children." Psalm 78:2-6

It blows my mind to think that He has so much belief in us that He trusts the proliferation of His Word for all future generations to be passed along through our lips! He makes it undeniably clear that no matter how difficult the strings of stress in our lives, we are commissioned to help alleviate those stresses by 'training up' our children in the truths of His instructions. And then He tops it off by giving us the promise that when we do, we will enjoy a long life. Following God's instructions does not limit us – it fulfills us!

Training vs Teaching

Since God uses the word *'train'* in reference to how we are to pass along His instructions, let us examine what it means to 'train' someone. Jesus was a great teacher to all who would listen. He also chose a few [12] to be His disciples. Those He *'trained'* to carry on His ministry after His ascension to Heaven. He closely related to His disciples, personally identifying with them and showing them by example how He wanted them to act and what they should expect from Him. He ate with them, dwelled with them, prayed with them, laughed and cried with them. Training goes beyond 'telling' into the realm of showing by example.

When a personal trainer helps their client, they show them how to stretch, exercise, lift, and run. When a coach trains a player how to handle the ball, he shows them the proper techniques through film and other means of example.

When we train our animals, we do so by showing them what we want them to do, and then rewarding them for their obedience. When we do this enough times we end up with an animal that follows our direction out of instinct, because they are well trained.

In God's wisdom, He used the word 'train' for clarification of His expectations. God doesn't just say 'teach' your children in the way they should go. He doesn't instruct us to just give them lip-service. He commands that we train up our children in the way they should go, knowing that if we do, when they are old they will not depart from it. There's nothing more valuable in the spiritual training of our children than for them to see us, on a daily basis, reading our Bibles and getting on our knees before God. We can tell them, and tell them, and tell them that God needs to be important in their lives and that Jesus Christ is alive and real; but unless they see us humble ourselves before the Lord and do the best we can to live out His instructions, our words aren't going to mean beans to them!

As we seek to lessen the strings of stress in our families through Biblically directed communications, discipline, and training, will our children always receive our instruction and discipline willingly? No, often they will not. We continue the process anyway. It has been wisely said, 'It's not only our objective in raising our children to have good children, but to prepare good adults.' Our children will not always respond joyfully to our redirection, but done with God's instructions in mind, He will always work through those attempts to mold them into who He Wills them to be. Remember, our kids don't have to like what we say; they just have to listen and do it. So pick your battles. Don't get caught up in the trap of demanding that they respond with a cheerful attitude of which they are incapable at the moment. Remember; if we will but kindle a fire towards God's nature in our children, in His good time He'll fan that fire, setting ablaze.

When Our Children Hurt - We Hurt

As we have unpacked the scriptures in this chapter we have become keenly aware that the responsibility we have as parents is huge in helping lessen the strings of stress for us and for our children. In the process of this responsibility, it is worth repeating once again that <u>our children are only on loan to us. They belong to God.</u> We need to lighten up a bit and unload our burden onto the One who has the ownership to carry it. God reminds us not to let our parental responsibilities loom over us so huge that we feel we are the only means to the end of our children's health and happiness. They are in His hands, and the strings of stress we create when we forget that weigh far too heavy for us to bear. Sometimes we just need to get out of the way and acknowledge that our kids are His. When we do, we release Him to do miracles. Allow me to share a couple of personal experiences.

Personal Reflection

When our oldest daughter was but four years old she began to have a problem with hearing. She had been having constant reoccurrences of ear infection from the time she was tiny. Up until now they had not resulted in any apparent loss of hearing. But all of the sudden this Friday afternoon it was different. We could stand right in front of her and nearly yell and she could not hear us. Needless to say, we were frightened and clueless of what to do. We allowed the situation to cripple our emotional well-being. We'd been praying, begging for a healing and trying to decide what to do next to help our precious little one. The week-end had already seemed like an eternity, and as we sat in our home on Sunday afternoon [drapes pulled - our daughter lying on the couch - somber and fearful] we felt an unbearable weight of the responsibility for her well-being.

Unexpectedly, a very dear friend came to pay a visit. As one of our prayer supporters, she had learned of our dilemma. When I opened the door she came bouncing in with her cheery 'God loves you' attitude, and walking over to the window she threw open the drapes and exclaimed, 'my goodness, you need to let some of that beautiful sunshine in.' I must admit we were a bit taken back and rather resentful of her upbeat persona, knowing that we were struggling with such a heavy spirit. But she continued: she turned to our daughter and encouraged her to get up and come to the table to have some of the treats she had brought. As she proceeded to put the cookies on a plate she exclaimed, "You need to remember that your daughter belongs to God and He loves her more than you ever can, so if you'll just let go and get out of His way He will be better able to touch her with His healing. You can't just surround her with all this gloom and doom and expect her to get better. Give her back to Him and let her get up and go out to play."

Our friend talked all the while our daughter quietly sat eating her cookie, and then opening the door and sent her out to the backyard to play. I wasn't at all sure under the circumstances that she should be out running around, but we sat silently trying to process this intrusion, not wanting to be rude, and sincerely wanting to be open to hear whatever it was God might be trying to tell us through this well-meaning friend. As we all visited she suggested we pray, and as we did we once again laid our daughter's health needs before God. In the process, we found ourselves humbly agreeing that we would try to let go of her and our feeling of defeat, acknowledging that she belonged to Him and that we believed that He was able to heal her. I have to admit that it was a relief to get the burden of effecting her healing off our shoulders and give it to God. After our prayer time we visited a bit longer and then our visitor went to the back door. Opening the door and calling in a very calm and quiet voice, she invited our daughter to come in and get a glass of Kool-Aid. To our amazement, she jumped up from the sand box [at the very back of the yard] and came running up to the house. She had heard! Even with her back to the voice that called her!

I can't explain miracles, nor why healing takes place on one occasion and perhaps not on another, but I'm here to tell you that on this occasion, getting out of God's way and giving Him His rightful ownership of our daughter allowed Him to bring about an unexplainable and total healing!

Yet even when we have witnessed His work, we are so human that we can easily forget the lessons we have learned, allowing fear and feelings of inadequacy about our parental roles to creep back in. When we find ourselves dealing with school issues, an unkind friend, an unfair teacher, and it hurts so much to see our kids hurt, we tend to take back ownership of their well-being time and time again. I have to admit that I have done this with my children. But God has always been there to meet me on my growing edge and gently move me to relinquish them back to His rightful ownership. Case in point…He met me at the hospital bedside of our critically ill daughter….

Personal Reflection
At twelve years old our daughter lay in her hospital bed, very ill. As a result of two days of intense internal bleeding, she had been put on the critical list. Following a 'routine' tonsillectomy, her stomach had perforated and she began upchucking and passing blood at an alarming rate. We hadn't left her bedside for two days, pleading with God for a healing and fearful that it was too late. Once again, God sent another dear Christian friend. He sat with me for awhile and as we visited he suggested that, though praying for a healing was certainly appropriate, perhaps it was time to let go and give God permission to reclaim her if He wished to. I was appalled! In other words, tell Him it was okay with me if she died! Are you kidding me! But after further discussion, it was so clear that what I was saying was, no God, I don't trust you with her. She belongs to me not you. So in a nearly impossible step of yielding, I got on my knees at her bedside and through my tears apologized to God for trusting my parenthood for her above His. I told him I was willing to let go of her if He wanted her with Him worse than I needed her with me. I acquiesced that He knew best, and I would not be resentful if He decided to take her home with Him. Even as I whispered 'amen' I could feel a flood of peace come into my soul. Within a few minutes she fell asleep, so sound that it was a bit alarming. She never threw up nor passed another spot of blood. She was released a couple of days later. To this day the hospital records declare, 'no explainable reason for the discontinuation of bleeding.' But we know!

Once again the Lord took this opportunity to teach me that He is serious when it comes to taking His responsibility for our kids, if we will but relinquish it to Him. When we plead with God to heal, will He always heal our loved ones while they remain here with us? Perhaps not. Sometimes, like with my dad, they receive God's full healing by going home to be with Him. I don't pretend to know why. I do know this; He does not author the tragedies and illnesses that steal our loved ones from us. These things are a result of living in this dying world. But He does know when it is time for them to come home and He awaits them with open arms.

Second Hand Faith

Sometimes we make an assumption. We assume that, since we have taken our children to church with us and done our best to instruct them, setting the example that God asks of us, that our child's faith has become their own. Sometimes not! It is common for a child's faith to actually be a 'second hand' faith....spawned by their exposure to our faith and fed by their belief in the integrity of our faith. But on their own, they are spiritually weak at best, their own faith having little root system to sustain them through the temptations and storms that inevitably come ....strings of stress abound for them!

As with our own faith, it is critically important that our children's faith becomes solidly rooted in a relationship with Jesus Christ, not just the religious experiences of their family. I will never forget the day our [then college] son came home after the first semester of his freshman year, and commented, *"I'm sure glad I have a clear understanding that it's a relationship with Jesus that makes me a Christian and not some religious philosophy, because if I didn't, my philosophy teacher would surely have me confused as to what Christianity is really all about."* I humbly praised God for that evening many years ago, when sitting on a little boy's bed and answering his questions led to the opportunity to explain to him the difference between 'religion' and 'Christianity' and to encourage him to ask Jesus to become his Savior!

A short while after our son's college break comment, I had one of those times that I have come to see as a 'divine appointment.' I was able to use his comment to bridge from something a friend said, to open up an opportunity to help her in a search for the deeper things of God.....

Personal Reflection
My neighbor and dear friend came to me asking help with a spiritual question. After searching together for God's answer she commented how she admired that I knew where to go in the scriptures to find answers. I shared with her that though I am grateful for having learned a great deal from wonderful pastors and other teachers over the years, it has been by reading the Bible for myself that I have been able to confirm what God Himself actually says, and that learning where to personally go to find His answers to my questions had made my faith my own.

My friend was fully committed to her church and its teachings, but she admitted that she had never really studied the Bible for herself. I encouraged her that the scriptures tell us that, as parents we really need to have it a priority in our lives to know as much as we can about God's Word so we can pass what we know along to our children. Then I shared our son's comment of how confused he would be if we hadn't helped him understand Christianity while he was at home, before being exposed to some of the teachings he was getting in college. I followed up with a question; "So, Kim, if Danny came home from school today and asked you, 'Mom, what really is a Christian?' How would you answer him?" After a moment of hesitation she said, "I'm not really sure. I guess I would tell him to go talk to the pastor or his teacher at school." [Danny attended a faith-based school.] I encouraged her that this would be good, but since her son loves and trusts her as his mother, why didn't she just tell him what she had done to become a Christian and invite him to do the same? She said she guessed all she could tell him was to 'try to love others, pray, go to church and learn all that he can, and hope that he can be a good enough person that God will accept him into Heaven after he dies.' I commended her for her obvious faithfulness to what she understood. I encouraged her that though she hadn't read a lot of the Bible, she didn't need to know 'all' the Bible says before she could use and claim that which she did know, warning her that Satan wants to discourage her from using any of the scriptures because she doesn't know all of them.

I invited her to allow me to help her mark her Bible with a few scriptures that would help her clearly point out God's instructions about what Jesus has done for us to enable us to become a Christian when we respond to Him, telling her that the scriptures we would mark would not be the only ones that help explain how we can become a Christian, but rather just one possible path that can help lead us to take that step. I encouraged her that once she had her Bible marked, she could sit down with her son and show him right from the Word of God how He defines a Christian. Later that day we did so. What a blessed time!

While in the Bible marking process Kim became extremely responsive to the fact that though she was very dedicated to her religion and to bringing her children up in the church, she didn't recall a time that she had ever really acknowledged Jesus as her Savior…didn't know she needed to. Now, the scriptures were making it clear to her that her trust was in the church and her ability to live a good life, and that she needed to transfer that trust to Christ. She became so anxious about doing so she could barely sit still long enough to finish the Bible markings before asking Jesus to become her Savior, transferring her trust to Him as the only reason for her being accepted into Heaven someday.

There isn't enough paper or pen on earth to relay the Heavenly experience and joy one experiences when they come to see the truth of their own salvation! This short personal reflection will have to suffice for now. The Bible tells us at that at that very moment all of the Angels in Heaven rejoice!

And God didn't stop there. I got a call about three hours later, with a very excited Kim on the other end, declaring, "I had to call and tell you what happened. When the kids [they have three] came home from school, I sat them all down in the front *room and talked to them like you did to me. I showed them all of the scriptures we marked and told them I had decided that I needed to pray for Jesus to become my Savior because I had never done that before. And I asked them if they wanted to trust Jesus as their Savior and become Christians too. They all said yes so I helped them pray, like you did me, and I wanted to call and make sure if I did it right."* WOW! What a testimony to the power of God's Holy Spirit...empowering a baby Christian of only hours to give witness to what God had done in her life, and to help her lead her children to the Lord!*

I assured Kim that there is no 'right' or 'wrong' way to start trusting Jesus as our Savior. For some it's a moment of sudden awareness. For others it's a slow revelation over many years. But the bottom line is, in order to become a child of God it must happen that at some point we transfer our trust from ourselves, our intellect, our church, our knowledge, or whatever we have been counting on to get us to Heaven, and trust in Jesus alone. Agreeing in our hearts that we are indeed all sinners, and therefore we all need a Savior, and that Jesus Christ is that Savior. That's the message to which we and our children need to respond – however that happens. Together that day and throughout the many years since, as we have shared the joys of our own and our children's faith walk with the Lord, we have rejoiced in His faithfulness!

We are never given permission to judge the spiritual condition of others. But we are given the command to *'Always be prepared to give reason for the hope that we have within us and do it with gentleness and respect.'* [I Peter 3:15] I am eternally grateful for the opportunities God has given me to pass along His instructions to others! In the chapter, 'Paying It Forward," you will see the pathway of scriptures Kim and I marked, along with some other helpful and proven insights as to how to share these important scriptures with those with whom God allows you a *'divine appointment.'*

Why did I determine to include Kim's story within the chapter discussing the strings of stress present in our families? Because of the extreme importance that the spiritual condition of our families plays in experiencing God's victory over life's stresses. I rejoice in the fact that Kim's husband came to know the Lord as well, and that with Jesus Christ living in the hearts of Kim's whole family they have been enabled by the power of the Holy Spirit within them to victoriously deal with the strings of stress caused by life's many difficult issues – with the stresses of marriage, children, and grandchildren, a daughter deployed on the battle field, a grandson lost at the state fair for hours, and serious illnesses of loved ones over many years. Today they and their children continue to follow the ways of the Lord, and as loving grandparents they continue to pass along to their grandchildren the truth of the Gospel. God is so good!

If your child [children] is not living a Christian life that God can bless, ask yourself, *"has anyone ever sat down with them and helped them to understand how to become a Christian, or are they trying to live the Christian life successfully on second hand faith – your faith?"* They cannot continue to live on your faith alone and still find God's plan for their lives. It is not enough. God has no grandchildren. No one is presented right before God because their parents or grandparents know and follow Him. To enter into the Kingdom one day they must have their own personal relationship with Jesus Christ. Trusting in Jesus will not only give them access to eternal life in the Kingdom one day, but also gives them the empowerment to endure the strings of stress that are inevitably present in this life.

In summary, the strings of stress are going to be present in our marriages and in our families because Adam and Eve ate that apple, we can't avoid it! But be sure of this: when we are willing to play out our roles as husbands and wives, and mothers and fathers as He instructs us, the blessings we gain will far outweigh the challenges!

In the next chapter we will take a more in depth look into what the scriptures have to say about the empowerment God gives His children to help us live victoriously, overcoming our strings of stress.

"Dear Lord
Sometimes the task seems too overwhelming, the mountain too high to climb, the valleys too low to transcend. The strings are all tangled up and the stress points too matted together even to be able to define them. Yet there are those other times, Lord. Those times when we move together like a well-oiled machine, times of joy and fulfillment, times of laughter and of a meaningful sharing of hearts. God we know you want us to bring all our stresses and lay them at your feet so you can help us serve one another in love, allowing your priorities to reign. Help us to give over ownership of our loved ones to you, while at the same time committing ourselves to protect, serve, and love one another as you Will us to do. Amen"

Personal Application

TRUTH:

As we live out the various rolls in which we serve, God is willing and able to bring joy, peace, and an over-riding love in the midst of the chaos, fear, and pain present within our relational complexities. He is able to untangle the strings of stress in our relationships.

1. Have you diagramed the *'strings of stress'* within your family relationships yet? If not, take a few minutes to do so. [If you are single, do so for your sibling family and/or significant others in your life, at home and/or in your career.] Once done, look at the stress points created within the picture and consider the following.

2. Have you given the Lord ownership of those in the complexity of your strings of stress? A tell-tale clue…how much do you need to be in control? Do you find there are times that, after having given God control you find yourself taking it back again? Note some of those times and what steps you will take to hand over control of the strings of stress in your life.

3. Discipline is a hard thing, both in our own lives and for us to apply with those over whom we have been given authority. Take a minute to review the discipline scriptures in this chapter. Ask the Lord to give you insights as to how you can carry out this monumental task, while yet making it clear to those you discipline that you love them anyhow.

4. Given the explanation in this chapter, which do you find more comfortable: Teaching? Or Training? What are steps you can take to more actively 'train in the ways of the Lord' those over which you may have responsibility and influence?

5. What personal action steps will you take to help alleviate some of the strings of stress in your relationships?

Journal entry at the end of a busy day: A Day in The Life of a Working Homemaker

My first awareness of dawn comes as I hear the water sloshing around the bathroom basin…Bob is shaving.

I stumble out of bed, eyes closed, and find my way to the basement to start the first load of laundry. Thank God for the simplicity of instant coffee makers that will give me just one quick cup so I can handle my next chore, getting myself awake enough to make the day's supply of coffee.

That chore completed, I find my way back to the now momentarily empty bathroom [oh for another one for this family of five – maybe someday]. I hold a nice hot washcloth to my face, hoping it will help convince my eyes that they must stay open to see what new and exciting things God has planned for us today.

Once opened, I check out the figure in the mirror. As I look at tosseld, tangled, unruly clumps of hair, I wonder, "Is there any way to tame it for the events of the day without completely redoing it?"

The melodious sounds of the kids alarms begin … one screeching … two buzzing, a simultaneous alert that would call the troops together for inspection! But no one here seems to hear them, so…..I'll need to visit each room!

Bathroom time is precious so there's no time to wash my hair, I'll wash the rest the best I can and try more 'good old hair spray.' It will just have to do for now or everyone else won't get their turn.

I really need to hurry now, the clothes are ready for the dryer, the coffee is ready to be transferred to the pump pot, the kids will be wanting breakfast soon, and Bob – "Oh my, he'll be leaving soon and I've hardly said hello!" I grab my clothes from my closet in the hall and while still dressing rush in to visit with him, but he's on his way out of the bedroom.

I hurry to slip into my shoes and rush out to have coffee with him, but he's now on his way out the door to the bus, "Bye honey…I love you….have a good day…." He's gone. Wish I'd had more time to connect with him, but wow - here's Con and Kev ready to eat and no breakfast is yet on the table. Better put something out good enough to sustain them.

"Yes, Kris, I'll be there in just a minute to help with you with your hair dear. Do you want breakfast now with the other kids or later? Kev will you answer the phone please? Okay everyone it's time to load up and head for school. Hustle so we won't be late."

"If you hurry and get in the car, we'll just make it to get you to early band on time…Do you have your horn? Lunch money? Books? What are you doing after school today? I love you ….bye"

Boy a cup of coffee sure sounds good! I never got around to drinking mine I guess. Wonder where I left it? It must still be sitting in the bathroom on the sink. Oh well, I'll have one when I get to work.

Work shouldn't be too tough today. Things are pretty organized. *"Hi Joan, I'm here, any messages?"* Five, really, already! Good grief I'll be returning calls for an hour. Okay, here we go....going on my third phone call when I remember...coffee....I'll sneak back and grab a cup before finishing up my return calls.

But on the way I'm confronted by two employees with issues that need immediate addressing. Better give them the time they deserve and finish the phoning after.

Hours later....still pushing, cold coffee, files clutter my desk begging for attention.... bedraggled and bewildered as to what happened to the day... I check out cause the kids will be home soon and I want to be there. Lunch?? Oh no, I forgot about lunch. Oh well I could stand to lose a few pounds. : = {

It's three now and the kids are going to beat me home. I really wanted to be there when they got there but I won't quite make it. Thank goodness they're understanding and so responsible. I need to pick up the cleaning and stop by the store. Oh yes...and those over-due library books must be returned!

"Hi kids. I'm here are you home? Did you have a good day? Sure I can help you with your homework, Kris, right after I cut Kev's hair. What are your plans for the evening, Con? Everyone better get to your homework while I put some supper together. Your dad will be home soon." Guess I'll run down and throw that last load of clothes into the dryer first.

Praise God for supper time. Here we are all together again. It's peaceful to talk to God together before we eat and to each other while we eat! God must have intended supper time to be for the nourishment of the mind and soul as well as the body. This is good!

Everyone's off again, meetings, hockey, babysitting, shopping. As soon as I get the kitchen cleaned up I have some other tasks to finish.

And now it's bed time. Boy am I tired! "Good night, honey. Glad your day at work went well. God bless!"

"Here I am again, Lord. It's been a good day. Please quite the stress that remains so I can sleep. Thank you for being with us all and protecting us as we've come and gone! I love you Lord. Thank you for loving me through all my busyness today. Thank you for bringing so many wonderful people into my life. Help me love them the way you want me to, Lord. Goodnight."

Lord Help Us - We Need You Now!

He hears me on this very dark day. As I cry out to Him and listen for His response, His love and guidance pours down through the holes in the floor of heaven directly into my troubled soul! He owns my loved ones and He is in charge!

There's a girl, Lord. She's not very old
She's brash and she's brave
She's stubborn, independent and bold!

That's all on the outside,
Anyway that's what I see.
But Lord could it just be that,
Underneath all that rebellion and anger,
Hides a frightened and frustrated girl,
Perhaps a whole lot like me?

One who cries out for acceptance and love,
For someone to see clear down inside to her needs.
Yet, while in the process, Lord, she makes it so
Utterly impossible for those to whom she pleads.

One who feels confused and lonesome,
Desperate to find a way to express her being,
For words that can say what she so longs to say.
For release from the fears and dark clouds in her day.
To find answers and get insecurities out of her way!

Does she long to believe in you?
Does she understand that you care?
That you know her so well that
You've counted every strand of her hair?

What's the key, Lord,
To releasing that trunk full of fear?
What suave Lord, to heal her hurt?
To open the door that will draw her near?
How to spark the reality of a God
Who comforts, who protects, and who cares?
Where are you God? Where? Where? Where?

Just who are we in your site, Lord?
In your high and lofty view,
Just what touches your heart?
What prayer motivates you?

Do you care when we hurt? When our hearts cry out?
When we plead and we beg and we finally shout,
For help and for guidance and just a little relief
From Satan's badgering, debilitating grief?

Where are you, dear Father and friend?
Does my cry fall on deaf ears?
Act now; it's been too many years.
Please - bring to an end all this craziness!

God, I'm a child of yours to be sure,
But how much more stress must I endure?
I'm human; I'm flesh; I'm blind and can't see.
I trust and believe, yet get laughed at and lied to.
I try to encourage and reach out with your word.
But am told, over-reacting, pushing, back off!

Dear God, what am I supposed to do?
Don't leave us in this desert place.
It's dry and it's parching, and
The heat chaps my tear stained face.
We need your help, your healing, your guidance,
Your deliverance, from these stresses of life!

Remove the scales from my eyes dear Lord.
Help me to see through this misty dim haze,
To feel the love flowing down from you, and
To sense your presence in these darkest of days.

Now, Lord, I feel the comfort of your rod and your staff.
I claim your promise; you restore my soul at last!
As you guide on your path of righteousness,
For your namesake, I will follow!

Yes, I feel your anointing just now, oh Lord.
The strength to go on, to claim your victory,
And surely goodness and mercy will follow us
All the days of our lives, and we will dwell
Forever together, in your house, oh Lord!

God, thank you. My cup runneth over!
And I believe you will claim the soul of this one,
So beautiful, and precious, and smart and young.
And together we'll rejoice when the day is done,
As through you, the victory will truly be won!

CHAPTER SEVEN
EMPOWERMENT

We all face multiple strings of stress in our lives, whether a result of our own inner conflicts, our growing families, school, vocation, or just merely surviving the ever increasing complexities of this world. In and of ourselves we are not equipped to overcome these stresses. But take heart, the victory is ours. God has not placed us here in the stresses of this world and simply abandoned us to sink or swim on our own. To the contrary, *He empowers us with His own Spirit and sends His Angels to guide and protect us.* No matter what we face we can confidently claim victory through God! He does not promise to deliver us from the storm, but He is committed to leading us through it.

Victory is not the absence of adversities, but rather peace in the midst of adversities! And this peace is not a surface kind of peace that comes from talking ourselves into some state of calmness through the power of positive thinking. Having said that, the Bible does encourage us to think on those things that are lovely, and pure, and true and right. Thinking on these things pushes out destructive negative thoughts. This effort in the training of our human thought process is a good thing. However, true peace comes only from the assurance that we will overcome by the power of the Holy Spirit within us. *The Holy Spirit is given as a gift to every child of God.* He indwells believers from the time they first trust Jesus as their Savior. In this chapter we will unpack the truths revealed in the scriptures related to two gifts through which God empowers us: the presence and purpose of His Holy Spirit and the guidance and protection of His Angels.

The Holy Spirit

Throughout the Old Testament we read of hundreds of occasions when the Holy Spirit came upon a particular person or event, at a particular time, for a particular purpose. With the death and resurrection of Jesus, all of that changed.

> *"On the last and greatest day of the Feast, Jesus stood and said in a loud voice, 'If anyone is thirsty, let him come to me and drink. Whoever believes in me as the Scripture has said, streams of living water will flow from within him.' By this he meant the Spirit, whom those who believed in him were later to receive. Up to that time the Spirit had not been given, since Jesus had not yet been glorified."* John 7:37-39

Through His life, death and resurrection Jesus paid the ultimate price for the forgiveness of sin, paving the way for an indwelling of the Holy Spirit within all who come to Him and receive Him as their Savior. Just 40 days after Jesus' ascension back to His heavenly home, the indwelling of the Holy Spirit for all believers came to be…just as Jesus prophesied.

> *"In my former book, Theophilus, I wrote about all that Jesus began to do and to teach until the day he was taken up to heaven, after giving instructions through the Holy Spirit to the apostles he had chosen. After his suffering, he showed himself to these men and gave many convincing proofs that he was alive. He appeared to them over a period of forty days and spoke about the kingdom of God. On one occasion while he was eating with them, he gave them this command: 'Do not leave Jerusalem, but wait for the gift my Father promised, which you have heard me speak about. For John baptized with water, but in a few days you will be baptized with the Holy Spirit."* Acts 1:1-5

> *"When the day of Pentecost came, they were all together in one place. Suddenly a sound like the blowing of a violent wind came from heaven and filled the whole house where they were sitting. They saw what seemed to be tongues of fire that separated and came to rest on each of them. All of them were filled with the Holy Spirit and began to speak in other tongues as the Spirit enabled them."* Acts 2:1-4

Shortly after the crucifixion and resurrection of Christ, the apostle Peter was addressing a huge crowd of people, telling them about who this 'Jesus' really is – the very man that their jeering had helped to put to death. They were devastated and ask, "What shall we do?" We find his answer in Acts 2:38 and 39….

> *"Peter replied, 'repent and be baptized, every one of you, in the name of Jesus Christ, for the forgiveness of your sins. And you will receive the gift of the Holy Spirit. The promise is for you and your children and for all who are far off – for all whom the Lord our God will call."*

Yes, even those whose selfish ugliness had helped nail Jesus to the cross were given an opportunity for forgiveness, salvation, and the gift of the indwelling of the Holy Spirit! After Peter God's willingness to forgive, nearly three thousand men, plus women and children were saved!

The Apostle Paul continually clarifies what he had heard from His teacher and Savior, that the gift of the Holy Spirit is available to ALL who realize their sin and come to Christ.

> *"For in Christ <u>all</u> the fullness of the Deity lives in bodily form, and you have been given fullness in Christ who is the head over every power and authority."* Colossians 2:9-10

> *"Don't you know that you yourselves are God's temple and that God's Spirit lives in you?"* I Corinthians 3:16

Having established through the scriptures, the undeniable fact that the Holy Spirit does come to live in every believer, what does that mean for you and me? How does that affect us in the middle of our adversities? How does His presence affect our relationships with each other? With God? The following pages help to reveal, at least in part, the functions of the Holy Spirit.

What the Holy Spirit Is Not

He is not a 'doctrine.' He is not some 'ghostly existence' – more than a cloud. He is not a super santa awaiting the opportunity to grant your every 'want.' He does not function separately from His counterparts in the Trinity, God the Father and Jesus His Son. He never empowers one contrary to the Father's Will.

I am a visual person, so it helps me when I can 'see' concepts in order to better understand them. Perhaps the following diagram will help to visualize the interactions of the Trinity with all believers.

Functions of the Trinity

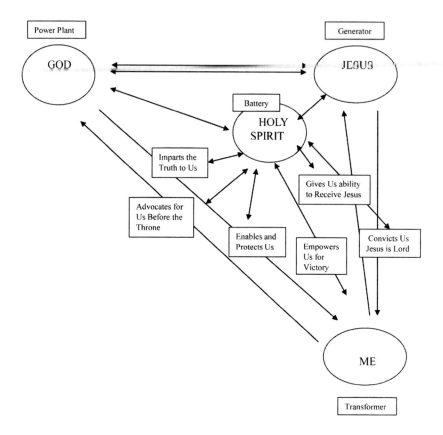

God the Father sent His Son to bring us forgiveness. The Holy Spirit is the power that convicts hearts of the Truth of Jesus. When Jesus comes into our hearts, so does the Holy Spirit. Like a 'battery' the Holy Spirit empowers the work of the Trinity in our lives. As though we were a transformer, His love and power flow through us, functioning like a conveyor belt, He carries God's truth to us and our needs to God.

Functions of the Holy Spirit

He is a holy person, a part of the Trinity. His presence and work are gifts from God the Father. Following are a number of scripture that clearly define the functions of the Holy Spirit. Peruse them carefully. Memorize them so that, as a child of God, you can quickly reference them and call upon Him to intercede for and empower you for victory.

He convicts us that Jesus is Lord:

> *"Therefore I tell you that no one who is speaking by the Spirit of God says, 'Jesus be cursed,' and no one can say, 'Jesus is Lord,' except by the Holy Spirit"* I Corinthians 12:3

He does not come to us as a result of our works but as a result of our relationship with Christ.

> *"You foolish Galatians! Who has bewitched you? Before your very eyes Jesus Christ was clearly portrayed as crucified. I would like to learn just one thing from you: Did you receive the Spirit by observing the law, or by believing what you heard? Are you so foolish? After beginning with the Spirit, are you now trying to attain your goal by human effort?"* Galatians 3:1-3

He convicts us of God's laws and testifies of God's forgiveness of our sins:

> *"The Holy Spirit also testifies to us about this. First he says; 'This is the covenant I will make with them after that time,' says the Lord. 'I will put my laws in their hearts, and I will write them on their minds.' Then he adds; 'Their sins and lawless acts I will remember no more. And where these have been forgiven, there is no longer any sacrifice for sin. "* Hebrews 10: 15-18

He testifies that we belong to the family of God:

> *"For you did not receive a spirit that makes you slave again to fear, but you received the Spirit of sonship. And by him we cry, 'Abba, Father,' The Spirit himself testifies with our spirit that we are God's children. Now if we are children, then we are heirs – heirs of God and co-heirs with Christ, if indeed we share in his sufferings in order that we may also share in his glory."* Romans 8:15-17

The Holy Spirit is our deposit that guarantees us of our heavenly home:

> *"Now it is God who makes both us and you stand firm in Christ. He anointed us, set his seal of ownership on us, and put his Spirit in our hearts as a deposit, guaranteeing what is to come.* II Corinthians 1:21-22

> *"Now it is God who has made us for this very purpose (to desire heaven) and then has given us the Spirit as a deposit, guaranteeing what is to come."* II Corinthians 5:5

> *"And you also were included in Christ when you heard the word of truth, the gospel of your salvation. Having believed, you were marked in him with a seal, the promised Holy Spirit, who is a deposit guaranteeing our inheritance until the redemption of those who are God's possession, to the praise of his glory."* Ephesians 1:13-14

He is our 'attorney' advocating for us before the throne:

> *"In the same way, the Spirit helps us in our weakness. We do not know what we ought to pray for, but the Spirit himself intercedes for us with groans that words cannot express. And he who searches our hearts knows the mind of the Sprit because the Spirit intercedes for the saints in accordance with God's will."*
> Romans 8:26-27

Jesus tells us that the Spirit will reveal truth, giving us an understanding of the things of God:

> *"If you love me, you will obey what I command. And I will ask the Father, and he will give you another Counselor to be with you forever – the Spirit of truth....But the Counselor, the Holy Spirit, whom the Father will send in my name, will teach you all things and will remind you of everything I have said to you."* John 14:15-17a, 26

> *"But when he, the Spirit of truth comes, he will guide you into all truth. He will not speak on his own; he will speak only what he hears, and he will tell you what is yet to come. He will bring glory to me by taking from what is mine and making it known to you."* John 16:13-14

Paul further stresses this truth to the Church at Corinth....

> *"....No eye has seen no ear has heard, no mind has conceived what God has prepared for those who love him, but God has revealed it to us by his Spirit. The Spirit searches all things, even the deep things of God. For who among men know the thoughts of a man except the man's spirit within him? In the same way no one knows the thoughts of God except the Spirit of God. We have not received the spirit of the world but the Spirit who is from God, that we may understand what God has freely given us. This is what we speak, not in words taught us by human wisdom but in words taught by the Spirit, expressing spiritual truths in Spiritual words. The man without the Spirit does not accept the things that come from the Spirit of God, for they are foolishness to him, and he cannot understand them, because they are spiritually discerned."* I Corinthians 2:9-14

The Holy Spirit Empowers Us to Pay it Forward:

> *"He said to them: 'It is not for you to know the times or dates the Father has set by his own authority. But you will receive power when the Holy Spirit comes on you; and you will be my witnesses in Jerusalem, and in all Judea and Samaria, and to the ends of the earth."* Acts 1:7-8

So what is a good measure to determine if we are allowing the Holy Spirit within us to function? Are we squelching the work of the Holy Spirit by our habits and attitudes, unwilling to reach out and share the love of God with those around us? Jesus declared that when we follow the Holy Spirit's lead we will not be able to keep quiet about who He is, but will be compelled to share with all nations what God has taught us.

As we share the story of Jesus, the Bible cautions us not to judge others. He does tell us, however, that we can discern the condition of those with whom we share, by their fruit. What kind of fruit does the Holy Spirit produce within those who give Him control? Take a look.....

"But the fruit of the Spirit is love, joy, peace, patience, kindness, goodness, faithfulness, gentleness and self-control. Against such things there is no law. Those who belong to Christ Jesus have crucified the sinful nature with its passions and desires. Since we live by the Spirit, let us keep in step with the Spirit. Let us not become conceited, provoking and envying each other." Galatians 5:22-26

Take a minute to consider if the attributes noted in this scripture are present in your life. Are you full of love, joy and peace? Are you patient, kind, good, faithful, gentle and self-controlled? As we daily search our hearts, we need to honestly ask God in which areas we need the Holy Spirit's help to better produce His kind of fruit in our lives.

Angels

Though we have let Him down time and time again, we have a Heavenly Father full of Grace and Mercy, who has provided every means to show us that He 'Loves Us Anyhow.'' One way He does this is through the gift and empowerment of the Holy Spirit. Another way He shows His love for us is by sending His Heavenly Host of Angels to minister to us, protect us, reassure us in times of crises, comfort us, and ultimately walk the transition with us from this home to our home in glory.

"And he will send his angels and gather his elect from the four winds, from the ends of the earth to the ends of the heavens." Mark 13:27

Though we plan our paths God guides our steps…He uses His Angels to help keep us from stumbling as we seek the path of His Will….

"For he will command his angels concerning you to guard you in all your ways; they will lift you up in their hands, so that you will not strike your foot against a stone." Psalm 91: 11-12

It is a fascinating study to learn of all the attributes and numerous ministries given to the Angels whom God has commanded on our behalf! We will touch on only some of these truths in this chapter. We will also take a look at the way

Satan [himself once an Archangel] enticed 1/3 of the Heavenly Angels to side with him against God, causing them to fall with him into eternal damnation.

This chapter contains only a few of the references, taken from approximately 300 scriptures found in the Bible about Angelic beings. Some of the various kinds of Angels are:

> Archangels: Jude 9 / Daniel 12:1
>   The highest level of Angels – in charge of the Angelic hosts and the fulfillment of their assignments. Three Archangels are mentioned: Michael, Gabriel and Lucifer. [Lucifer falling from Grace and becoming Satan]
> God's Messengers: Daniel 8:15, 16, 9:21 / Luke 1:9, 26
>   Gabriel is also referred to as a messenger, used to proclaim the messages of God.
> Seraphim: Isaiah 6:1-6 [meaning 'love' in Hebrew]
>   These Angels are referred to as beautiful. They are found constantly praising God, depicted above the throne of God and sending out His praises.
> Cherubim: Psalm 99:1, Genesis 3:24
>   They have to do with the glory of God, often used to symbolize His glory (as with the Ark of the Covenant). They are found to be guarding the throne, the gate to the Garden of Eden, and the way to the tree of life.

We will take a look at God's origin of the Heavenly Angels who serve the Lord, their purpose, habits, and assignments. As mentioned, the information here will be but an introduction to the fascinating subject of the Angels on assignment from God. I pray that through this glimpse of the reality of their existence you will be compelled to continue your own study of Angels, beyond that which is referred to in this book. Now a few 'Angel' facts.....

Though God created the Angels, He is not referred to as their Father. There is no provision for forgiveness for the sin of the thousands of Angels who chose to side with Lucifer in his bid to become wiser than God. Thus, these fallen Angels cannot be reinstated to their Heavenly home. The scriptures tell us that the rebellious activities of those fallen Angels will continue on earth until the end of time. Those fallen Angels [referred to as demons] are continually moving to and fro throughout the earth, tempting us and doing Satan's bid for evil.

Lucifer – The fallen Angel
It is also imperative that we become aware of the fallen Angels – who they are and how they daily interact in our world. Led by Lucifer, these fallen Angels [referred to in the Bible as demons] labor together to keep

the lost from knowing Christ and discourage the saved from growing and serving Him.

We have reference to three Archangels in Heaven, Michael, Gabriel, and Lucifer. There was a great battle as Lucifer [who became Satan] and the rebelling Angels fell. Though we don't get any specific account of 'when' the Archangel Lucifer fell, it was *likely* sometime between the 7th day of creation (when God pronounces that all He has created is good) and the temptation of Adam and Eve in the Garden, when Lucifer is referred to as the 'serpent.'

"And there was war in heaven, Michael and his angels fought against the dragon, and the dragon and his angels fought back. But he was not strong enough, and they lost their place in heaven. The great dragon was hurled down – that ancient serpent, called the devil, or Satan, who leads the whole world astray. He was hurled to the earth, and his angels with him. Then I heard a loud voice in heaven say: 'Now has come the salvation and the power and the Kingdom of our God, and the authority of his Christ. For the accuser of our brothers, who accuses them before our God day and night, has been hurled down." Revelation 12:7-10

"All your pomp has been brought down to the grave, along with the noise of your harps; maggots are spread out beneath you and worms cover you. How you have fallen from heaven, O morning star, son of the dawn! You have been cast down to the earth, you who once laid low the nations! You said in your heart, 'I will ascend to heaven; I will raise my throne about the stars of God..... I will make myself like the most High...But you are brought down to the grave, to the depths of the pit." Isaiah 14: 11-14 [excerpts]

"This is what the Sovereign Lord says: 'You were the model of perfection, full of wisdom and perfect in beauty. You were in Eden, the garden of God, every precious stone adorned you: ruby, topaz and emerald, chrysolite, onyx and jasper, sapphire, turquoise, and beryl. Your settings and mountings were made of gold; on the day you were created they were prepared. You were anointed as a guardian cherub, for so I ordained you. You were on the holy mount of God; you walked among the fiery stones. You were blameless in your ways from the day you were created. Through your widespread trade you were filled with violence, and you sinned. So I drove you in disgrace from the mount of God, and expelled you, O guardian cherub, from among the fiery stones. Your heart became proud on account of your beauty, and you corrupted your wisdom because of your splendor. So I threw you to the earth;..." Ezekiel 28:12b-17a

For Angels, sinning is unforgiveable.....
"For if God did not spare angels when they sinned, but sent them to hell, putting them into gloomy dungeons to be held for judgment....." II Peter 2:4

"And the angels who did not keep their positions of authority but abandoned their own home – these he has kept in darkness, bound with everlasting chains for judgment on that great Day." Jude 6

Satan's plan for him and the fallen Angels........
From the time of their fall it has been the purpose of Satan and his demons to destroy our faith in God. Satan's attempts to lead all of mankind into sin started began in the Garden of Eden. He continued his evil attacks when confronting Jesus in the desert, and according to the Bible, he will continue to tempt us to reject God's truths throughout history until the final judgment. Many scriptural references confirm that these demons move about this earth doing all they can to thwart the work of God. In the tenth chapter of Daniel we read of how the fallen Angels hindered God's work for three weeks, by preventing a task from completion.

Take Heart: Though Satan and his demons are powerful enough to wreak havoc, they have no authority over God!

One of Satan's most devastating ploys is to plant seeds of 'if' in our minds. He started with Adam and Eve....'*if*' you eat of the fruit of this tree ye shall not surely die.' Genesis 3:4. He would have us to believe that '*if*' we follow him instead of God, we will be happier. Be careful when '*if*' enters your thinking regarding anything that may turn you away from God's principles.

Before we have Christ, we are slaves to sin and Satan has control....

"As for you, you were dead in your sins, in which you used to live when you followed the ways of this world and of the ruler of the kingdom of the air, the spirit who is now at work in those who are disobedient." Ephesians 2:1-2

With Christ we have access to God's armor to shield us against the demons....

"Put on the full armor of God, so that you can take your stand against the devil's schemes. For our struggle is not against flesh and blood, but against the rulers, against the authorities, against the powers of this dark world and against the spiritual forces of evil in the heavenly realms." Ephesians 6:11-12

The attributes and ministries of God's Heavenly Angels....
So what about the 'good' Angels who remain a part of God's army of Angelic Hosts? How many are there? What empowerment have they been given? What assignments do they have regarding our well-being? Take a look....

Hebrews 12:22 and Revelations 5:11-12....There are millions of Angels and their numbers in Heaven never change because they never die....

"But you have come to Mount Zion, to the heavenly Jerusalem, the city of the living god. You have come to thousands upon thousands of angels in joyful assembly, to the church of the first-born, whose names are written in heaven."......"Then I looked and heard the voice of many angels, numbering thousands upon thousands, and ten thousand times ten thousand. They encircled the throne and the living creatures and the elders. In a loud voice they sang, "Worthy is the Lamb, who was slain, to receive power and wealth and wisdom and strength and honor and glory and praise!"

Angels do not marry.... Humans will never become Angels, but like the Angels, we will not marry in Heaven. .....Matthew 22: 30... *"At the resurrection people will neither marry nor be given in marriage, they will be like the angels in heaven."*

They rejoice when sinners repent. *"In the same way, I tell you, there is rejoicing in the presence of the angels of God over one sinner who repents."* Luke 15:10

They deliver us from harm. Examples: II Kings 6:14-17 – Elisha's deliverance – Acts 27:23-25 – Paul's deliverance

They are assigned to be ministering spirits. *"Are not all angels ministering spirits sent to serve those who will inherit salvation?"* Hebrews 1:14

They are God's messengers to us. *"The revelation of Jesus Christ, which God gave to him to show his servants what must soon take place. He made it known by sending his angel to his servant John, who testifies to everything he saw, that is, the word of God and the testimony of Jesus Christ."* Revelation 1: 1-2

God gives Angels a ministry of empowerment for the purpose of our well-being
Some basics... Angels are not the Holy Spirit, so they do not indwell people nor convict them of sin. They are not a part of the Trinity. They receive their assignments from God. They always come from God to man. They are not omnipresent, thus can only be in one place at a time.

We have each been given a guardian Angel to watch over us... *"See that you do not look down on one of these little ones. For I tell you that their angels in heaven always see the face of my Father in heaven."* Matthew 18:10

For the most part Angels are invisible (probably to guard us against misplaced worship) **however we have reference to them having been seen ministering here on earth...**

I Kings19:5...fed Elijah / Genesis 18:1-2...fed Abraham / Genesis 19...ate with Lot / Matthew 28:3... guarded the tomb of Jesus / Genesis

32:1-2 "And Jacob went on his way and the angels of God met him. And when Jacob saw them, he said, "this is God's host..." / Daniel 10:6 and Revelation 10:1...Daniel and John describe the glory of the angels

Do you believe Angels are present and ministering today?

Even though we read all of these truths about the reality of Angels, have you ever asked yourself, *'Do I really believe Angels are real and present in the midst of my battles?'* If your answer is, *'Yes,'* do you think you may have ever encountered an Angel? You actually may have you know! There are scriptures that admonish us that we may be entertaining Angels 'unaware.' Since we read so many Biblical accounts of Angelic appearances on earth, why wouldn't they still be moving about the earth today? Allow me to share a bizarre but true incident, involving myself, my son and my youngest daughter....a true story of an Angel encounter.

Personal Reflection

Let's start the story a few months after the 'incident,' while attending a typical Wednesday night Bible study. As I take my seat, while others engage in the usual early evening small talk, I am more than anxious for our scheduled lesson time to begin. Tonight's assignment?...to delve into the topic of Angels.

'Angels,' a mystery seems to surround even the very word. Several years ago, I read Billy Graham's book, "Angels Angels Angels" as well as "Angels on Assignment" by Charles Frances Hunter. Afterwards I did a pretty exhaustive word-study on 'Angels' as they were referred to throughout the Bible. And yet, it was still an evasive subject to me, until, well until that balmy summer night about four years ago now! That night when, with my son and my youngest daughter, we came face to face with the reality of Angels....or did we?

I vividly remember the frightening darkness of the night as we hurried along a deserted road, returning home from the opposite side of town, where our eldest daughter lived. It was 1 AM and my youngest daughter was asleep in the back seat, while my son and I chatted in the front. We missed dad, we agreed, and sure would be glad when he returned home from yet another of his many business trips.

As I drove along in the darkness we almost missed it, but suddenly we observed a truck jammed into the embankment and hopelessly lodged between the hillside and the steepness of the shoulder. As we slowed to check it out, then moved on past, my son shouted, "Mom go back. There's a person in that truck." I hesitantly drove on a little farther, my mind racing with thoughts of all I had heard about the potential dangers of stopping at such a scene, especially when after dark and alone. Fear gripped my thumping heart, and I wished all the more that my husband was there with us. He would know what to do. I did not. He would take over and manage the situation in his usual very capable take-charge manner. But he wasn't there, was he. My mind raced on, 'what should I do?' Cell phones didn't exist yet, but maybe I could find a place enroot to call 911.

My son's pleading voice broke through my thoughts, "Mom, you've always taught us that God is in charge and will turn everything into good. We have to help. Please, there's someone in there slumped over the steering wheel. Please go back!"

He wasn't thinking of anything but the motionless body he had observed, and what we might be able to do to help. [Thank you, God, for your work in this young man's life - for making him a compassionate soul after your own heart.] We turned around, pulling cautiously along side of the road at the scene of the accident. With my heart still thumping as if it would surely penetrate the walls of my chest at any moment, I prayed while he investigated the accident.

I could see him only dimly as he climbed down the ravine, through the window and into the cab of the truck. He found a bleeding man, and a CB. He began trying to call for help. No one came. Confident by this time that the situation was a legitimate accident, I got out and stood roadside, praying that God would somehow send one of those Angels that I had been studying about, to help us. Little did I know the events that were about to take place!

After about ten minutes, my hope for help quickened as I saw headlights in the distance. They were coming our direction! I muttered, 'Dear God who will it be? Will they be friendly? Helpful? Or at 1:30 in the morning, will they be coming home from some nearby bar, drunk and ugly? Please help us!"

Soon, the vehicle I had observed headed our way, pulling over and stopping behind our car. It was an ancient battered, broken down brown and white truck. The door creaked open and out stepped a man. But not just any man...would you believe it...a policeman!

Perhaps it was just the eeriness of the night or the lateness of the hour, but for whatever reason this policeman was not like any I had ever talked with before. His eyes were kind and penetrating. His spirit was gentle and quiet as he calmly reacted to my explanation of our dilemma.

He explained that he was off duty but would be happy to help. Walking to the front of the wedged-in truck, he kneeled down beside the window by the injured man. My son remained in the seat beside the man, wiping the dripping blood from his head and assuring him that we were doing everything we could to get him some help; neither seemed to be slowed by the unbecoming odor of the mixture of liquor and uncleanliness.

As I observed them ministering to his needs, I thought of the story told in the book of Mark, the story of the Good Samaritan. I've read and taught that story to Sunday school classes a dozen times, always supposing…if I had been the Samaritan, I would surely have stopped to aid the beaten Jew. Now I wondered, would I have? I hadn't been so quick to stop tonight, had I! Without my son's prompting and pleading, I most certainly would have gone right on and at the least made a phone call….as soon as it was convenient. But God had intervened because He had a blessing in mind for us. And I'm quite certain, because the injured man must have had loved ones praying for God to send his Angels to protect him from harm.

Feeling more comfortable now, with our new found policeman friend on the scene, I sped quickly away to find a phone from which to make a 911 call. Shortly after I got back to the scene we were engulfed with police cars, an ambulance, and a fire truck. All of the commotion kept me near my car on the opposite side of the road from the accident, and nearly as soon as I got out of my car, our policeman friend came over to join me. Why hadn't he stayed over with the others, I wondered? Why did it seem there was no interaction between him and his policeman co-workers? They seemed oblivious to the fact that he was a policeman brother, even though he had on his uniform. It just seemed strange to me.

His warm sympathetic eyes searched me momentarily, as if he sensed my weary yet anxious spirit. For some reason I felt like I wanted to explain to him how it happened that we were out there so late at night, and how I almost hadn't stopped, and that when we did I had pleaded with God to send an Angel. Up until this point nothing had been mentioned about our faith-based life, but in a loving authoritative voice that I shall never forget, he responded, "As a Christian we must always be willing to stop and aid another who is hurting." Though He spoke a truth that drove home my wrong decision in hesitating to stop, He spoke with the compassion and understanding I would have imagined Christ to have used with the woman at the well, whom He lovingly instructed, forgave and restored.

It wasn't until I lay in bed later thinking about the dynamics of our experience that I wondered about the name of the man Angel in uniform whom God had sent to us. And I thought about how he had disappeared without a sound when I had turned to answer the questions of the accident investigator who had joined me beside my car. Why? Where had he gone? He could have helped corroborate my story if I needed him to, but he was nowhere to be found. And why, when I recounted the story of the sighting of the accident, my son's insistence on checking it out, and the off-duty policeman in the old truck who had come to help, had the investigator looked at me as though I was incoherent? He kindly informed me that there was no battered old truck, no off-duty policeman in a uniform, and no one else aside from myself and my kids anywhere around the accident, either when they arrived or while they were there. WOW!

Suddenly I am snapped back from my reflections to the reality of the present, with a cup of hot coffee being thrust into my hand by our Bible Study host as she quipped light heartedly, "Where on earth was your mind? You nearly missed out on a very interesting discussion. Come on now; you surely have some opinion as to whether Angels exist today and whether or not they can be seen. We'd like to hear from you. So do you believe Angels exist today?"

"Oh" I hesitantly mutter, "All I know is if they really do exist and God really does still assign them to help His people, I think mine drives an ancient, battered up, old brown and white truck."

From the puzzled looks I'm receiving, I realize the story of our Angelic encounter might be better left to another time. In the meantime, I will continue my habit of calling upon God's Angelic hosts for inspiration and protection from the evils of this world. Try it. You may soon find yourself writing your own Angel story!

As I pen the reflection of this incident, just recalling it again still brings goose bumps! It is mind boggling to realize the extent to which God is willing to go to share Himself with us!
We have so great a God! He sends His most powerful, wise, and dedicated beings – His own Holy Spirit and the Angels – to bring us to Christ, then to uplift, instruct, protect, and empower us to share His love through carrying out His ministry of reconciliation!

Perhaps as with the disciple Thomas, you feel compelled to say, 'Lord, I believe, help thou my unbelief.' These truths are matters of the Heavenly realm! Will you join me in committing to allow our whole mind and soul to be open to the mysteries and joys of the empowerment that God has given us!

"Thank you Father God for all your provision for us…for your Holy Spirit and for your ministering Angels. We accept the truth of the Word about your provision and we pray for your continuing wisdom as we live out your calling to become all that the Holy Spirit empowers us to become. Remind us to call upon the Angels you've assigned to protect and guide us, as we follow your calling to serve you by loving those whom you have placed in our lives. Lord as you empower us, help us to be wholly committed to live the life you've called us to live. We know we need to grow up in our faith in order to experience the victory of soaring above the challenges. Today we ask for the assurance of the Holy Spirit's presence in our lives and acknowledge your Angelic hosts that surround us. Thank you! Amen"

Personal Application

TRUTH:

God has not left us alone to sink or swim in the world of sin. He empowers and guides His children through the presence and power of the *Holy Spirit* and the *Angels* He has assigned to each believer.

1. As you reflect over your life have you ever felt overwhelmed and in need of a power beyond yourself in order to survive? Is the concept of the Holy Spirit indwelling you a new concept for you? How does that make you feel?

2. Before this reading, how have you envisioned the Holy Spirit - An *'it?* ' Or a *'person'* with whom you can have a relationship? An advocate pleading your case before the Lord? A purveyor of the Truth? How do you perceive Him now?

3. In order to let the Holy Spirit do His work in our lives we have to let go and believe that He can and will. Take a minute to examine your heart...are there areas in your life where you feel powerless to seek victory? Give these areas to the Holy Spirit now and ask Him to advocate for you before Almighty God regarding them.

4. Since God has assigned Angels to you, have you ever called upon them for guidance and protection? Take a minute right now to invite them to occupy each room of your home, to ride on the fenders of your car, and to go with you throughout your day. I have. The results would fill another book!

CHAPTER EIGHT
COMMITMENT AND GROWTH

While reviewing this writing thus far, just sitting and soaking in all of God's golden nuggets of truth and being moved by the victorious stories of others, we have taken only a small beginning step in our own personal journey. Personal growth comes when we step out in faith and put into action what we have learned.

Knowing things in your head doesn't change you. Knowing things in your heart only begins to move you toward your goal of a victorious life in Christ. Allowing all these truths to creep so deep within your soul that you are compelled to take personal action steps and apply them in your life enables you to embark on an incredible journey of your own personal relationship with God, through His Son, Jesus Christ. This type of journey moves us to become who we've really always been since our very creation. As we embark on our own walk to personal commitment and growth, God is there to guide us. As He recorded in His Psalms, chapter 139, He not only created us, He walks every step of the way with us.

> *"O Lord, you have searched me and you know me. You know when I sit and when I rise; you perceive my thoughts from afar. You discern my going out and my lying down; you are familiar with all my ways. Before a word is on my tongue you know it completely, O Lord. You hem me in – behind and before; you have laid your hand upon me. Such knowledge is too wonderful for me, too lofty for me to attain. Where can I go from your Spirit? Where can I flee from your presence? If I go up to the heavens, you are there; if I make my bed in the depths, you are there. If I rise on the winds of the dawn, if I settle on the far side of the sea, even there your hand will guide me, your right hand will hold me fast."*

Again in Philippians 1:6b we see evidence that it is God's intention to help us work out His plan for us....

"...he who began a good work in you will carry it on to completion until the day of Christ Jesus."

Walking the walk that enables us to reach God's intended purpose for our lives takes commitment and growth in the knowledge and application of His ways. It takes a growing awareness of 'who' we really are and 'whose' we really are. During this process we begin to get in sync with God's plan for our lives, finding a purpose and fulfillment far beyond anything this world can ever offer us.

"For we are God's workmanship, created in Christ Jesus to do good works, which God prepared in advance for us to do." Ephesians 2:10

God prepares us for a 'ministry of reconciliation.' As we mature and embrace the empowerment of the Holy Spirit and receive the guidance of His Angels, we begin to experience the joy and fulfillment of that ministry, a ministry through which we find new meaning to life, new depth in our relationships, and a new partnership with the Lord.

"All this is from God, who reconciled us to himself through Christ and gave us the ministry of reconciliation: that God was reconciling the world to himself in Christ, not counting men's sins against them. And he has committed to us the message of reconciliation. We are therefore Christ's ambassadors, as though God were making his appeal through us. We implore you on Christ's behalf: Be reconciled to God." II Corinthians 5:18-20

As we continue this journey together, we will take a deeper look into how we can successfully reach the Christian maturity for which we strive and which God commands. Let us start at the beginning. First, in order to grow, we must be born.

In order for anything to grow well it must have a solid root system, anchored in its life's origins. It is no different with a child of God. We start out life as 'newborns,' having been birthed through our mothers and carrying forward the genes of our parents, grandparents and ancestors. The same is true in our spiritual lives. As Christians, we also start out as newborns, 'born again by the Spirit of God,' inheriting the genes of our ancestry - the Trinity, God, Jesus Christ, and the Holy Spirit. We are babies in Christ.

We Are <u>Born</u> into the Family of God

When we transfer our trust from ourselves to Jesus, believing He is who He says He is, and that His death on the cross was sufficient to make atonement for our sins; we are <u>born again</u> - this time born of the Spirit. For some, taking this step of placing their trust in Jesus seems too simple a spiritual birth process. But the scriptures make it undeniably clear that when we believe and receive Jesus Christ as our Savior, we are given the right to become 'a <u>child</u> of God.' [John 1:12] This is our starting place; whether we slowly come to this realization through years of 'sittin' and soakin' in a church pew [as our pastor terms it as 'a crock pot Christian'] or whether one day it comes as a sudden revelation that we have never taken this step, however it happens, the TRUTH is that we are born into the family of God when we place our trust in Jesus and Jesus alone for our salvation.

For those who lack assurance that they have taken this step, why not do it now? Perhaps it will help to liken it to a bride and groom exchanging their wedding vows. When a bride and groom approach one another for their marriage ceremony they come as single people, each loving and believing in the other, but still single. After they have exchanged marriage vows with one another they are introduced by the official who performed the ceremony as Mr. and Mrs...... The exchanging of their vows changed their status from single to married. In a similar manner, we exchange vows with Christ, trusting Him with our lives. We do so because we love and believe in Him. But unlike the devils who also believe in Him, we determine to trust Him as our Savior. Christ already said His vows to us while hanging on a cross. Even as He faced excruciating pain and death because of mankind's injustice to Him, He willingly declared, "Father forgive them for they know not what they do." He vowed to love us anyhow. And then just before He breathed His last breath, He uttered "It is finished," declaring that when we respond to His invitation to trust Him, the work of our sanctification is finished – because of His bloodshed on the cross. As with a bride and groom, though we may love and believe in Him, He still awaits each of us to 'receive' Him.....offer our vows to Him. In essence - transfer our trust to Him for our salvation.

> *"Yet to all who <u>received</u> him [Jesus], to those who <u>believed</u> in His name He gave the right to become children of God – children born not of natural descent, nor of human decision or a husband's will, but born of God." John 1:12-13*

This whole process is what Jesus referred to when telling Nicodemus that he must be 'born again' to become a child of God. This man called Nicodemus came to Jesus in the night [so as not to be seen by his peers] to seek answers from this miracle healer, Jesus. But he wasn't really prepared to hear what Jesus had to say. Let's peek in on their conversation as recorded in John 3:1-6....

> *"Now there was a man of the Pharisees named Nicodemus, a member of the Jewish ruling council. He came to Jesus at night and said, 'Rabbi, we know you are a teacher who has come from God. For no one could perform the miraculous signs you*

are doing if God were not with him.' In reply Jesus declared, 'I tell you the truth, unless a man is born again, he cannot see the Kingdom of God.' 'How can a man be born when he is old?' Nicodemus asked. 'Surely he cannot enter a second time into his mother's womb to be born. Jesus answered, 'I tell you the truth, unless a man is born again, he cannot see the kingdom of God.' [and so Nicodemus pushes back] 'How can a man be born when he is old? Surely he cannot enter a second time into his mother's womb to be born." [Again Jesus declares the truth] 'I tell you the truth, unless a man is born of water and the Spirit, he cannot enter the kingdom of God. Flesh gives birth to flesh, but the Spirit gives birth to spirit."

As Spiritual Babies We Start Out On Formula

When babies are born, they start out being nourished on mom's milk [or baby's formula]. If they were to stay on this limited nourishment as they grew older, their bodies would not become strong. As they grow, they need something more. Our spiritual bodies are no different. When Jesus becomes our Savior, since we become new creatures 'born again of the Spirit,' we are like spiritual babies. We start out on the equivalent of spiritual baby formula, but eventually we require spiritual meat in order to grow up as healthy children of God, capable of carrying out the ministry of reconciliation He has prepared for us. Sadly, we often continue sucking on the formula of a spiritual baby, unwilling to seek grown up food that will strengthen us enough to take on the responsibility the spiritually mature. Too often Christians are contented just to know that someday when they die they will be going to Heaven. I would lay down the challenge that we need to do a better job of focusing on the journey to which God calls us, not just the destination.

The truth is that our 'eternal' life starts the moment Jesus comes into our lives. He lives in us and begins His work in us, to give us healing, victory, and ministry. Not grasping this truth, too often as spiritual babies we live our lives as paupers, spiritually poor and defeated, not understanding that the minute we received Christ we were given an eternal inheritance consisting of ALL of the good things God has for us. Our spiritual bank account is full and overflowing with truths and strengths that empower us to be strong, healthy, and productive spiritual adults!

Yet we are contented to stay babies, wailing away at the pain of our circumstances! This was true of many who made up the early Church as well. Paul laments over the immaturity of those to whom he ministers...

> *"I gave you milk, not solid food, for you were not yet ready for it. Indeed, you are still not ready. You are still worldly"* I Corinthians 3:2-3a

> *"We have much to say about this, but it is hard to explain because you are slow to learn. In fact, though by this time you ought to be teachers, you need someone to*

teach you the elementary truths of God's word all over again. You need milk, not solid food! Anyone who lives on milk, being still an infant, is not acquainted with the teaching but righteousness. But solid food is for the mature, who by constant use have trained themselves to distinguish good from evil." Hebrews 5:11-14

"Like newborn babies, crave pure spiritual milk, so that by it you may grow up in your salvation, now that you have tasted that the Lord is good." I Peter 2:2

Even as the Apostle Paul exhorted the early church to grow up, he knew full well that even though he was striving to be all that God wanted him to be, he often failed because he was not perfect and the evil one was continually pulling on him as he does us!

"We know that the law is spiritual but I am unspiritual, sold as a slave to sin. I do not understand what I do. For what I want to do I do not do, but what I hate I do....What a wretched man I am! Who will rescue me from this body of death? Thanks be to God through Jesus Christ our Lord!" Romans 7:14,15,24,25

What Paul understood is that our righteousness is found <u>only</u> in the perfection of Jesus Christ and never in our own ability to achieve it! That doesn't mean we ever stop striving to be all God calls us to be. It just means that God understands our human imperfection, so He sent Jesus. If we could achieve perfection on our own, Christ died for nothing. We can't. And He didn't. It is through His death that we are cleansed and empowered to grow up in our stature with God.

Part of the rewards of growing up in our salvation as Paul talks about in these scriptures is that we begin to realize that when we were born again, we claimed our rightful heritage, inheriting the image of God. Take a minute right now to look into a mirror. What image do you see looking back at you? Is it a glowing picture of a child of God, confident, joyful, and filled with love and purpose? Or is it a bedraggled and beaten image of, 'I can't do life anymore?' or 'I'm not good enough?' 'I'm a failure?' Or 'I am not worthy of being loved the way I need to be?'

His Image – My Image

When you are on the mountain top, what image do you see? When you are in the deepest valley, what image do you see? When you are ridiculed, criticized, and insecure, what image do you see looking back at you? Do you struggle with maintaining a secure *'self-concept?'* To understand the truth of *'self-image'* vs *'self-concept'* helps to unlock a clearer vision of who you really are.

It is critical to your sense of well-being to realize that when you were created, you were made "in the image of God." When you trust Christ as your Savior you claim that image. In Him, your *self-image* cannot be marred, damaged, nor destroyed by any negative force, because it is an inherited image, inherent in <u>whose</u> you are.

"Then God said, 'Let us make man in our image, in our likeness...'" Genesis 1:26a

"So God created man in his own image, in the image of God he created him; male and female he created them." Genesis 1:27

So then, as a child of God, it is our inheritance to carry on His image. The truth often missed is that assuming His image doesn't just start when we get to Heaven; it begins here on this earth, right where we are. As a born again child of God, we have inherited the right and freedom to claim God's truth, that our *image* is His *image* – right now!

Since the Bible solidly establishes that my image is His image, no one can mar my image...God won't let them. My roots are solid in my spiritual family. Though this is true, people can still say or do unfortunate things that may cause me to suffer from a poor *'self concept.'* Satan loves to attack our sense of *'self concept,'* confusing us into believing that the results are a reflection of our true 'self image.' NOT TRUE! Our true image remains in the likeness of Christ! If we are to experience the freedom of our spiritual heritage, this is an important and liberating truth to which we must cling.

Yes, our 'self-concept' may suffer great pain at the hands of the narcissistic, unkind world around us, or even worse at the hands of our own failures that lead us to entertain the thought that we are 'not good enough' to come to God or to expect His to love and forgiveness. Whenever we feel our 'self-concept' starting to suffer insecurities, we need to deny the attacks and declare the truth that no matter how anyone or anything tries to tear us down (including our own judgment of ourselves) we must stand firm on the fact that we are precious to God and we remain 'in His Image.' That doesn't change, even when we have let Him down. The Bible repeatedly confirms that when we humbly turn to Him, agreeing that we've blown it, He stands anxious to forgive us and restore our sense of the reality that He 'Loves us Anyhow!' He will pick us up, stand us on our feet, and guide us on His path of righteousness...because He loves us too much not to do so!

As born again Christians, no more can we disclaim our heritage of being created in our Heavenly Father's image, than can we determine not to be 'seed of our birth parent's seed.' It just can't happen. This golden nugget of truth is elementary to our spiritual growth. The evil one would like nothing better than to use the circumstances of our life's experiences to convince us otherwise, claiming that we deserve the poor self image we imagine to have.

Christian speaker and motivator Josh McDowell has carried out a mighty ministry to thousands of youth and their leaders over many years. Josh understands how important it is to claim this truth of being made in '*His image.*' He has made this truth the foundation of his teaching series entitled, *His Image – My Image.* This powerful teaching series is changing lives worldwide; I know…I am one of them. I can't encourage you strongly enough to seek out this series!

Josh tells the story of how, when traveling he often calls ahead and has a dozen roses delivered to his hotel room so that they are there when he arrives. Why does he do this? He confesses that just seeing them sitting there when he comes into his room is a needed reminder that he is 'special' - a child of God - made in His Image. During the series, Josh reveals his story of how his childhood was riddled with heartaches, insecurities, and pain. He gives testimony that once he was able to accept Jesus Christ as his Savior and understand that he was a reflection of God, made in His image and no longer subject to all his past mess, he was released from the pain of the past and empowered to minister to others. This truth is one of the most liberating truths you will ever experience! Believe it! Accept it! Act on it and live it to the fullest! When we used Josh's *"His Image My Image"* series as a teaching tool, it was so thrilling to watch as many young people grasped this truth, becoming liberated from their insecurities! Likewise I encourage you, as you continue your journey of Christian commitment and growth, look in the mirror daily and see *HIS IMAGE* reflecting back at you.

God's Instructions Help Us Grow Up

Why is it that we are so content to remain helpless babies? And yet, as such, we continue to complain because life is so tough? The question may well be answered with the insights of a small boy responding to his mother's inquiry as to why he continued to keep falling out of bed every night…His answer: '*Well, mommy, I guess it's because I keep falling asleep too close to where I got in.*' From the mouths of babes!

Dear friend, do you keep falling asleep too close to where you got in - with the maturity and security you seek eluding you at every challenge? Do you feel like you are on a continual uphill hike with no summit in sight? You are not alone. In order for us to not continue falling asleep too close to where we got into our new lives as Christians, it is essential for us to take some action steps and to grow beyond feeding only on the milk of babes!

As God guides us in our Christian lives He provides us with everything we need to be victorious in the ministry to which He calls us. Spending the time needed to discover God's golden nuggets of truth, as recorded for us in the Bible, and then taking the action steps required to live them out as best we can, provides us with the meat of maturity that will bring us victory – no more falling out of the bed! The Apostle Paul shared some helpful insights with the early church as to how they could grow up into mature Christians. His words are also for us ...

"You were taught with regard to your former way of life, to put off your old self, which is being corrupted by its deceitful desires, to be made new in the attitude of your minds; and to put on the new self, created to be like God in true righteousness and holiness....Be imitators of God, therefore, as dearly loved children and live a life of love, just as Christ loved us and gave himself up for us as a fragrant offering and sacrifice to God." Ephesians 4:22-24 and 5:1-2

Knowing that the early church was missing so many blessings by remaining such immature babies in Christ, Paul implores them to grow up so they can enjoy their rich inheritance of holiness and Christ-like love. Since they could not gain the victory they desired, in and of themselves, Paul instructs them that it is 'by the authority of the God-head' that all things are possible.

"For in Christ all the fullness of the Deity lives in bodily form, and you have been given fullness in Christ, who is the head over every power and authority." Colossians 2:9-10

We have re-visited this scripture a number of times throughout this writings because this truth is so critical to our victory. We simply <u>cannot</u> overcome the challenges on our own, because the battle is beyond us! Once again...the battles we fight are battles over which we have no authority accept that which we can claim with the power of the name of Jesus.

"For our struggle is not against flesh and blood, but against the rulers, against the authorities, against the powers of this dark world and against the spiritual forces of evil in the heavenly realms. Therefore put on the full armor of God, so that when the day of evil comes, you may be able to stand your ground, and after you have done everything, to stand." Ephesians 6:12, 13

"Be self-controlled and alert. Your enemy the devil prowls around like a roaring lion looking for someone to devour." I Peter 5:8

As Christians, we have been given the full armor of God for our protection. [Ephesians 4:13-18] Putting on God's full armor gives us: the assurance of salvation in Jesus, a revelation of God's truths, an open communication with Him, and a passion to actively pray for others. These disciplines drive away the evil one with the authority that is ours in Christ! Putting on the full armor of God keeps us from falling out of bed too close to where we got in! Even with the protection of the full armor of God, our human nature remains vulnerable to the pulls of this world and the challenges it presents. Recognizing those challenges, and what we can do to face them, will help prepare us for victory over them. One of the biggest is that of 'fear.'

Fear

Satan is alive and well, mocking our failures. Nothing serves him better than for us to remain spiritual babies. He is the great LIAR, presenting us with *false evidence* that we need to fear the truth of our own salvation and ability to serve the Lord. Fear paralyzes. It creeps into our sub-conscious and renders us ineffective to overcome the struggles in our own lives, let alone supposing there is some way God could use us in helping others to overcome theirs.

Claiming the *authority* of the Trinity that lives within us helps us see fear for what it really is, thus giving us the strength to overcome it. This acronym defines FEAR pretty clearly. Fear is:

> **F** - alse
> **E** - vidence
> **A** - ppearing
> **R** - eal

Overcoming this 'false evidence' is a matter of the Spirit. As we prayerfully meditate on God's instructions, turning our fears over to Him, He will give us the victory. Along with victory over our fears, He will also guide us to specific steps we can take to alleviate the problems which spawn our fears. We need to give our fears to God and listen to His instruction about how to overcome them.

Prayer

Effective prayer is our lifeline to God's presence in our lives. He is a friend upon which we can depend. And as such a friend, we would do well to be in communication with Him like we would be with a 'best friend.' To coin a phrase from today's electronic texting vocabulary, how do we become someone's BFF [best friend forever]? We spend inordinate amounts of time getting to know each other, learning what makes each other happy, sad, laugh, cry. What causes one to hurt causes both to hurt. Our day is not complete without a thought of each other, sharing a communication, a smile and a hug. Sharing our deepest thoughts with each other becomes some of the most fulfilling moments of our lives. That's what God wants with us. He wants to be our 'BFF!'

You may think it impossible to get that close to one whom you cannot see, but in reality the opposite is true. Sometimes the physical actually gets in the way of true communication between two souls. Though we can't see God, it is possible to build a deep spiritual connection with Him. The purity of communications without body language or outside interruptions can sometimes draw us into a 'soul mate' kind of relationship which face-to-face communications often cannot. It is inadequate at best to try to compare our relationship with God to any earthly relationship, however I think of one possible example that may help us conceptualize the truth of this principal...

Personal Reflection

After much persuasion on my part and that of my, then boyfriend-now husband, my sister and his brother, finally agreed to a blind date. It happened like this....

My boyfriend's brother was to be home on military leave the same week as a really big party my friend was having. Of course we had been planning on attending, but much to my dismay my boyfriend decided he could not abandon his brother during his only week at home on leave. I devised a plan to salvage the evening...we could invite my sister and his brother to go to the party with us, on a blind date with each other. :0) Ingenious, right? They didn't think so. OR at least she didn't. Having never met one another, she was not interested! However after a number of adamant 'nos' on her part, she finally acquiesced to my pleadings.

We had a great evening, laughed and talked and thoroughly enjoyed one another. The 'blind date' had been even more successful than we could have hoped for. I had no idea how successful! They saw each other every day for the rest of his leave time, followed by writing to each other every day for the next year, while she finished up her high school senior year and he continued with his commitment to the Air Force. Every now and then they called one another, but back then [before cell phone long distance freebees] long distant calls were not altogether too affordable.

Though they didn't see each other face-to-face throughout that entire next year, they came to know each other's every thought, like, dislike, music preferences, religious preferences, irritants and joys. They were able to share their hearts and sincerely considered each other's thoughts – without the interference of interruptive body language. They became each other's BFF. And they fell in love. They planned a lifetime together. And after that year, on his next leave home, they were married.

Forty-nine years later, upon his death, my sister shared with me, "Through all our communications that first year, I got to know him so well that I never once questioned but what we would have a good marriage, and given a chance, I would do it all over again." What a convincing testimony of the love and commitment that can result from taking pure unfettered time to get to know each other – even unseen!

It's like that with God. The more we communicate with Him, the greater our connection and commitment. And the more we know His thoughts, likes, dislikes, and those things that bring Him joy, the more we will be prepared to enter into that great and wonderful day when we will be seated at the wedding banquet of the Lamb, celebrating our eternal marriage to Christ!

So, how do we get to know God that well....by reading His letters to us [the Bible] and communicating with Him often through prayer. Remember that communication is two-way...we *talk* AND we *listen*.

Have you ever given up on a conversation when realizing that the one to whom you are speaking has quit listening and is in no way interested in what you have to say? I have. But, we never have to worry about that with God. He listens all the way through what we have to say. But do we? He is interested in what's going on in our hearts and our souls, and He wants to respond.

> *"This is the assurance we have in approaching God: that if we ask anything according to his will, he hears us."* I John 5:14, 15

> *"Let us then approach the throne of grace with confidence, so that we may receive mercy and find grace to help us in our time of need."* Hebrews 4:16

> *"For the eyes of the Lord are on the righteous and his ears are attentive to their prayer..."* I Peter 3:12a

Prayer is not only a pouring out of our own heart; it is also 'listening' for His response. In my early Christian life God nearly had to hammer this principle into my head in order to get this important truth drilled into me!

Personal Reflection

As I bumbled through my early Christian walk I had so many things to learn, so many things to let go of. I was fortunate to be among wonderful caring Christians, but I soon learned that we can't function victoriously from second hand faith. The faith of others encourages us and helps us to believe in ourselves, but it is in our own understanding and application of God's truths that we find victory. I was soaking up all the spiritual mentoring I could get and talking to God often, reading my Bible, and attending every Christian function that came along. But I was still struggling with letting go of some of my own harmful ways and I didn't understand why. In desperation one night I cried out to God 'Why?' 'Why?' I determined I would refuse to end my time in prayer until He made it clear to me just what more it was that I needed to understand. After much crying out, His voice penetrated my thoughts...

"You talk to me but you never take time to listen to me. But when your friend calls, after pouring out your heart to him, you don't just hang up on him. You listen diligently while he shares the truths from my word with you. On the other hand when you come to talk with me, after pouring out your heart and asking for my help, you

just quickly say 'Amen' and are off and running to the next thing. You don't hang up on your friend before listening to what he has to say, so - why do you hang up on me?"

It hit me like a ton of bricks. That's exactly what I was doing. Though I talked to God often, I didn't listen much. This revelation changed my Christian life. I committed to giving God His fair share of time....each prayer time....listening to Him as long as I had talked to Him. If I talk to Him 10 minutes, He gets His 10 minutes – 20 minutes, He gets His 20 minutes. It was hard at first. My mind would immediately start wondering to all kinds of things, what I was going to fix for supper, how would I approach my 'to do' list that day, what calls did I need to make, etc. It took practice to learn to sit quietly and listen, but it has been so well worth it! Sitting quietly after pouring out my heart to God in prayer, and then listening for God's voice in my head and heart, has become one of the biggest blessings of my life! I have had to learn to take a pencil and paper with me when I pray so I can jot down the things that He says, because God gives me so many thoughts as to what He wants me to know about Him, and things He wants me to do for Him, that I otherwise would never be able to remember it all! Over the years there has been story after story of wonderful ministry opportunities that it has been my blessing to experience, all as a result of listening and responding to the thoughts God places into my head and heart during the 'listening' portion of my prayer time. I love hearing His compassionate instruction.

Prayer Is Spiritual Breathing

Prayer gives life to our spiritual body, as breathing air gives life to our physical body. We breathe out our praise and petitions and we breathe in the wisdom of God.

> *"...The wisdom that comes from heaven is first of all pure; then peace-living, considerate, submissive, full of mercy and good fruit, impartial and sincere."* James 3:17

Even Jesus – the Son of God – felt that talking with His Father and listening to His instruction was so important that during His last days on earth He made it a priority to take time to pray, for Himself, His disciples, for us, and for all who would believe through us. Take a look at some excerpts from His prayer, recorded in John 17:1-4 & 15-21....

> *".....Father, the time has come, Glorify your Son, that your Son may glorify you. For you granted him authority over all people that he might give eternal life to all those you have given him. Now this is eternal life; that they may know you, the only true God, and Jesus Christ, whom you have sent. I've brought you glory on earth by completing the work you gave me to do."*

"My prayer is not that you take them out of the world but that you protect them from the evil one. They are not of the world, even as I am not of it. Sanctify them by the truth; your word is truth. As you sent me into the world, I have sent them into the world. For them I sanctify myself, that they too may be truly sanctified. My prayer is not for them alone. I pray also for those who will believe in me through their message, that all of them may be one, Father just as you are in me and I am in you. May they also be in us so that the world may believe that you have sent me."

How blessed are we that, in those last days the Son of God counted us worthy of spending time in prayer petitioning God on our behalf! I sincerely encourage you to take a look at all of Jesus' prayer recorded in the seventeenth chapter of John. You will see that scripture is never clearer than in this prayer, regarding the ministry to which we are called. His petitions to God clearly declare that He prays for 'all who will believe because of us.' How will they believe 'because of us' if we do not tell them? That's why we must grow up to a level of maturity that equips and empowers us to participate in helping reconcile the world to Jesus Christ!

Scriptural Prayer

Numerous scriptures instruct us on how to pray effectively. Prayer is not meant to be a hap hazard shout out, 'hey how are ya...thanks for meeting me here ....here's my list of wants for today.' It is a serious and precious time with almighty God. So what does scriptural prayer look like?

We are assured that we can go to the throne of God with confidence....
"Let us then approach the throne of grace with confidence, so that we may receive mercy and find grace to help us in our time of need." Hebrews 4:16

He wants us to humbly *verbalize our desires*....
"Ask and it will be given to you; seek and you will find; knock and the door will be opened to you. For everyone who asks receives; he who seeks finds; and to him who knocks the door will be opened." Matthew 7:7-8

Pray with the *right motives* in mind....
"When you ask, you do not receive, because you ask with wrong motives, that you may spend what you get on your pleasures." James 4:3

Pray in *Faith*....
"...faith is being sure of what we hope for and certain of what we do not see." Hebrews 11:1

"And the prayer offered in faith will make the sick person well; the Lord will raise him up. If he has sinned, he will be forgiven. Therefore confess your sins to

each other and pray for each other so that you may be healed. The prayer of a righteous man is powerful and effective." James 5:15-16

Pray in *Jesus' Name*...
"I tell you the truth, my Father will give you whatever you ask in my name. Until now you have not asked for anything in my name. Ask and you will receive, and your joy will be complete." John 16:23b-24

Believe *He hears* you.... And first *forgive others*....
"Therefore I tell you, whatever you ask for in prayer, believe that you have received it and it will be yours. And when you stand praying, if you hold anything against anyone forgive him so that your father in heaven may forgive you your sins." Mark 11:24-25

Be *Persistent*....
"...Suppose one of you has a friend, and he goes to him at midnight and says, 'Friend, lend me three loaves of bread.....Then the one inside answers, 'Don't bother me. The door is already locked...I tell you, though he will not get up and give him the bread because he is his friend, yet because of the man's boldness, he will get up and give him as much as he needs. So I say to you: Ask and it will be given to you; seek and you will find; knock and the door will be opened to you." Excerpts from Luke 11: 5-9

Have confidence that *God is listening and will respond*.....
"For the eyes of the Lord are on the righteous and his ears are attentive to their prayer..." I Peter 3:12a

"Devote yourself to prayer, being watchful and thankful." Colossians 4:2

The Key to Effective Prayer?....*PRAY ACCORDING TO HIS WILL*
"This is the assurance we have in approaching God: that if we ask anything according to his will, he hears us. And if we know that he hears us – whatever we ask - we know that we have what we asked of him." I John 5:14, 15

Pray with a *prayer partner*....
"Again, I tell you the truth, that if two of you on earth agree about anything you ask for, it will be done for you by my Father in heaven. For where two or three come together in my name, there am I with them." Matthew 18: 19-20

As you exercise your spiritual lungs, breathing out your thought to God daily and breathing in His blessings and instructions, I pray that you will experience the power of a growingly effective prayer life. When we lift our heart to Him in prayer, it is the **faith** to believe that He hears us that brings peace and healing into our lives.

Faith

Faith is the foundation of our Christian life, yet sometimes even just the word FAITH is daunting. How do you get faith? How much faith does it take to move God on our behalf? How can we make our faith grow? Allow me to encourage you to put your concerns aside about somehow developing a huge amount of faith in order to experience a victorious Christian life.

Jesus said we need only a 'mustard seed' of faith – remember? When I was in Israel I had the opportunity to see many mustard seed plants. Their seeds are so tiny they look like sprinkles of pepper. Jesus says just that much…that's all we need to move mountains!

> "….I tell you the truth, if you have faith as small as a mustard seed, you can say to this mountain, 'Move from here to there' and it will move. Nothing will be impossible for you." Matthew 17:20b

So why are there so many times when we feel inept in our faith walk? I would suggest that it is not because our faith is too small but rather because, in our minds eye, the 'object' of our faith is too small. How big is the object of your faith? How big is your vision of God? Do we so underestimate His omnipotence and power that we limit His work in our lives, and then assume that it's because our faith is too small? God is accessible. He is able. And He is willing. We only need a 'mustard seed' of faith in a BIG God in order to gain that intimate healing relationship with Him that we seek! Once we understand this, we are on our way to a path of Christian maturity. The first step toward Christian growth is the faith to trust that Jesus is who He claims to be.

A Stairway to Christian Maturity

We all want to grow up – to reach our full potential – to become who we were created to be – to love others deeply as God commands. But how on earth do we get there? Seems with all the efforts we make it is still such an uphill battle sometimes, doesn't it? Perhaps it's because we try to reach that ultimate goal [the top of our ascension to spiritual growth] by jumping from the bottom step [the beginning – faith] to the top [loving others deeply so that we can be fruitful and useful to the Lord]. Ever try that while on a physical set of steps? It just does not work. Without taking the climb one step at a time, we will just keep slipping back down. And spiritually speaking, depending on the circumstances we face, even when we begin to move upward in our spiritual maturity one step at a time we may stumble back from time-to-time.

So, what are these '*steps to spiritual maturity?*' Let's start with II Peter 1: 2-4 [as paraphrased in The Living Bible] This scripture records Peter's compelling invitation to us regarding the great and wonderful gifts God wants to give us in reward for our obedience....

> *"Do you want more and more of God's kindness and peace? Then learn to know Him better and better. For as you know Him better, He will give you, through His great power everything you need for living a truly good life; He even shares His own glory and his own goodness with us. And by that same might power He has given us all the other rich and wonderful blessings He promised; for instance, the promise to save us from the lust and rottenness all around us, and to give us His own character. But to obtain these gifts..."*

Consistently throughout the Bible God rewards us for following His instructions. Such is the case with the wonderful promises noted in this scripture from the first part of II Peter, in which Peter continues to further outline the stair steps of Christian growth. Following His statement 'But to obtain these gifts,' He reveals the path and the rewards of 'growing spiritually strong and becoming fruitful and useful to the Lord.' Take a look.....

> *"But to obtain these gifts, you need more than faith [step 1]. You must also work hard to be good [step 2], and even that is not enough. For then you must learn to know God better and discover what he wants you to do [step 3]. Next learn to put aside your own desires [step 4] so that you will become patient and godly [step 5] gladly letting God have his way with you. [step 6] This will make possible for the next step, which is for you to enjoy other people and to like them, [step 7] and finally you will grow to love then deeply. [step 8] The more you go on this way the more you will grow strong spiritually and become fruitful and useful to the Lord [step 9]"* II Peter 1:5-8

Since the first step Peter mentions in this 'stairway to learning to love others deeply and becoming fruitful and useful to the Lord' is FAITH, let's take another couple minutes to review what faith is and what it is not....

> *"Now faith is being sure of what we hope for and certain of what we do not see."* Hebrews 11:1

> *"And, without faith it is impossible to please God, because anyone who comes to him must believe that he exists and that he rewards those who earnestly seek him."* Hebrews 11:6

Faith *is*, believing that God will do what He says He will do. It is *not* conjuring up some kind of 'power of positive thinking' that relies on our own ability to rise to the occasion. Otherwise, God would be dependent on our ability, rather than us on His, and we would all be in one heap of trouble!

Once we have a firm grip on what faith is, the first step on our journey to Christian growth is applying our faith in Jesus Christ, believing He came to set us free from the evil one. We cannot experience Christian maturity without first becoming a Christian – not just a religious person. So the first step is placing our faith in Jesus. Then we are ready to take the next step, living the sort of virtuous life Jesus asks us to when we become a part of His family. He knows that we may make mistakes as we sincerely seek to become mature in our love and service to Him, but He will be there to pick us up and set us back on our stairway to Christian growth.

Divinely inspired, Peter clearly outlines these nine spiritual 'stair steps,' and when we climb them, we reach a level of maturity that compels us to love others deeply enough to become useful and fruitful to the Lord in their lives, declaring, *"I Love You Anyhow!"*

I have developed the following graphic in an attempt to help us visualize these stair 'steps to Christian maturity' that have so helped me in my journey to systematically move beyond feeding on baby's milk, to feeding on the true spiritual meat that God offers. As you read these wonderful instructions, start at the bottom of the page [on step one] and move your way up to the top. In addition to the scriptures Peter records for each step, I have included some additional supportive scripture for each level.

Vs 8 – SERVE….. *"The more you go on this way the more you will grow strong spiritually and become fruitful and useful to the Lord."*

I Corinthians 5:20a …*"We are therefore Christ's ambassadors, as though God were making his appeal through us."*

Vs 7 –LOVE…. *"and finally you will grow to love them deeply."*

I John 4:7 *"dear children do not just say you love others show it by your actions."*

Vs 7 – BROTHERLY KINDNESS… *"This will make it possible for the next step which is for you to enjoy other people and like them."*

Romans 12:18 … *"In as much as it is possible for you; be at peace with everyone."*

Vs 6 – GODLINESS… *"… and Godly, gladly letting God have His way with you."*

Philippines 2:13… *"for it is God who works in you to will and to act according to his good purpose."*

Vs 6 – PERSEVEARANCE…. *"…so you will become patient"*

II Timothy 1:12… *"I know in whom I have believed and I am convinced that he is able to guard that which I have entrusted to him for that day."*

Isaiah 40:31… *"…those who hope in the Lord will renew their strength. They will soar on wings like eagles; they will run and not grow weary, they will walk and not be faint."*

Vs 5 – SELF CONTROL…. *"Next, learn to put aside your own desires…"*

Romans 8:6 … *"The mind of sinful man is death (separation from God), but the mind controlled by the Holy Spirit is life and peace."*

Vs 5 – KNOWLEDGE…. *"For then you must learn to know God better and discover what he wants you to do."*

Psalm 19:9-11…*"How can a young man keep his way pure? By living according to your word. I seek you with all my heart; do not let me stray from your commands. I have hidden your word in my heart that I might not sin against you."*

Vs 5 – GOODNESS [Virtue]…..*"You must also work hard to be good, and even this is not enough"*

Ephesians 2:10 --*"God prepared good works for us to do long ages ago."*

Vs 5 – FAITH ….*You will need more than FAITH   [The journey must start with faith in Jesus]*

I John 5:11-13 -- "And this is the testimony; he who has the son has the father. He who does not have the son does not have the father. I write this to you who believe in the name of the son of God, so that you may know that you have eternal life."

As you study this diagram, which step are you on in your journey to Christian maturity? This is not baby's milk we are ingesting! This is the 'meat' that Paul tells Christians to chew on in order to reach the maturity to declare, *'I Love You Anyhow!'*

Or perhaps this whole concept of Christianity is totally new to you. Perhaps you are like I was, you've been in the church as long as you can remember, wanting to love others deeply and serve the Lord willingly, trying to reach that top step. But somehow you sense that you are missing something essential to get you there. Perhaps you too have been so inoculated with *'churchianity'* that you have been unable to catch *'Christianity.'* Remember the first step is a simple step of 'FAITH' - transferring your trust to Jesus alone for the forgiveness of your sins and your adoption into the family of God. Has this truth eluded you as it did me? You've thought it all depended on you – your ability to deliver – instead of it all depending on what Jesus has *already delivered* – taking your sins to the cross so you can be forgiven, declaring a message of *'I Love You Anyhow,'* and inviting you to spend eternal life with Him! If you have not yet taken this first step of transferring your trust to Jesus, take a minute right now to declare your awareness of the price He paid to erase your sin. Transfer your trust to Him for your eternal salvation.

Perhaps you are more like the *'crock pot'* Christian mentioned. You have slowly, through many, many years, learned more and more of the truths of Christianity – believing who Jesus is and knowing that He died on the cross for you. But you still wonder, *'Where am I with the Lord? If I were to die tonight would I go to heaven?'* Perhaps you just need the assurance of your own salvation. Be sure to pay close attention to the next chapter, *'Pay It Forward.'* You will see a clear Biblical path of the assurance of your salvation in Jesus.

You may want to post a copy of Peter's 'spiritual stairway to maturity' somewhere where it can be a constant measure for you as to where you are in your spiritual growth, and what action you will take to move to the next step on your journey to Christian maturity. I trust this discipline will prevent you from *"falling out to close to where you got in!"*

Unfortunately, though I took the step of placing my faith in Jesus many years ago, my walk is still not always a consistent journey of ascension to Christian maturity. My stair treads are nearly worn through from my journey up and back down and back up and back down again! And I have a feeling I'm not alone. But I never give up. One day I feel full of assurance regarding my relationship with Jesus, working hard to be good, spending time to get to know Him better, and persevering in my relationships, striving to serve God by loving others. On another day it is all I can do to just muster up enough faith to believe God really could love such a creature as me! But I have been to the top and I have experienced the joy that it holds to be fruitful for the

Lord, and I will forever continue with my commitment to seek His face every day, as He helps me continue on my path to Christian growth and maturity.

Thank God He never moves away from us, never gives up on us! His plan to help you grow up and empower you to serve Him has been in place from the moment He formed you in your mother's womb and will continue to be in place throughout all eternity. He has gifted each of us with our own special gifts of service....

> *"It was he who gave some to be apostles, some to be prophets, some to be evangelists, and some to be pastors and teachers, to prepare God's people for works of service, so that the body of Christ may be built up until we all reach unity in the faith and in the knowledge of the Son of God and become mature, attaining to the whole measure of the fullness of Christ."* Ephesians 4:11-13

And so this is what our journey of commitment and growth is all about: placing our trust in Christ, committing ourselves to daily moving up the steps of Christian maturity, with the goal in mind of fulfilling God's plan for our lives to serve Him in a ministry of reconciliation. And He is always, always there lovingly available to meet us on our growing edge, helping lift us up to that next step on the path of becoming all He has planned for us to be. At every difficult juncture we can be assured that He will be there declaring, *"I Love You, Anyhow!"* I wouldn't trade my journey of Christian commitment and growth for anything this world has to offer!

We have inspiring examples of the perseverance of many Biblical characters as they committed themselves to growing in their faith and 'paying it forward.' For a modern day example:

Personal Reflection:
I had a dear friend, spiritual soul-mate and prayer partner, that I shared a lot of life with over many years. He spent the last eight years of his life diagnosed with terminal cancer. Though we lived on two different sides of the country, spawned and nurtured through our common vocation of Christian film production, our attendance at an annual film production conference, and the magic of computer technology communications, for over 30 years he continually inspired me to grow up in Christ. He set a great example of serving the Lord with every part of his life. When first diagnosed with cancer, he was told he probably had less than a year left on this earth. Yet he had reached such Christian maturity that he persevered in his Christian witness for eight more years. Throughout these eight years his diagnoses continued to reveal more and more tumors throughout his body. But spurred on by his determination to pay forward the incredible blessings the Lord had given to him, his family, and his film production/distribution company, he refused to let the circumstances rob him of his opportunity to share the lessons he was learning about

the sustaining strength of the Lord. He surely was at the top step of his 'steps to Christian growth,' loving others deeply and being fruitful and useful for the Lord. And he had a heartfelt desire to pay it forward to the thousands whom he could potentially reach with his films. As a result, during this very difficult time he continued his commitment to ministry as a walking testimony of the power of the Holy Spirit and the guidance of the Angels in his life. He found the strength, focus, and compassion to continue his film production. With his devoted son by his side [personally and in their film business] they produced unbelievably beautiful stories, filmed in the Holy Land, stories emphasizing how Biblical instructions given in The Lord's Prayer, The Beatitudes, and The 23rd Psalm, give us strength to face the uphill climb – even, and especially, for those with cancer. In those days he diligently sought out the Lord's direction, & through the power of the Holy Spirit and the protection and guidance of his Angels, he traveled with his son throughout the Holy Land producing these inspiring dramatic films.

As I helped to edit his journaling through this walk with cancer, I asked him one day how he found the courage and encouragement to carry on – especially in those days when he was really ill and weak. He said, "I just wake up every day and keep asking, Lord what do you want from me today?" And then he told me about how [though he was not Catholic] for years he had admired Mother Teresa's strength and her commitment to ministry, even though she served most of the time in very difficult and poor conditions. He said that in following her ministry he became inspired to pray daily one of the prayers she had written, and prayed regularly herself. He said this prayer helped him find great strength in just simply trusting God enough to place himself in the Lord's hands every day, seeking His direction as to how he could still 'pay it forward' even in the midst of unfathomable physical challenges. I have included that prayer at the end of this chapter and I challenge you, as he did me, to be bold enough to pray it daily.

What a modern day example of a Christian's commitment to growth, commitment to 'pay it forward!' And even now in death he continues to pay it forward, as the Holy Spirit continues to work through his powerful film productions, still being distributed by his company, Vision Video [now directed by his son]. Because this dear man so dearly loved God and loved people, he was wholly committed to 'pay it forward' and truly showed it by his actions! As a result, all over the world in private homes, doctor's offices, hospice homes, care centers, and everywhere there are DVD players, people are witnessing live testimony of God's ever present love, strength, compassion, and commitment to His children - even through devastating illness! They are witnessing the truth of His promise in Jeremiah 29 that God has a plan for us - a plan for good and not for harm, for hope and a future. Yes, His plan for my dear friend stayed intact throughout cancer, and his hope for a future is now a reality as he walks – fully healed - with Jesus!

Once again.....as you read Mother Theresa's heart tugging prayer, following the 'Personal Application' section at the end of this chapter, I encourage you to ask God for the bravery to pray it, trusting as my friend did that no matter what challenges you may face as you commit to grow and seek opportunities to 'pay it forward,' God will empower you.

Dear Lord,

Help us, through the power of your Holy Spirit, the guidance of your Angels, and effective two-way communication with you in prayer, to persevere up the steps of Christian growth, so that we may be fully empowered and equipped to be consistently strong enough to love others deeply and serve you effectively. Help us to realize what we've really always been since you created us - a reflection of your image. Help us to see ourselves as you see us. Help us to be deliberate in our commitment to grow up spiritually. Help us to let go of our fears, that we might take a step of faith in getting outside of ourselves and serving you. You have given us so much! And, Lord, like so many who have gone before us, we want to pay it forward! With your help we will! Amen"

Personal Application

TRUTH

God gives us clear instructions as to how to grow up in our journey with Him so that we can become mature Christians through whom He can reconcile the world to Himself, through Jesus Christ.

1. As you reflect on the material in this chapter, what are some of the tell-tale things that you experience which may indicate that you have *gone to sleep too close to where you got in* to your Christian life?

2. Look over the things you've noted and in each case ask yourself, *'when these things happen, how do I react? What steps can I take to allow God to help me get back on track?*

3. Have you developed prayer habits that help keep effective *two-way* communications in your time with God? What steps will you take to make this special time better?

4. Are you on the way up the stairway to Christian growth? Have you exercised the 'Faith' to take that first step – transferring your trust to Jesus? If not: Is there any good reason why you cannot do that right now? If your heart if prompting you that you need to take this step, talk to Him. He is standing at the door and knocking. Let Him in.

5. Once we know the assurance of your own eternal destiny, we need to determine which step we are on in the *steps to Christian growth*. Take a look and determine which step is next for you. Ask God to help you in moving on to that next step toward the ultimate goal of loving others deeply and becoming fruitful and useful for Him.

A Prayer From Mother Teresa

I am yours, and for you I was born.
What do you want from me?

O sovereign Majesty,
unending wisdom
and my soul's greatest goodness,
the one supreme and good God,
you see one who in her unworthiness
sends her love to you today.
What do you want from me?

I am yours because you created me,
yours because you redeemed me,
yours because you bore with me,
yours because you called me to you,
yours because you also waited for me
and did not have me condemned.
What do you want from me?

* * * * * * * * * *

See, here is my heart,
I place it in your hands,
together with my life, my body and my soul,
my inmost feelings and my love;
dear Husband and Redeemer,
since I have given myself to you,
What do you want from me?

Give me life or death,
health or sickness;
give me honor or dishonor,
conflict or sublime peace,
weakness or full strength;
I will accept it all.
What do you want from me?

It may be poverty or wealth,
consolation or distress:
it may be joy or sorrow, or heaven or hell;
for I have surrendered completely to your will,
my sweet life, my shining sun,
What do you want from me?

If it pleases you, grant me the gift of prayer,
but if not, give me dryness;
give me piety and abundant grace,
or give me sterility.
O sovereign Majesty,
with you alone I can find peace.
What do you want from me?

In your love, then;
give me wisdom, or give me ignorance;
let me have years of plenty,
or years of leanness and hunger,
let me be in darkness
or in the bright of day;
send me wherever you wish.
What do you want from me?

If you want me to rejoice,
then out of love for you I will rejoice.
If you lay burdens upon me;
then I shall want to die bearing them.
Tell me where, when and how;
just tell me, my sweet love;
What do you want from me?

* * * *

Whether I speak or am silent;
whether I produce fruit or none at all,
let the Law proclaim to me my guilt
or the Gospel its sweetness.
Let me be in the midst of trouble or of joy,
if you will only live in me.
What do you want from me?

I am yours and for you I was born;
What do you want from me?

CHAPTER NINE
PAY IT FORWARD

We have a dear friend that is a learned and dynamic Bible teacher. His knowledge of the scriptures and the lives and claims of the prophets, throughout history and to the present day accounts of Israel, may be unparalleled! We attend the same church while in the south at our winter retreat. He has always shared so many great insights during our Pastor's Wednesday Bible Studies, but due to the unavailability of our Pastor for this particular year's Bible study, they asked Dale to lead a study. It is such a privilege to sit under his tutelage! Yet I was unbelievably humbled, when in the midst of his study one morning, he stated: *"I am very honored and pleased to have been asked to lead this year's Bible Study, but I have to tell you, after attending Marge's study last year I was a little disappointed that, due to the fact that she is in the midst of writing a book we weren't going to get to hear her again this year. I loved just sittin' and soakin' up all she taught us last year. But I know there are times for sittin' and soakin' and there are times when God asks us to be willing to pay forward all that He has taught us, so this year it's your turn to just sit and soak, Marge."*

Well, I have to say my dear Dale; I loved sittin' and soakin' throughout your classes on the state of affairs of the Holy Land! I was like a dry sponge, soakin' and soakin' and soakin'! Thank you for your kind words of encouragement regarding the ministry God has allowed me to share while at our wonderful church there, and thank you so much for your willingness to share all your incredible wisdom, knowledge and inspiration with us!

I haven't included Dale's comment in this writing to somehow glow in his pat on the back [though I sincerely appreciate it]. Rather, I include it because I want to make a very important point here. You see - I am not a scholar of theology. I am not an ordained pastor. I am simply one who loves the Lord and seeks to pay forward the many opportunities He has given me to learn and grow and serve. Much of the material to which Dale referred, that I was privileged to teach at Grace Church, is found tucked within this manuscript.

When we use the gifts God has given us to share the Gospel with others, allowing Him to use us for His purposes, His Holy Spirit enables us to share effectively. This all works because as Paul said, *"I am not ashamed of the gospel, because it is the power of God for the salvation of everyone who believes; first for the Jew, then for the Gentile."* Romans 1:16 So you see it is that the power unto Salvation is in the Gospel itself - not in the communicator of the Gospel.

I lay this challenge before you as you near the end of this writing. Whatever truths and inspiration you have gained from sittin' and soakin' up the truths communicated herein, it is now time for you to *pay it forward!* Jesus said it first. Before He left this earth to re-join His Father in Heaven, He gave us a commission, with a promise....

> *"Therefore go and make disciples of all nations, baptizing them in the name of the Father and of the Son and of the Holy Spirit, and teaching them to obey everything I have commanded you. And surely I will be with you always, to the very end of the age."* Matthew 28:19

In the original language of this command 'therefore go' reads, '<u>as</u> <u>you</u> <u>go</u>.' Sharing the story of Jesus should overflow from us 'as we go,' as though we can't help it because we are so full of Him.

> *"But thanks be to God, who always leads us in triumphal procession in Christ and through us spreads everywhere the fragrance of the knowledge of him."* II Corinthians 2:14

This 'great commission' is for everyone who knows Jesus, not just for a select few. Do you love Jesus? Love His people. After Jesus' resurrection He pressed this point with His disciple, Peter, in saying to him multiple times, *"Peter do you love me? Feed my sheep."* In chapter one we read of this account. If we are to join Peter in Jesus' challenge to *'feed His sheep,'* we must pre-determine to love them first. ...

> *"This is the message you heard from the beginning: We should love one another. – Dear Children, let us not love with words or tongue but with actions and in truth."* Excerpts from I John 3:16, 23

It is time that the Church - big 'C' [i.e. all who belong to Christ] moves out and declares to the world around it, with boldness and in love, the truth about Jesus Christ....

> ➤ that, as the Son of God, He came to earth to reconcile man to God
> ➤ that in doing so He died a sacrificial death on the cross, giving His life to pay the price for man's sin, so that we may be forgiven and redeemed to spend eternity in Heaven
> ➤ that after His crucifixion and burial, He rose again and ascended back to Heaven
> ➤ that He will come again someday to gather those who belong to Him and take us all to our Heavenly home
> ➤ And that we all need to be ready!

How many people do you suppose have died since you started sittin' and soakin' up God's wonderful truths contained in this book? Millions! How many of them died without Christ? Way too many! Even one is too many! How many of those who died without Christ are among those you and I have passed by on our daily journey through life, which we may have been able to reach for Christ – but just didn't?

It is so easy to think and believe and strategize…with all the good intentions in the world…that we <u>should</u> share our faith <u>someday</u>….but then never do anything about it. Satan is alive and well and he will throw every possible deterrent into our pathway to keep us from telling of the sweetness of life in Jesus. There is a tendency on our part to feel inadequate to the task, but the truth is that the effectiveness of doing so lies in the Gospel itself, not in our wisdom nor our oratory abilities. It may help release us to share our faith when we realize that we can never 'lead anyone to Christ' – the Holy Spirit alone leads people to Christ. We cannot take the credit when someone decides to transfer their trust to Christ. Of course the opposite is then also true, we cannot beat ourselves up whenever we have shared the Gospel and someone chooses not to respond. It is all guided by the ministry of the Holy Spirit and the willingness of those who do not yet know the Lord to respond to His claims. We need only tell our own story, the story of Jesus' love and redemptive work in our lives. He will do the rest.

Recall the scripture that we read in the Empowerment chapter, confirming the Holy Spirit's work….

> *"Therefore, I tell you that no one who is speaking by the Spirit of God says, 'Jesus be cursed,' and <u>no one can say</u>, 'Jesus is Lord,' <u>except by the Holy Spirit</u>."* I Corinthians 12:3

Paul understood this well, realizing throughout his ministry that it is the work of the Holy Spirit through the Gospel story that convicts one to respond to Jesus. It is worth repeating…

"I am not ashamed of the Gospel, because it is the power of God for the salvation of everyone who believes, first for the Jew and then for the Gentile." Romans 1:16

Be Active

After God turned Saul around by blinding him in order to get his attention, He forgave him for his persecution of thousands of Christians and commissioned him to go out and tell the truth about Jesus. In response, Saul became the Apostle Paul, stopping his attacks on Christians and 'actively' witnessing for Jesus Christ, giving all he had – ultimately even his life – to pay it forward for Jesus' sake. He realized that this was not a passive calling, thus devoted his life to *action* in sharing his faith - not his perfection - in Jesus. Likewise we must realize it is not a calling to which we can take a 'wait and see' attitude. God instructs each of us to be *'active'* in sharing the good news of the Gospel. In fact He tells us that, if we want to know all of the good things He has for us, it is imperative that we be *active* in telling His story.

> *"I pray that you may be active in sharing your faith, so that you will have a full understanding of every good thing we have in Christ."* Philemon 6

The Apostles got it! Through their bold witness in *actively* paying it forward, we have many accounts of the work of the Holy Spirit......

> *"Peter replied, 'Repent and be baptized, every one of you, in the name of Jesus Christ so that your sins may be forgiven....Those who accepted his message were baptized, and about three thousand were added to their number that day."* Acts 2:38, 41

> *"They [the religious leaders of the day] were greatly disturbed because the apostles were teaching the people and proclaiming in Jesus the resurrection of the dead. They seized Peter and John and because it was evening, they put them in jail until the next day. But many who heard the message believed, and the number of men grew to about five thousand."* Acts 4:4

In fact, there was just no stopping them. They had a plan and that plan was to, if necessary, give their very lives for the sake of the Gospel....

> *"Having brought the apostles, they made them appear before the Sanhedrin to be questioned by the high priest. "We gave you strict orders not to teach in this name, he said. Yet you have filled Jerusalem with your teaching and are determined to make us guilty of this man's [Jesus] blood." Peter and the other apostles replied: "We must obey God rather than men!"....They called the apostles in and had them flogged. Then they ordered them not to speak in the name of Jesus, and let them go. The apostles left the Sanhedrin, rejoicing because they had been counted worthy of suffering disgrace for the Name. Day after day in the*

temple courts and from house to house, they never stopped teaching and proclaiming the good news that Jesus is the Christ." Acts 5:27-29, 40-42

Wow, talk about determination to be *active* in sharing one's faith! There really is no good reason not to *pay it forward*. If it is our intention to share our faith, we will have a plan to do so and we will become *active* in doing so. I have heard it said that is just not natural to talk about Jesus in our normal daily conversations outside the church, but I would disagree. When we truly understand how much Jesus loves us and what He has done in paying a huge price for our sins, it becomes as natural a way of life as anything else we do. When He becomes the love of our lives and the object of our affections there is no way to keep it a secret.

One thing to note….as we *intentionally* become *active* in sharing our faith *it is critical that we do so with humility and grace*. Too many who determine to 'actively' share their faith become so overly zealous in their approach that they actually do more harm for the Gospel than good! Be careful to share the Gospel for Jesus' sake and not for your own glory, or because you are looking down on and judging those without Christ. Instead, as you share for the sake of the Gospel, honor others above yourself. God clearly cautions us about *how* we share, imploring us to share the Gospel with a compassionate heart….

"Be devoted to one another in brotherly love. Honor one another above yourselves." Romans 12:10

"Do not judge, or you too will be judged. For in the same way you judge others, you will be judged, and with the measure you use it, will be measured to you." Matthew 7:1-2

"Always be prepared to give an answer to everyone who asks you to give the reason for the hope that you have. But do this with gentleness and respect…" 1st Peter 3: 15-16a

It isn't always easy to share with the gentleness God asks us to. Satan doesn't like it. He would be happy if we would get distracted and angry when others want to argue with us, but we must remember souls hang in the balance so we cannot be dissuaded from the calling.

"Don't have anything to do with foolish and stupid arguments, because you know they produce quarrels. And the Lord's servants must not quarrel; instead, he must be kind to everyone, able to teach, nor resentful. Those who oppose him he must gently instruct, in the hope that God will grant them repentance leading them to a knowledge of the truth, and that they will come to their senses and escape from the trap of the devil, who has taken them captive to do his will." 2 Timothy 2:23-25

As we commit ourselves to 'pay it forward' we are committing to bathe ourselves in prayer, seek God's wisdom and guidance, not allow a judgmental attitude, and hold the utmost of respect for those with whom we share, doing so with _gentleness_ and _respect_.

God has not given us this all-important assignment and then left us to sink or swim on our own. He has a plan. His pre-determined plan for us is that we partner with Him in a **'ministry of reconciliation'**...reconciling ourselves to each other and to Him. As Christ's Ambassador's He is there with us all the way, and He has our backs.

> "_For if when we were God's enemies, we were reconciled to him through the death of his Son, how much more, having been reconciled, shall we be saved through his life! Not only is this so, but we rejoice in God through our Lord Jesus Christ, through whom we have now received reconciliation._" Romans 5:10-11

> "_All this is from God, who reconciled us to himself through Christ and gave us the ministry of reconciliation: That God was reconciling the world to himself in Christ, not counting men's sins against them. And he has committed to us the message of reconciliation. We are therefore Christ's ambassadors, as though God were making his appeal through us. We implore you on Christ's behalf: Be reconciled to God._" II Corinth 5: 18-20

Wow - '_as though God were making his appeal through us!_' Once again He stresses that it is _HE_ who is doing the reconciling – through us. This call to a ministry of reconciliation is not reserved for those who go to Seminary. I know we've covered this before but it is such an important truth. Do you get it? Do you hear Him calling you? We who know Jesus are God's children, commissioned to carry His message of salvation to the world. If we will only be willing, He will enable us for the job, just as He did when He called a common man named Moses to lead His enslaved people out of Egypt. Moses pushed back, declaring that he was not a good speaker, thus he didn't feel equipped for the task. God exhorted him to go anyway, sending his brother, Aaron, along to help him. He assured Moses that He would be with him and enable him to victory. And we read in the book of Exodus that indeed God's Spirit was with Moses, telling him what to say to Pharaoh to ultimately cause him to let the people go, and then sending His Spirit to guide Moses as He led the people out of Egypt, through the Red Sea, over the desert and to freedom in the Promised Land.

We read story after story like this, revealing how God's Holy Spirit equips His children for ministry, even giving them the words to speak. One example: when the Apostle Peter was called before the Sanhedrin to defend himself for preaching the Gospel to the crowds, the Lord encouraged him not to worry about what he would say....

"But when they arrest you, do not worry about what to say or how to say it, for it will not be you speaking, but the Spirit of your Father speaking through you." Matthew 10:19

"Whenever you are arrested and brought to trial, do not worry beforehand about what to say, just say whatever is given you at the time, for it is not you speaking, but the Holy Spirit." Mark 13: 11

In Luke's writings he also confirms:

"...for the Holy spirit will teach you at that time what you should say." Luke 12:12

God stands by us in our witness. We do not have to know all there is to know about the Bible in order to share what we do know. Our confidence cannot be in ourselves; it must be in the power of the Gospel. As God has allowed me to share Jesus with people of all faiths He has proven to me over and over again that He will give me the words to say.

I don't know a lot about the Jewish faith, but I have attended services at the Synagogue from time-to-time, and I hold great admiration and awe for those who share the lineage of my Lord and Savior, His chosen people. If you would have asked me, *"How do we share our faith in Jesus with a Jewish person and what do we say?"* I would have had to say: *"I'm not sure. I guess we just rely on the same Biblical truths, but how one would couch this truth in sharing with a person of Jewish faith, I would have no clue."* But the Holy Spirit does. Allow me to share an experience of His doing....

Personal Reflection:
Returning home from an International Christian Visual Media conference, I found myself sitting on a plane beside a kind gentleman. Being one not to want to interfere with another's private time and thoughts, I decided to turn my thoughts to reading my Bible, and give my seat partner his peace and quiet. After a few minutes, he asked me, "Are you a religious person?" "No," I quickly replied. "I used to be, but religion never did anything for me accept give me a list of dos and don'ts that I could never live up to. It seemed I constantly failed to be all that was expected of me."

He looked quisikly at me, and questioned, "So why are you reading a Bible?"

My reply? "Well, I may not be religious but I am a Christian. So, how about you; are you a religious person?"

He replied, "I am a Jewish Rabbi."

201

Whoops…had I offended him declaring that I was a Christian? I hoped not. But I wasn't sorry. He continued our conversation. "So what do you mean when you say that you are not religious but you are a Christian?"

"I don't want to offend you, sir, but I have to be honest with you….you see one day awhile back in the midst of failure after failure I learned that God loved me anyhow, and that He yearns for a real relationship with me, and that He sent His Son Jesus to invite me into that relationship. I learned that I had only to trust the truth that, because God loves me so much, He sent Jesus to come and die to pay a huge price so that my sins could be forgiven. Then afterwards Jesus actually rose again and went back to Heaven to wait for me to open my heart to Him and receive His free gift of eternal life. And that's very different than religion. You know, I actually have a little Bible with me here that I have marked with some of the scriptures that really explain all this better than I can. I sure don't want to offend you but, if you would allow me to, I would love to share with you some of the places I have marked that have helped me so much to understand just how much God loves us. Would that be okay?"

His comment? "Sure, of course I have done a lot of studying of the Old Testament myself, but in my religion we don't really accept the New Testament as a part of our beliefs. But I am always interested in what others have found to be helpful to them."

For the next wonderful hour in flight, I had the rare and precious opportunity to present the Gospel story through the scriptures I had marked. He listened respectfully and with what appeared to be interest. I was grateful, knowing that whatever he might do with the information presented, God promises that the Word will not return void. The plane landed and we each offered our warm goodbyes as we headed in opposite directions down the concourses to our connecting flights. I had a 2-hour layover before my next flight, was a bit thirsty and it was lunch time, so I decided to stop at a food counter before my gate. As I sat eating, I suddenly became aware of my new Jewish Rabbi friend hurrying down the concourse towards me.

He caught his breath while saying, "I'm so glad I caught you before you left. I wanted to say thank you. Thank you for taking the time to so lovingly explain what you believe about the scriptures you showed me. For so long I have really wondered but not truly understood why it is that so many people – some Jews even - seem to believe that Jesus was the Messiah we were all waiting for. It just didn't make sense that He would not come as the King that my people were looking for. Reading the scriptures that you marked really helped me see some missing pieces and [hesitation] well - I just really want to be who God wants me to be, so I decided to pray the little prayer that you wrote in the back and …. if Jesus is really who the scriptures say He was when He was here, then I have asked Him to help make it clear to me. I don't know why but for some reason I feel like it all makes more sense now. I'm sorry but I really have to run now or I'll miss my plane connection - just wanted to say thank you again."

We bid each other goodbye with a holy hug and tears in my eyes. My heart was racing fast and my Spirit even faster. I knew without a doubt that the Holy Spirit had taken over the conversation for Jesus' sake. God is so good!

Who knew plane ride home could turn into an opportunity to share the love of Jesus with one of His chosen people! The Holy Spirit knew all along, and He used the Word and a simple willing servant to reconcile a new child to God. My part was the easy part....just love Jesus and love others the way He asks me to...with a love greater than human affection...a love that puts Jesus before my fears, my judgments, and my insecurities.

Love Comes First

If we don't first sincerely love those around us, finding reason to affirm them, we will have no inclination to share the Gospel with them. As the love God has placed in the *rooms full of love in your heart* pours out to each of those whom He sends you, it will be a natural and effective sharing, producing the fruit of the Holy Spirit. This cannot be a manipulation for the purpose of adding one more notch to our 'Gospel preachin' belt.' To truly love others is to take whatever *action steps* are needed to prepare ourselves to share the Gospel with them. Knowing how to share directly from the scriptures will help those with whom you share to be assured that it is God's message to them – not just yours. They will walk away from their experience of receiving the truth about the Gospel declaring, 'God says' and not 'she said or he said.'

Be Intentional

Pray for God to use you and then move about your daily life *'intending'* for Him to do so – as you go. When we *intentionally* bridge our conversations to open up an opportunity to share the Gospel, it will happen. It is no different than when we bridge our conversations in order to open up opportunities to talk about other things that we want to talk about – like our kids, our jobs, etc. I can bridge from almost any conversation to tell wonderful cute stories about my grandkids whenever I want to. Why? Because it is what I want to and *intend* to share. When we *intend* to talk about Jesus, we will.

Share with Courage and Confidence

It takes *courage* to step out in faith expecting Jesus to use us. Satan wants us to fear that we will do it wrong; but God is not the author of fear. He tells us that when we share the Gospel with those He sends our way, we need not fear failure.

> *"For God did not give us a spirit of timidity, but of power, of love and of self-discipline."* 2 Timothy 1:7

Of course the evil one is not happy with us when we step out in faith to share what we know about Jesus, so he puts all kinds of obstacles in our way. As we touched on earlier, the battle is not with flesh and blood but rather with the spirits and principalities of darkness. But just as when Joshua was about to go into battle on God's behalf, we also can claim God's promise that He will be with us as we go in His name.

> *"Have I not commanded you? Be strong and courageous. Do not be terrified; do not be discouraged, for the Lord your God will be with you wherever you go."* Joshua 1:9

> *"Never will I leave you. Never will I forsake you…"* Deut 31:6, Joshua 1:5, Hebrew 13:5

Be *courageous*, humbly and gently meeting people where they are and remembering that *love comes first* - repentance, restitution, and reconciliation follow. No one is willing to be vulnerable to a know-it-all, Bible thumping, holier-than-thou witness. Die to self as Christ did, and allow His love to overtake your agenda, as He allowed His love for us to drive Him even to the cross. God has said *'the fields are ripe unto harvest, but the harvesters are few.'* Are you willing to join the Old Testament character, Job, in his willing offer: *"Here am I Lord, send me"* or do you instead tend to declare, *'send him/her?'* There was the time when I really didn't want to say *'yes Lord.'* I am so glad He drove out my fear and hesitancy one day and replaced it with the conviction and courage to go where He led. Here's the story….

Personal Reflection:
It was a night when my dear friend called at 10PM, crying and fearful of what was happening with her husband. He had been taken to the hospital with a heart condition and she was concerned about his eternal life. He was stable and they had scheduled him for an Angiogram in the morning. She wanted me to go talk to him before the procedure, for fear he might not make it through. I didn't want to go. I encouraged her that she could share the Gospel scriptures with him herself. After all she had led her three children to the Lord just hours after having received Christ herself [remember the story in the Strings of Stress chapter]. But as often is the case, it's sometimes harder to share the deeper things of life with our spouses than with anyone else, for fear of pushing them away. But if I did go and it upset him, what might happen with his heart. I very fearfully agreed to go to the hospital in the morning, asking the Lord to open up the opportunity to share with her dear husband, while protecting him from getting upset and having it affect his heart condition.

I was up bright and early, begging God all the way to the hospital for His Grace and wisdom. When I walked into the room Jim was propped up in his bed and looking like death warmed over…very pale and sullen. I greeted him, visited for a few minutes, and assured him that we were praying for him and that the procedure they were going to do on his heart would go well. He was appreciative but not at all talkative at this point. I understood. I told him that I understood from my own experience how long it can seem while awaiting a Dr's procedure, so I had brought a little gift for him that might help him pass the time while he was waiting. [Where did that come from? Had to be God speaking!] I pulled a small pocket Bible out of my purse, asking him if I could show him a few scriptures I had marked in it that had helped me to have the assurance that someone greater than I is watching over me in tough times. He said "Sure." I briefly showed him a couple of the scriptures and then encouraged him that perhaps it would help him to pass some time by while he was waiting for the procedure, if he would take a look through the rest of the ones I had marked. I told him that he could just follow the page numbers I had noted that would help direct him through the path of scriptures I had underlined for him. Then I very briefly showed him a quick glimpse of a prayer I had written at the back, encouraging him that it had been a meaningful prayer for me to turn everything over to the Lord and let Him carry the anxieties this life throws at us. Then laying it on his night stand, I asked permission to take a minute to pray for him before I left. [Was I shirking my calling? I had never shared quite like this before – just leaving the Bible for someone to find their own way through the markings. But it felt right and after all hadn't I prayed for God's guidance and wisdom…so I just left it at that. This was 6:30AM. His Angiogram was to be at 10AM.

Later that afternoon I returned to his room to get a report on how the test had gone. He was sitting straight up in bed, good color, and a bright smile. I commented on my way into the room, "My do you look better. You must have gotten great news from your test!"

"No" he replied, haven't had it yet. The Dr. has been tied up all day with emergencies."

"Wow, I'm so sorry. I just thought it was all over since you look so much better."

"That's okay. I am doing better" he said, as he leaned over and picked up the New Testament off the night stand. "I did read all the scriptures you marked in here. And I did read the prayer you wrote in the back. And I prayed that prayer and gave my life to Jesus." Then he patted the Bible cover, confidently declaring, "Now and it really doesn't matter how the test comes out cause I know where I am going."

God is so faithful! Had I let my human fear of perhaps not doing it right stand in the way, I would have let Him [and my very good friends] down. Thank you Lord for the courage to love your way!

Ask Permission

You may have noticed throughout this reading that there is one prevailing principle present whenever I have had the opportunity to introduce someone to the marked scriptures....*ask permission*. People are not interested in us pointing fingers at them and declaring that we have been called to tell them what they need to know about how It is with God. But they are nearly always interested in hearing our story. As we seek to *give reason for the hope we have within us, doing it gently and with respect*, people will not be offended if we first ask *permission* to use the Bible to help us in telling them our story.

Will You Prepare Yourself To *Pay It Forward?*

Someone has asked God to empower you to tell others how His story of forgiveness and redemption has affected your life – His name is Jesus. He died on a cross to make way for your redemption and the indwelling of the Holy Spirit in your life, and He is there with you just now, pleading for you to be *active* in *paying it forward*.

> *"As the scripture says, everyone who trusts in him will never be put to shame. For there is no difference between Jew and Gentile – the same Lord is Lord of all and richly blesses all who call on him, for, "Everyone who calls on the name of the Lord will be saved." How, then, can they call on the one they have not believed in? And how can they hear without someone preaching to them? And how can they preach unless they are sent? As it is written, "How beautiful are the feet of those who bring good news."* Romans 10-11-15

Will you be one of those whose feet will be *active* in bringing good news to the lost? Would you like to be *prepared* to be able to share the story of Jesus, directly from the Bible?

On the following pages you will see an explanation of the marked scriptures to which I have referred several times in these writings. Years ago I worked with others to help develop this particular Gospel pathway for the purpose of counselor training for Mustard Seed International's Film Evangelism ministry. We trained thousands around the world to use this method in sharing their faith in Jesus, following showings of dramatic Christian films. If you are interested in obtaining Christian films you may call Mustard seed International at 515-270-2080.

Though the scriptural pathway shared in the next section is a proven effective way to help others receive Jesus as their Savior, it is important to remember that these scriptures are but a few of the dozens that one can use to help reveal the story of Jesus. The truth is that it doesn't matter exactly which of the many possible scriptures you use to explain the truths about Jesus' purpose for coming to this earth. I know one gentleman in Ireland who has marked thirty different possible paths through his Bible to help him present the Gospel of Jesus. The important thing is that you are prepared in some way to navigate through the scriptures in order to back up your claim that: We are all sinners, sin separates us from God, Jesus came to pay the price for our sin so that we can be redeemed from it, He was crucified, dead, buried, and rose again, and He is coming back again to receive those who have placed their trust in Him. The story of the Gospel is simple. It is we who complicate it.

The first few pages of the next section will simply be instruction on the logistics of marking some scriptures to which you can refer in telling the Gospel story. Once you have read through the directions of how to mark the scriptures, you will see some bridge comments in between each that I have found helpful in navigating from one scripture to the next. This is just one way to use them. It is not the only way. You will develop your own style and your own 'bridge' comments out of your own experiences with which you feel comfortable. The important thing is that, once done, you will have a Bible marked with a scriptural path to easily present the claims of Jesus Christ. We have purchased boxes of small New Testaments from International Bible Society, so that we have a supply marked ahead of time, in anticipation of giving them away every chance we get. We also take every opportunity to teach other Christians how to mark a Bible for themselves, so that they also can easily share the Gospel with those whom God brings their way.

May He richly bless and empower you as you look for opportunities to *pay it forward*. Remember, it is the Holy Spirit in you who will guide and empower you.

> *"And of the Gospel I was appointed a herald and an apostle and a teacher. That is why I am suffering as I am. Yet I am not ashamed, because I know whom I have believed, and am convinced that he is able to guard what I have entrusted to him for that day."* 2 Timothy 1:11-12....

What a powerful claim! I know in whom I have believed and I am convinced that He is able to guard that which I have entrusted to Him [those people whom I am praying for, that need Jesus]. Thus I can go in confidence that it is His work, done in His time, empowered by His Holy Spirit, and I am only the funnel through which He will pour out His love!

Following a moment for prayer, you will find the details for marking the scriptures to which we have been referring. God has given you so much! It is time now for you to *personalize* your response by *equipping* yourself with a marked Bible so that you are prepared to *pay it forward*. As you mark your Bible carefully follow the instructions. First, a few minutes to talk to the Lord about our desire to tell the story of His Son, Jesus....

Thank you, Lord, for never giving up on us and for counting us worthy to carry your message of reconciliation to the world. Thank you for preparing us a heavenly home and for your promised return to bring us to you for all eternity! Help us to overcome our fears and become prepared and committed to pay it all forward. We want to follow your direction to, be prepared to give reason for the hope that we have within us, and we want to do it with gentleness and respect. We love to tell your story, dear Jesus, because you mean everything to us! Amen"

Introduction to Marking a Bible

In the marking process you will be writing page numbers at the bottom of each page of scripture that you present to indicate which page you will go to next.

Once again a reminder - this first step of marking the scriptures will be just the mechanics:

- noting the page numbers as to where to find certain scriptures
- underlining those scriptures and noting a few comments that support them
- writing a prayer and assurance section in the back

After you are finished with the mechanics of marking the scriptures, you will read some insights about how to effectively navigate through these scriptures when sharing the Gospel story.

Since noting page numbers is an integral part of effectively moving through the scriptures, if given the opportunity to help a group of people to mark their Bibles all at the same time, you would want to have enough of the exact same New Testaments that everyone's scriptures will be on the same pages. Small pocket New Testaments are available through many Christian bookstores, directly from many publishers, and as well through the International Bible Society.

As you now move through the marking process, follow the directions carefully and you will have a fully prepared, effective tool to help you tell the story of Jesus!

Marking Your Bible for the Purpose of Sharing the Gospel

Now it's time …. Get your Bible and a pen with which to mark the scriptures. Find a comfortable table top spot where you can work.

Turn to the front blank page and in the upper right hand corner write the page number on which you will find Romans 3:23. Then turn to Romans 3:23.

**At the top of the page on which you find Romans 3:23 write: "All Are Sinners"
- Underline Romans 3:23
"For all have sinned and fall short of the glory of God"
At the bottom of this page write the page number for Romans 6:23 [then go there....]

**At the top of the page on which you find Romans 6:23 write: "The Results of Sin"
- Underline Romans 6:23
"For the wages of sin is death, but the gift of God is eternal life in Christ Jesus."
At the bottom of this page write the page number for John 3:16 [then go there.....]

**At the top of the page on which you find John 3:16 write: "God's solution"
- Underline John 3:16
"For God so loved the world that He gave His one and only son, that whoever believes in Him shall not perish but have eternal life."

At the bottom of the page write the page number for John 14:6 [then go there....]

**At the top of the page on which you find John 14:6 write: "Only Through Jesus"
– Underline John 14:6
"Jesus answered, 'I am the way the truth and the life. No one comes to the Father except through me."
At the bottom of the page write the page number for Acts 2:38a [then go there....]

**At the top of the page on which you find Acts 2:38 write: "Repent"
– Underline Acts 2:38
"Repent and be baptized, everyone of you, in the name of Jesus Christ, so that your sins may be forgiven."

At the bottom of the page write the page number for John 1:12 [then go there....]

**At the top of the page on which you find John 1:12 write: "Believe and Receive"
>   - Underline John 1:12
>   "Yet to all who received Him, to those who believed in his name, he gave the right to become children of God."

At the bottom of the page write the page number for Revelation 3:20 [then go there....]

**At the top of the page on which you find Revelation 3:20 write: "Jesus Is Waiting"
>   - Underline Revelation 3:20
>   "Here I am, I stand at the door and knock, if anyone hears my voice, and opens the door, I will go in and eat with him and he with me."
>   At the bottom of the page write: 'next pg ' [and then go there....]

** At the top of the next page write:
>   "Is there any good reason why you could not receive Jesus right now?"

At the bottom of this page write: "Back Page" [then go there....]

*NOTE: If the Bible you are marking does not have a blank page in the back, use a blank index card on which you can write the prayer on one side and the assurance statements on the other. Then slip it in the back of the Bible after preparing it.

** On the front of the last blank page write:

>**Prayer**
>"Dear Lord Jesus,
>I confess to you that I am a sinner [Romans 3:23]
>I am sorry and I believe that you died for my sins [John 3:16]
>I want to open the door of my heart and let you in [Rev 3:20]
>I want to transfer my trust to you to be my Lord and my Savior
>So that I can become your child [John1:12]
>Amen

At the bottom of this page write: "Does this prayer express the desire of your heart today?"

"Over"

**Turn the page over and write:

Assurance
Did you sincerely ask Jesus to become your Savior?
Then where is He right now? [Rev 3:20]
What does that make you? [John 1:12]

At the bottom of the page write the page number for I John 5:11-13 [then go there]

**At the top of the page on which you find I John 5: 11-13 write... "Hope? Think? Guess€?"
- Underline I John 5:11-13 - boxing in the word '**know**'
"And this is the testimony: God has given us eternal life, and this life is in his Son. He who has the Son has life; he who does not have the son of God does not have life. I write these things to you who believe in the name of the Son of God so that you may know that you have eternal life."

At the bottom of the page write: 'Thank You Prayer'

You have now completed marking a proven effective scriptural pathway through which you can share your faith in Jesus. Keep it handy. Pray that God will bring people into your life with which you can share it. Mark more than one so you can give one away every time you share it.

On the next and final pages of this 'Pay it Forward' chapter, you will read some helpful hints as to some possible ways you may wish to bridge from one marked scripture to another. Once again keep in mind, these are only suggestions. You will have many more idea of your own as to how you will bridge from one to another.

Effectively Bridging Between Your Marked Scriptures

Now that your Bible is marked, here are some possible phrases that you may want to use to bridge from one scripture to the other. The scriptures remain the truth – just as they are – but much of how you will present these special scriptures will depend on your own experiences and the specific circumstances of the one with whom you are sharing. These are the personal application areas that make the presentation real and shared with feeling.

Bridging statements should not be too lengthy nor detract from the scriptures that they are supporting…only short explanations that will help the listener to better personalize the meaning of the truth being presented. So, here we go……

After reading the *"All are sinners"* scripture [Romans 3:23]…..
> *"When I heard this scripture one of the first things I had to come to grips with was that I am a sinner. Even though I've never killed anyone or stolen anything, or any major thing like that, I know I have thought, said, and done things that have made God sad and that makes me a part of the 'all' referred to in this scripture. And I know that the Bible tells us that because of Adam and Eve's sin we have all inherited a sinful condition. What about you…do you have any trouble accepting the fact that you are also a part of the 'all' who have sinned?" [pause for their answer] This puts us in a vulnerable position, doesn't it?…Now that we've agreed we are both included in the sinners referred to in this scripture, what do you think the results of our sin might be…let's take a look at what God tells us about this."* [turn to Romans 6:23]

After reading the *"Results of sin"* scripture [Romans 6:23]………
> *"What are wages?" [wait for answer] Then in comparison what is a gift? Help facilitate this thought by explaining that when the two of you are done reviewing the scriptures you are going to give them a gift of the marked Bible. Ask: as a gift, would you have to pay for it? [pause for their answer] Then, likewise, since God says here that eternal life is a free gift would we have to pay for it? No, because Jesus Christ paid our fine for us! This scripture says 'the wages of sin is death and we have both just agreed we are part of the 'all' that have sinned, but we are not dead are we….this is referring to the fact that we are dead in our sins – separated from God for all eternity. Mankind needs a solution to this dilemma and God provides it – let's take a look at His provision….."* [Turn to John 3:16]

After reading the *"God's Solution"* scripture [John 3:16]………
> *"Take just a minute here and close your eyes and focus your thoughts on the one most important person in your life….ok, now ask yourself….could you willingly sacrifice that person for someone else's wrong doing? I cannot imagine asking my son to willingly die for someone else's wrong doing. Especially someone who is in rebellion against him! But God so loves us that, that's exactly what He did! So*

we see here that God has taken the initiative for <u>ALL</u> people to be reconciled to Him, because Jesus died for <u>ALL</u> people. Perhaps you, like me, would like to ask, 'what about people who believe they can be reconciled to God in some other way other than Jesus?' Let's read Jesus' own words ...." [Turn to John 14:6]

After reading the *"Only through Jesus"* scripture [John 14:6]....

"This has been a difficult scripture for me to accept...and for a lot of people....because I want to think that every good person will be in Heaven. But either Jesus is a liar or no one goes to Heaven accept through Him. Since I have chosen to believe that Jesus truly is God's son, I have to believe that He would not lie, and so this means exactly what it says...it's only through Jesus. So... how do we 'go <u>through</u> Jesus'? Let's take a look." [Turn to Acts 2:38]

After reading the *"Repent"* scripture [Acts 2:38]....

"What does the word 'repent' mean to you? [listen] Sometimes I think people believe that repent means just being sorry – maybe just sorry they got caught. But God explains throughout the scripture that repent means to turn around from a sin and go the other way, not continuing to repeat the same sin over and over again. Once we have decided we really do believe that Jesus Christ is God's son, and we repent from our sins, we are invited to receive the gift of eternal life that God offers us through Jesus. Let's look at what God tells us in the book of John about this step." [Turn to John 1:12]

After reading the *"Believe and Receive"* scripture [John 1:12]....

Our ultimate goal is to become a child of God, knowing Him and His love and spending eternity with Him. In this scripture He clearly shows us how to become His child. When Jesus died on the cross He proclaimed, "It is finished," leaving no doubt that the work of our salvation was complete the day He died. Believing this is the first step, but did you know that in the book of James the Bible tells us that that the demons also believe? And I don't believe they will be in Heaven, do you? So how else does God ask us to respond to His 'gift' of eternal life? See the word 'receive?' Like any gift, it is only when we 'receive' it that the gift of eternal life that Jesus Christ offers us becomes ours. I can sit here forever and hold this Bible out as a gift to you, but it will never become yours until you take it. Today we use many various terms when referring to the step of 'receiving Jesus Christ as our Savior.' Some call it 'receiving' Christ, some being 'born again,' some 'being saved' [saved from our sin and condemnation to hell]. For me, I refer to my experience in 'receiving' God's gift of Jesus as 'transferring my trust' from myself to Jesus – acknowledging that it is the only way I will ever become a child of God. Whatever we call it, the Bible clearly tells us that receiving Jesus free gift of salvation is essential. Many people with whom I have shared cannot recall a time when they have 'received' God's free gift of eternal life. They love Him. They have grown up in the church, believing and receiving the truth about Jesus throughout their churched experience, but they lack the assurance of their salvation. They just aren't sure if they died today whether or not they would go to Heaven. The Bible tells us that we can be sure! No matter who we are or what we may have done in our lives, Jesus is waiting for each of us to receive Him into our hearts. Let's look further at what the Bible tells us about how we can receive Him....[Turn to Revelation 3:20]

After the *'Jesus is Waiting'* scripture [Revelation 3:20] .....
"I believe that just by virtue of the fact that you have been so gracious as to have allowed me to share these incredible truths with you today [name] that Jesus is knocking at the door of your heart. He wants to come in. I don't know where you might be in all of this right now, but if you do not have the assurance of ever having ever received God's free gift of eternal life, I have an important question for you; it's written here on the next page... It says here: 'Is there any good reason why you cannot receive Jesus right now?' [listen]

"If you have any question in your heart as to whether you have ever done this, I encourage you to seriously consider that this is the day that God is calling you to receive His precious gift of salvation. Perhaps it's all too overwhelming right now for you to grasp what you would even want to say to Him.....May I show you a prayer I have written for you in the back of this little Bible that might help...This is a simple prayer similar to the one I and many others have prayed to let God know we were ready to 'receive' His gift of salvation. Understand here that it isn't the words that are so important – they only help us to recall the scriptures we have just looked at and give us the opportunity to tell God that we personally agree with them." [Turn to the Prayer]

Show the listener the *Prayer* as you read.....
"Let me just read it and see what you think...notice that after each line here I have noted a scripture that we have already read...reminding us that the prayer an agreement of those scriptures."

After reading the *Prayer*
I've written a question here for you to consider... "Does this prayer express the desire of your heart today?" [listen!]

If they say 'yes'.... [later we'll cover if they say 'no']
"It would be my privilege to help you pray it...perhaps I could read it one line at a time and you could repeat each line after me...remembering that you are praying the prayer to God...not to me...kind of like when a bride and groom repeat their wedding vows following their pastor's reading of them. Remember as you repeat each line, you will be exchanging your vows with Jesus. He has already said His to you, on the cross, when He said "Father forgive them for they know not what they do"...and followed with... "It is finished." Would you like to say your vows to Him now, transferring your trust to Jesus and receiving His gift of eternal life? ..... If the answer is still 'yes'....

Praying the Prayer.....

> Help them in praying to invite Jesus into their heart by praying the prayer one line at a time, giving them the opportunity to repeat each line after you.

After the Prayer....

> After their 'amen,' welcome them into the family of God – reminding them that I John has declared them a child of God. Tell them that you just have a couple of more pages you'd like to share with them to help cement in their minds what they have just done and what God has done. Note that Satan is alive and well and will likely try to discourage them that this has not been real nor necessary, so it's important to have the assurance that God has done exactly what He said He would do. Turn the page over....

Assurance

> Use these Assurance questions to help them confirm what they have done, and what God has done in response. When you read 'Where is He right now?' be sure to encourage them to verbalize for themselves where Jesus is … 'in their heart!' If need be refer back to the Revelation 3:20 scripture to help them clearly see that Jesus came in just as He said He would. And what does that makes them… 'A child of God!'

> *After reviewing the Assurance page questions, ask them, "Did you know that God tells you that once you have trusted Jesus to be your Savior you can know for sure right now that you have eternal life?"* Let's look at just one last scripture that will confirm for you that you can trust this incredible promise.... [Turn to I John 5:11-13]

Read I John 5:11-13......
While reading this scripture, insert the word '*Hope*' where the word '*know*' appears...

Read the sentence again and insert the word '*Think*' - and again with the word '*Guess.*' In doing this you will help your listener to connect with the awesome truth of the word '*KNOW.*'

> *i.e. "...so that you may 'hope' you have eternal life?....so that you may 'think' you have eternal life?...so that you may 'guess' you have eternal life? NO! So that you may 'KNOW' you have eternal life! And it begins right now! This is such important confirmation because no 'hope so' – 'think so' – 'guess so' – Christian will ever share their faith with others....they aren't going to share something of which they aren't really sure. And that gift of eternal life that God has given you starts right now! You don't have to wait until you get to Heaven's door to begin to live your life as a child of God! What a gift!"*

Take a moment to close in prayer
> Ask: *"What do we usually do when someone gives us a gift?"* ['Thank you'] *God has given us a wonderful gift, shall we take the time to tell Him thank you? Why don't you pray and then I'll pray after you.* [If it appears this scares them, or they question whether they can pray out loud you might follow with...] *Let's just suppose Jesus were sitting here with us; what would you want to tell Him?* [Give them an opportunity to express their answer, and then follow with] *Now just say 'amen.' You just prayed. That's all prayer is, expressing our thoughts to God.* [You have just encouraged them that they actually can pray out loud.] *Now may I pray?"* [Match your prayer with the simplicity of their expression least you discourage them from feeling they will ever be able to pray as adequately as you do.]

Praise the Lord you have now completed telling the story of Jesus. God bless you!

<u>IMPORTANT NOTE</u>: What if at the point of asking them *"Is any good reason why they cannot receive Jesus right now?"* they had said they were not ready? **PLEASE <u>DON'T</u> PUSH!**

We do not do people a favor when, because of our intensity or insistence, they pray to receive Jesus just to get us off their back, when it isn't sincerely from their heart! We put them in the position of never knowing for sure whether they actually received salvation or not.

Here is a suggested approach under these circumstances .....
"I respect that. I encourage you never to allow anyone to harass you into receiving Jesus. This is a deeply personal spiritual step and it must be taken only when you feel the Holy Spirit is moving you to do so! I really do believe though, that God is speaking to you, and that someday you <u>will</u> be ready to trust Jesus as your Savior. I'll tell you what, may we continue through just a couple of more pages, and then I want to give you this Bible so that someday when you feel your heart is ready invite Jesus in, you will have it handy to review once again what God's promises are to you. And when that time comes the Bible says that 'all the angels in Heaven will rejoice over your decision. So, is it okay if we just finish these last couple of pages?" [If they say 'no' graciously give them the marked Bible and assure them that whenever they are ready, they will be able to follow those last steps themselves.]

If they do then give you permission to finish:
Follow through with the rest of the markings. As you do, use the approach: *'someday – when you are ready to receive Jesus – you will want to....'"* Give them the gift of the Bible when you finish [as you earlier said that you would] and ask them if they would mind if you would pray. Make it a short and simple prayer, thanking God for the graciousness of your visitor in allowing you to

share these precious few minutes, and thanking Him for His apparent work in their heart.

Reflection: Recall the story of my nephew earlier in this writing....not yet ready to give his life to Jesus when we shared a marked Bible, but tucked it into his dresser drawer as I had suggested. Then called at 3AM three years later to let me know he had just prayed to receive Jesus after visiting with some Christian friends, and was now looking at his marked Bible. God is good!

Personal Application

TRUTH

Those who have received Jesus have received a great gift - the gift of His presence here on this earth and the gift of eternal life in Heaven with the Trinity! This is so great a gift that *'paying it forward'* must become a priority for which we *prepare* and *intentionally* seek opportunities to *actively* share its message. In doing so we put a smile of the face of God!

1. This chapter is chucked full of *'action'* steps. The first step of 'personal application' is simply to work through the process of marking your personal Bible and some additional New Testaments that you can give away as you *'pay it forward.'* Do it now! :=)

2. Once marked, give time and prayer as to how you will personalize it for your own use. Choose 4-5 people [family, friends, Christians or non-Christians] with whom you can practice your Gospel presentation. Ask if they would be willing to help you with an assignment by just listening to you for a few minutes. **Note**...It may seem a bit stilted as you practice but that's okay...it is giving you the opportunity to own it, and you will put a smile on God's face. I know several who have received Christ while someone was 'practicing' with them!

3. Make a list of those you know whom you sense may not have yet received God's free gift of eternal life. [Remember we are not to judge – only praying for discernment of one's spiritual need.]

4. Commit to diligently pray over your list every day, telling God that you are willing to be used in His *ministry of reconciliation*. Be aware, prepared, and willing to respond when a door opens.

Journal Entry: **Life A Can**

Today I saw a can, randomly rolling across a lot.
I thought of how often life also just rolls along,
much like that little can, pitching to and fro,
lazily meandering along, blown by the winds,
changing directions with each strong gust,
and adjusting its course with each stone in its path.

It rolled along into an obstacle too big to climb,
And, as often happens in life, it just lay there –
unable to get the momentum to move around.

Then someone came along
and saw that can stuck there,
and kindly picked it up and took it home.

I thought of how that abandoned can
would have just laid there - all alone,
for who knows how long,
through winter's wind and storm.
Or perhaps not…it might have become
victim of a kick from an angry foot,
at which time it would have just
begun its journey all over again,
aimless, tossing and pitching
with each stone in its path.

Life can be much like that you know,
aimlessly tossing and pitching,
adjusting its course with each bump in its path.
Blowing about with the winds of time,
and experiences, and acquaintances…
Stopping now and then with the lack of momentum,
or desire, to climb the obstacles before it.

And then God sends someone along to pick it up
And take it home and give it rest,
where storms and strife and life itself
can no longer kick itself around and dent it up,
and where the mountains are easier to climb,
because someone cared enough to pick it up
and help it find its way home!

**Journal Entry: National Religious Broadcasters Convention - 1988
Reflections from a hotel lobby corner**

Hustle – Bustle
Papers that rustle
Greetings and handshakes
Dear friends, old and some that are new
"Hello, it's been a long time;
And so, how are you?"
Personalities from TV, radio, and film makers too,
All whole heartedly agreeing, a change is long overdue.
But alas, the critical question is posed;
"Who needs to change – is it me?
Or perhaps could it be you?"

While we ponder the issues, let us all pause,
Let's play Hollywood, just for awhile,
cause heaven know we all like applause!
As one by one, each winner is called,
We proudly march up on the stage, graciously
receiving our awards and expected due praise,
responding with a nod and exuberant smile.

"A perfect producer!" – "An outstanding man!"
"A wonderful leader!" – "Best show in the Land!"
Let's all stand up and give them a hand!

One would hardly believe we were ever aware,
that once, when Christ was called 'a good man'
He responded with a questioning stare;
"Why do you call me good?" he posed,
For you see only God is truly good…
Not you and not me.

If only we were as good as we believe that we are,
I think our conventions might be different by far.
And maybe the money, the tons that we spend,
would be spent on the lost, the more workers to send!
Not for conventions and halls and the games that we play –
But for hearts who despair and who've perhaps lost their way!

I wonder, the housekeepers, desk clerks and servers we've used,
If Jesus would come just now to call His children home,
who all would there be that could go with Him there?

Would He have spent this week as we have?
From meeting to meeting and applause to applause?
Or would He have risen each God-given day,
Divinely inspired by a much holier cause?
To share with those housekeepers and desk clerks and servers,
His love and His life - His death on the cross,
The price that He paid for all of the lost?

Here comes the dear housekeeper from up on my floor
I've so enjoyed getting to know her story, and
I just know if there's time, she'll share so much more.
"Hello, off work now you say?
Would you have time to just sit a spell
and share some more of your day?

Your country sounds great and your family swell.
I wish I could meet them and know them as well.
Yes, we're all here for a convention – it's for our work
We are all devoted to telling stories – stories about Jesus.
About His love and His gift of eternal life,
How His presence helps in distresses and strife.
Do you know of Him too?
No – I would love to tell you about Him – may I?

I have His story all marked in this Bible of mine.
It would just take a few minutes, if you have the time.
Let's look at some key scriptures here underlined....

Now she is gone – my new sister in Christ.
Thank you Lord for your faithful advice...
To just sit quietly and ponder your Grace,
while the world around me keeps up their pace.

This time has been precious and your presence felt
While all around new media Agreements are dealt.
Guess there's a place for both...a time to do business
and a time to be still...to let our love so shine through
that all of the business deals in the world will pale
Compared to the main deal....on the cross,
That was signed in blood, and delivered by you!

EPILOGUE

And so this has been the journey....one in which God has been ever faithful, and one in which the truth and healing process of giving and receiving an "*I Love You Anyhow*" kind of love has reigned true and powerful!

Thinking about and pouring my heart into this manuscript for over forty years has been an incredible mission. Getting it all to come together has been a bit like giving breach birth to a very special baby! Exciting, painful, and when finally holding the baby in your hands, very very worth it! To God be the glory. It is a dream come true, one that though penned by me has most certainly been authored by the Lord.

He continues to teach me more of His truths every day. In the winter of my life I am ever so grateful to look back and rejoice over His love and leadership throughout the ups and downs of this life. At the time of this writing I am blessed with good health, a continued marriage to a faithful husband, and enjoying children, grandchildren, great grandchildren, and a myriad of greater family and friends with whom I am privileged share life's joys. As I look forward, I have no idea what life will have in store, but I know one thing for sure - He does! And He is my strength and my portion. When I have Him He is all I need.

I believe it is no accident that you are holding this book in your hands. It is an answer to years of prayer that it will find its way to all whom the Lord has chosen to bless with its contents. I encourage you to keep it nearby, allowing God to use it as a constant resource and reminder of:

- ✟ True God-driven Love...Are you experiencing the fulfillment of '*I Love You Anyhow?*'
- ✟ How are you doing at applying the principles of affirmation and vulnerability?

✝ Are you allowing your vertical/horizontal communications to be God led?
✝ Have you accepted forgiveness through Christ, forgiving others as He has forgiven you?
✝ Are you committed to living out your God given roles as He has designed them to be?
✝ Are you giving God ownership of relationships so He can unravel the strings of stress?
✝ Are you claiming the presence of the Holy Spirit within and the guidance of His Angels?
✝ Have you stopped feeding on baby's milk and started moving up the stair steps to Christian maturity - or are you still falling out too close to where you got in?
✝ When is the last time you shared Christ, paying forward the *'I Love You Anyhow'* kind of love that He has offered you?

I pray that you have been encouraged and inspired by God's presence throughout this reading and that He will use the *golden nuggets of truth* within to convict your heart to apply them in your life, for Jesus' sake.

It is my heartfelt prayer that all who read its message will experience a revolutionary change in their relationships, becoming inspired to give up the limitations of offering I love you *'when'* or *'if'* in exchange for the indescribable fulfillment and joy of offering *"I LOVE YOU ANYHOW,"* all for Jesus' sake!

My vision for this book: Having been blessed with over fifty years of participation in the leadership of such activities as Small Group gatherings, Alpha, Sunday School and Bible studies, youth group, women's and couples retreats, I long for this book to find its way to becoming a resource for such groups. I pray that, through distribution to book stores and church libraries, it will find its way to the homes of those who are searching for deeper relationships with God and with others. Thank you reading my book and for joining me in prayer to this end!

Even as I commit this manuscript to this vision, I acknowledge that the results – as with all of life's journeys - must be left to the Lord.

"There is no wisdom, no insight, no plan that can succeed against the Lord. The horse is made ready for the day of battle, but victory rests with the Lord."

Proverbs 21:30-31

I LOVE YOU ANYHOW!

INDEX

A

all have sinned....Romans 3-20 67

all things are possible with God....Mark 10-27 85

all things are possible....Philippians 4-13 32

always be prepared....I Peter 3-15 to 16a...199

angels are God's messengers....Revelation 1-1&2 161

angels are ministering spirits....Hebrews 1-14.................................161

Angels deliver us from harm....II Kings 6 - Acts 27 161

Angels who fell from Grace are in everlasting chains for judgment....Jude 6 160

Angels rejoice when one sinner repents....Luke 15-10....................161

Angels will not marry....Matthew 22-30 161

Apostles actively paid it forward 198

aproach Him with confidence....Hebrews 4-16 179

as far as the east is from the west....Psalm 103-8to12 68

ask according to his will....I John 5-14&15 179

Author Merlin Carothers 87

authority on earth to forgive sins....Matthew 9-5&6 97

B

be active in telling His story....Philemon 6 198

Be Persistent....Luke 11-5to9..182

be quick to listen-slow to anger...James 1-19&20 73

begin with Faith 183

believe He hears-and forgive others....Mark 11-24to25...............182

boat was in the middle of the lake....Mark 6-46to51a....................56

body does not belong....I Corinthians 7-3&4 114

Bradley family - Role Reversal 110

bridging the scriptures...213

brothers, what shall we do....Acts 2-36 to 39 & 41 ....*xxxiv*
Bruce Larson-Hello out there, world...*64*
by this he meant the Spirit....John 7-37to39 ....*152*

C

children obey....Ephesians 6 1to3 ....*132*
children obey-Fathers don't embitter....Colossians 3-20&21 ....*132*
correction and training are Godly *133*
crave pure spiritual milk....I Peter 2-2 ....*173*

D

devil prowls around like a roaring lion....I Peter 5-5to8 ....*176*
do not grieve the Holy Spirit....Ephesians 4-30...................................*73*
do you truly Agape me....John 21-15to17..*3*
don't quarrel....2 Timothy 2-23to25 ....*199*
Dr. Barbara DeAngelo - Real Moments *103*

E

endure hardship-God's disciplines are good....Hebrews 12-7to11 ....*133*
Esther's story *29*
everything comes from God....I Corinthians 11-11&12 ....*117*
everything each one does effects the other *128*

F

Father speaking through you....Matthew 10-19 ....*201*
fathers, do not exasperate....Ephesians 6-4 ....*132*
FEAR *177*
filled with the Holy Spirit....Acts 2-1to4...*152*
fix these words in your heart....Deuteronomy 11-18to21.......................*137*
Forgive as the Lord forgave....Colossians 3-13 ....*85*
fruit of the Spirit....Galatians 5-22to26 ....*157*
Functions of the Trinity *154*

G

go and make disciples....Matthew 28-19 ....*196*
God created man in his own image....Genesis 1-27 ....*58, 174*
God did not give a spirit of timidity....2 Timothy 1-7...........................*203*
God did not spare sinful angels....II Peter 2-4 ....*159*
God disciplines us for our good....Hebrews 12-7to13 ....*12*
God is love....I John 4-7,9,12,16 ....*13*
God is not unjust....Hebrews 6-10to11 ....*10*
God works together for good....Romans 8-28 ....*22*
God's Spirit lives in you....I Corinthians 3-16.....................................*153*

H

have a prayer partner....Matthew 18 - 19&20 182
have you eaten from the tree....Gensis 3-10&11 66
He has risen....Mark 16-6 to 7 2
He hears us....I John 5-14&15 179
He is able to guard what I have entrusted to him....2 Timothy 1-11&12 207
He wants to be our BFF.............177
He who began a good work....Philippians 1-6b 170
He will command his angels to gaurd you....Psalm 91-11&12 157
He will make your paths straight....Proverbs 3-5&6 23
He will send his angels....Mark 13-27 157
here I am I stand at the door....Revelation3-20 28
him who had no sin to be sin for us....II Corinthians 5-21 95
his ears are attentive....I Peter 3-12a 179
His image - my image 175
hold anything against anyone....Mark 11-25 85
honor one another....Romans 12-10 199
how beautiful are the feet....Romans 10-11to15 206
how do we share with Jewish people 201
how do you know whether you will save....I Corinthians 7-16 107
how many times shall I forgive....Matthew 18-21&22 93
Howard Hendricks - We Really Do Need Each Other 75
HS comes with Christ....Galatians 3-1to3.............155
HS of God lives in all Christians....Romans 8-9to10 93
HS empowers us....Acts 1-7&8 156
HS helps us in our weakness....Romans 8-26 55
HS gives us the words to speak....Mark 13-11, Matthew 10-19 24
HS intercedes for us....Romans 8-26&27.............156
HS guarantees our heavenly home....II Corinthians 1-21&22 155
HS guarantees our inheritance....Ephesians 1-13&14 155
HS convicts....I Corinthians 12-3 155
HS is a deposit, guaranteeing our heavenly home....II Corinthians 5-5 155
HS is the Counselor that reveals truth....John 14-15to17a & 26 156
HS testifies we belong to God....Romans 8-15to17.............155
humbly *verbalize your desires....Matthew 7-7&8*.............181
husband is the head....Ephesians 5-22to24 114
husbands love your wives....Ephesians 5-25,28,31,33 116

I

I can do all things....Philippians 4-13.............32
I do not understand what I do....Romans 7-15to 25 xvii
I gave you milk....I Corinthians 3-2to3a.............172
I know in whom I have believed....II Timothy 1-12 xlii
I know the plans I have for you....Jeremiah 29-11 to 13 xxxiii
I will never leave....Hebrews 13-5.............130

231

I will not take my love from him....Psalm 89-30to33 ....*11*
If we confess our sins....I John 1-9 ....*81*
if you do not forgive....Matthew 6-14 ....*85*
impress them on your children....Deuteronomy 6-5to9 ....*137*
in Christ all the Deity lives....Colossians 2-9&10..................................*xxiii*
in the beginning....John 1-1to5...*81*
is in Christ, he is a new creation....II Corinthians 5-17 to 20.....................*xlix*
it is unforgivable to reject Him....Mark 3-28&29 ....*84*

J
Jesus prayed for us....John 17- 1to 4 & 15to21 ....*180, 181*
Josh McDowell ....*175, xxx*

K
keep his decrees and commands....Deuteronomy 4-40 ....*136*
keep reminding them....II Timothy 2-14 ....*74*
keeps no records of wrong....I Corinthians 13-4&5...................................*90*

L
let no debt remain except love...Romans 13-8&10 ....*5*
let us make man in our image....Genesis 1-26a.......................................*174*
live a long life....Deuteronomy 5-33to6-2 ....*136*
live at peace with everyone....Romans 12-9to17 ....*13*
Lord is compassionate....Psalm 103-8to13 ....*12*
love covers over a multitude of sins....I Peter 4-8......................................*10*
love God - love your brother....I John 4-19..*98*
Love never fails....I Corintians 13-1to8a...*12*
love one another deeply....I Peter 1-22 ....*10*
love will never be taken away....II Samuel 7-12to15a *133*
love with actions and truth....I John 3-18 ....*97*
Lucifer cast down to the earth....Isaiah 14-11to14 excerpts *159*
Lucifer's heart became proud....Ezekiel 28-12bto17a *159*

M
man reaps what he sows....Galatians 6-7...*75*
many parts form one body....I Corinthians 12-12to26 excerpts..................*106*
Marking a Bible...*210*
members of one body....Ephesians 4-25-32 excerpts *74*
ministry of reconciliation....II Corinthians 5-17to20 ....*xlix*
Mother Teresa's prayer *193*

N
not ashamed of the gospel....Romans 1-16 ....*196*
not good for the man to be alone....Genesis 2-18to24 ....*112*

O
overlooks an insult....Proverbs 12-16 74

P
plans to prosper you....Jeremiah 29-11to13 ....23, xxxiii
pray in *Faith....Hebrews 11-1 and James 5-15&16* 181
pray in *Jesus' Name....John 16-23bto24* 182
pray with confidence....Hebrews 4-16.................................179
Pray with the *right motives....James 4-3* 181
prayer brings heavenly wisdom....James 3- 17 180
prayer is spiritual breathing 180
prepare God's people....Ephesians 4-11to13 188
pride only brings quarrels....Proverbs 13-10..........................74
put on the full armor of God....Ephesians 6-11&12 160
put on the new self....Ephesians 4-22to24 & 5-1&2 176

R
receive the gift of the Holy Spirit....Acts 2-38&39..................152
reckless words pierce....Proverbs 12-18 61
Reuben Welch - *We Really Do Need Each Other*......................xxii

S
second hand faith 141
so the next generation would know....Psalm 78-2to6 137
solid food is for the mature....Hebrews 5-11to14 172
spur one another on toward love....Hebrews 10-17to24 91
steps to Christian maturity 186
struggle is not against flesh and blood....Ephesians 6-12&13............xxxviii, 176

T
teach them to your children....Deuteronomy 4-9 136
That's my soul..44
the Angel Lucifer falls....Revelation 12-7to10..........................159
the faith of a mustard seed Matthew 17 - 20b 183
the gift is not like the trespass....Romans 5-15to19 95
the head of Christ is God....I Corinthians 11-3.....................117
the Lord is my shepherd....Psalm 23 134
the right to become children of God....John 1-12....................xli
the serpent deceived me....Genesis 3-13................................67
think about such things....Philippians 4-8 105
thousands upon thousands of angels....Hebrews 12 & Revelations 5 160
to all who _received_ and believed....John 1-12&13 ....xli, 68, 171
tongue 61

U

unless a man is born again....John 3-1to6 171

Unless I go away, the Counselor....John 16-7bto11 84

V

victory rests with the Lord....Proverbs 21-30&31 227

W

wages of sin is death....Romans 6-23 68

wait for the gift....Acts 1-1to5 152

was justification that brings life....Romans 5-18&19 68

Wayne Jacobsen...give up serving your reputation ....xxxi, 94

we are Christ's ambassadors....II Corinthians 5-18to20 ....34, 170

we are God's workmanship....Ephesians 2-10 170

we each have a gardian angel....Matthew 18-10 161

we were reconciled to him....Romans 5-10&11 34

when you and your children return....Deuteronomy 30-2to3a 136

which is the greatest commandment....Matthew 22-36to40 5

who are you to judge....Romans 14-4 75

who takes the offense to the cross 93

wife of noble character....Proverbs 31-10to31 113

will not take my love from them....Psalm 89-30to33 ....11, 133

with you there is forgiveness....Psalm 130-3&4 82

wives be submissive....I Peter 3-1,2,7 107

woman at the well....John 4-19to26 35

Y

yoked together with unbelievers....2 Corinthians 6-14to16a 107

you created my inmost being....Psalm 139-13to16 103

you may know that you have eternal life....I John5-11 to 13 xlii

you were dead in your sins....Ephesians 2-1&2 160

you were once darkness....Ephesians 5-8 73

you will surely die....Genesis 2-15to17 66

your iniquities have separated you....Isaiah 59-2 67

CPSIA information can be obtained at www.ICGtesting.com
Printed in the USA
LVOW07s0755280514

387579LV00025B/1220/P